Praise for *Louisiana Coushatta Basket Makers*

"The methodology and analysis that went into writing *Louisiana Coushatta Basket Makers* offer a marvelous example for future work in Native American studies. This book resulted from close collaboration with the Coushatta Tribe. Weavers tell their own stories, with tribal members collecting and translating interviews with them. By anchoring Coushatta history 'through the lens of basketry,' this book adds significantly to our understanding of the dynamic and complex ways in which Indigenous communities have put their material culture to use. Each chapter features a dimension of the Coushattas' production and marketing of baskets across time and space, demonstrating along the way their resourceful adaptation to environmental and economic circumstances."

—Daniel H. Usner Jr., author of *American Indians in Early New Orleans: From Calumet to Raquette*

"This is an amazing book. The authors offer us the voices of the Coushatta basket makers, telling of their art and their culture. The Coushatta language sews the chapters together, just as raffia sews the baskets. The political history of the Coushatta so entwines with these basket makers, their families, and friends that one learns it in the traditional way, like sitting in a group sewing baskets listening to the stories as people work and talk. It takes the Coushatta into the hearts of the reader. This is not another book on baskets; it speaks with the Coushatta artisans and their culture in ways that are themselves exciting."

—Hiram F. "Pete" Gregory, coauthor of *The Historic Indian Tribes of Louisiana: From 1542 to the Present* and coeditor of *The Work of Tribal Hands: Southeastern Indian Split Cane Basketry*

"As my father, Ernest Sickey, advocated for and successfully ensured our Native American rights and federal re-recognition throughout the 1960s, '70s, and '80s, he consistently arrived at various politicians' offices and negotiation tables with one of our handcrafted pine-needle

Coushatta baskets. Like myself, his father raised him to know that the Coushatta were citizens deserving of the same public education, health care, and access to employment opportunities afforded to all American citizens. The Coushatta, our culture, and legacy would survive the struggles we faced and make us stronger. Then and now, every Coushatta basket collected or given continues to represent our tribal members' social identity as well as our political strength. They were and are a role not only in the path to a better life and justice but a beautiful illustration of how the Coushatta recognize the many roles necessary within our community. We are an Us."

—David Sickey, chairman, Coushatta Tribe of Louisiana

Louisiana Coushatta Basket Makers

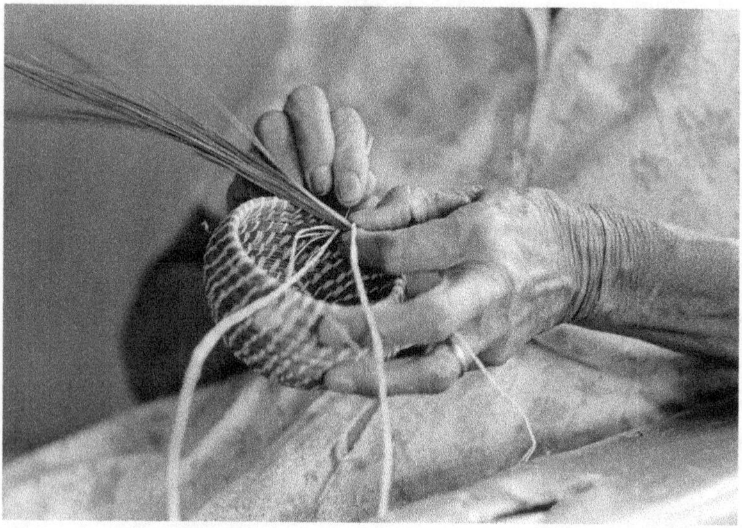

Louisiana Coushatta Basket Makers

TRADITIONAL KNOWLEDGE, RESOURCEFULNESS, AND ARTISTRY AS A MEANS OF SURVIVAL

LINDA P. LANGLEY and DENISE E. BATES

Louisiana State University Press
Baton Rouge

Published by Louisiana State University Press
www.lsupress.org

Manufactured in the United States of America
First printing

Designer: Laura Roubique Gleason
Typeface: Minion Pro

Cover and frontispiece photo: Basket held by Coushatta weaver Minnie Obe. Image from Princeton University, William Byler Collection, Photo by Sam Guillory.

Library of Congress Cataloging-in-Publication Data

Names: Langley, Linda P., author. | Bates, Denise E., author.
Title: Louisiana Coushatta basket makers : traditional knowledge, resourcefulness, and artistry as a means of survival / Linda P. Langley and Denise E. Bates.
Description: Baton Rouge : Louisiana State University Press, [2021]. | Includes bibliographical references and index.
Identifiers: LCCN 2020036835 (print) | LCCN 2020036836 (ebook) | ISBN 978-0-8071-7124-0 (cloth) | ISBN 978-0-8071-7525-5 (pdf) | ISBN 978-0-8071-7526-2 (epub)
Subjects: LCSH: Koasati Indians—Louisiana—Allen Parish—History. | Indian basket makers—Louisiana—Allen Parish—History.
Classification: LCC E99.K77 L36 2021 (print) | LCC E99.K77 (ebook) | DDC 976.3/580049738—dc23
LC record available at https://lccn.loc.gov/2020036835
LC ebook record available at https://lccn.loc.gov/2020036836

Yok oiyaak inchaakak Koasati immo̲, hoiisahchoto,
ya-iistilka, hoiisaahi̲

For all the Koasati people, past, present, and future

Contents

Illustrations

MAP

FIGURES

Acknowledgments

THE AUTHORS WOULD LIKE to extend our sincere gratitude to several people who were integral to this book, including the Koasati Language and Cultural Committee and the Coushatta Tribal Council for supporting this project. Special thanks go to the many weavers, past and present, who provided us with interviews and oral histories, and who answered countless questions, made valuable suggestions, and served as reviewers and editors. They are the people who have truly made this work possible.

We also want to recognize Arina Melkozernova for developing the map, Andrea Layton and Hiram "Pete" Gregory for helping to survey and identify museums to gather data about Coushatta basketry collections, and tribal members Alisia Sylestine, Gwyneth Thompson, and Raynella Fontenot for helping to plot out the family connections of basket makers. Thanks also to Coushatta Tribal Archivist Marianna Luquette, for her endless patience in searching for and finding photographs, documents, bills of sale, and other basketry records, as well as her ability to translate "Linda-speak." We also would like to extend our gratitude to those, such as Dan Usner, Susan Gray, K. Tsianina Lomawaima, and Katherine M. B. Osburn, who offered invaluable feedback to the manuscript. To the folks at LSU Press, particularly Jenny Keegan and Margaret Lovecraft, we appreciate your support and belief in this project. You have been a joy to work with.

For their countless hours of assistance, we would like to thank Lorenda Poncho, Loretta Williams, Bertney Langley, and Raynella Fontenot for checking and double-checking the accuracy of Koasati spellings and translations. We would be remiss without recognizing the contributions of two individuals in particular: Mr. Ernest Sickey, the first chairman of the Coushatta Tribe of Louisiana, who always maintained that the basket makers were the true unsung heroes of tribal resilience and survival, and Bertney Langley, who suggested numerous manuscript ideas over three decades, answered endless questions, read multiple revisions, and encouraged us with unwavering support.

It takes the determination of an entire tribe to tell their story. Thank you all for choosing us to facilitate this telling.

Louisiana Coushatta Basket Makers

Introduction

Aba Chokkooli maat yon choiyi hatchalichiskatohon choiyi hissi wiilok chin thiffhiliik schabachasaakahiik stachayoop. Akkaamos!

Dear God, thank you so much for giving us this pine tree, for planting and growing this pine tree to provide us with these needles. I am so grateful to look for and collect these pine needles that you grew!

—Blessing given by Coushatta elder and weaver Jeanette Celestine Langley before picking pine needles, 2008

IN MAY 2016, A BEAUTIFULLY crafted pine-needle basket—made by Coushatta weaver Margaret Williams John and sold at the tribally run Trading Post in Allen Parish, Louisiana, a half-century earlier—made its way back home to the tribal community.[1] Like other Coushatta baskets sold or traded throughout the twentieth century, it likely sat on a shelf in some family's home among other works of art before ending up for sale on eBay so that it might be reacquired by the tribe years later.[2] The timing of the basket's return home was particularly fortuitous given that the weaver's only son, Ben John, was going through a long and debilitating illness. Rather than being cataloged and put into storage along with the rest of the tribe's growing collection, the basket was immediately given to the family, who put it in a prominent place in Ben's house so that it could provide him with joy and comfort for the remainder of his life.

Margaret Williams John's basket was among a series of Coushatta baskets that have found their way home in recent years. Although some are being purchased, others have been returned from sources both near and far. When you talk to most Coushatta tribal members about baskets, their eyes light up. Everyone has a favorite story to share about a woven treasure made by a favorite basket maker, relative, or friend.

The conversation might even generate a fond memory about gathering pine needles, learning to sew baskets, or watching others sew. Baskets are among the most meaningful gifts shared within the community for major life events like graduations, weddings, and birthdays. They are so integral to Coushatta life that basket making is quite literally woven into the very fabric of Coushatta identity. The practice of using baskets for trading, gifting, and other forms of exchange has unquestionably been the single most critical element in Coushatta cultural, political, and economic survival for countless generations.

While the commonly used Coushatta expression "the struggle has made us stronger" has a broad application, it also aptly reflects the tribe's weaving tradition through its many migrations from the Tennessee River Valley to the tribe's present home in Allen Parish, Louisiana.[3] Every Coushatta family has a history to share about weathering hard times by making, trading, and selling baskets. Shifting historical and geographic contexts and circumstances have required weavers to be versatile in the techniques they employ and the materials they use. Drawing on both woven and coiled techniques in the production of baskets, the Coushatta basket tradition primarily is based on using river cane and longleaf pine needles. However, additional materials have either been traditionally used or later incorporated as a result of resource accessibility or to achieve a specific style or aesthetic. The knowledge of basket making has persevered because weavers not only committed to working together to teach the younger generations, but they innovated along the way to strategically create a commercial market for what quickly became considered "the showpiece of Louisiana Indian art."[4]

This book anchors Coushatta history through the lens of basketry. Incorporating the ideas and words of tribal basket makers themselves—as well as insights from non-tribal archaeological, historical, and contemporary sources—we explore the production, multiple uses, teaching, and innovations in basketry across several centuries. Like Indigenous pottery, basketry has always had both utilitarian and decorative attributes. Far beyond the utilitarian function of baskets for storing or processing food, baskets are a platform for cultural transmission, relationship building, and community cohesion. There is a strong social aspect to basket production, which involves several generations, often with elder weavers providing guidance for younger ones while children play at their feet and learn by watching. Weaving also provides opportunities for artisans to curate individual styles and artistic signatures by incorporating new designs or materials. This is a practice that dates far back in the tribe's history, but also defines the approach of the current generation of tribal weavers. While there are consistent themes that have come to characterize Coushatta basket-making practices over time, this book is organized chronologically. Beginning with the tribe's migration journey and early use of river cane for basketry (chapter 1), it details the transition to using longleaf pine needles in response to environmental shifts, factors of accessibility, and market demands (chapter 2). Basketry may have served as a trade commodity and source of income since the tribe first settled in southwest Louisiana, but by the 1960s basketry took on an increasingly important role as the tribe opened a Trading Post and basket makers regularly participated in public education demonstrations to bring greater attention to the tribe (chapter 3). In spite of these efforts, however, like other cultural traditions, such as ceremonial dancing, different forms of weaving seemed to have taken a temporary dip in participation, only to seemingly reemerge full blown after being reawakened when the time was right (chapter 4).

There are several dominant threads throughout this book. For one, baskets have played—and continue to do so—a strategic role in securing allies or reaffirming relationships with non-Coushattas. It is no coincidence that over the tribe's history those who held leadership positions on the tribal council or within one of the community's churches also played prominent roles in supporting and promoting the basket industry. From gifting farmers and landowners baskets as an expression of gratitude for sharing crops or permission to collect pine needles, to selling baskets to tourists and engaging in a form of what one tribal leader coined "basket diplomacy" within the political realm as a way of reaffirming Coushatta identity, the tribe has a long tradition of leveraging the use of its unique art form that is not only world-renowned, but distinguishes them as Indigenous people within a racially and culturally diverse region. Although the tribe also manufactured ceramics and other cane implements such as blowguns, these never took on such an integral position in negotiating personal and tribal identity. The strategic effort to use baskets as a "calling card" for the tribe among American politicians played a vital role in achieving reinstatement of federal recognition in 1973, after the tribe was unofficially "terminated" without legislation in 1953.[5] What permitted Coushatta leaders to advocate for the tribe within the political realm was the "basket activism" of the weavers themselves who worked behind the scenes to ensure a positive outlook for the future.

Basketry is a community industry. As a result, over the years, pricing has become communally regulated, following standards recognized by all weavers. Every basket maker has a unique style, so that each one's baskets are recognized by other weavers for a distinctive stitch, pattern, or decorative element. Innovation is celebrated, and weavers are encouraged to develop unique traits that distinguish their own signatures. Even in the hardest times, as a way of showing respect to the individual weaver, the baskets of someone who passes away are no longer sold or traded. While basket making is often associated with women, in the Coushatta community there is no concept of basketry being either "men's work" or "women's work." In fact, there is no way to express this in the Koasati language, which does not have gender markers. Numerous observers over several centuries have recounted an egalitarian division of labor in which Coushatta men were just as likely as women to make baskets; however, in the decades when tribal women had difficulty securing jobs in agriculture and the timber industry alongside their male counterparts, many of them turned to sewing baskets to supplement the family income. Baskets also are frequently associated with tribal women since clan affiliations are passed through the mother. Interviews integrated throughout this book demonstrate the prominent influence of Coushatta women who are more likely to serve in roles as caregivers and teachers, passing along traditional knowledge and basketry techniques that are tied to a specific family or clan lineage.

Basket making also serves as a prism through which to observe Coushatta values. For one, the community places great emphasis on helping one another, yet never taking more than one needs. So, when a situation necessitates borrowing something, such as pine needles, the expectation is that the lender will be repaid the exact amount borrowed. The Koasati term for this concept is *malmaamin*, which is translated by weavers as "same for same."[6] Another cultural value is the emphasis placed on always being active and productive, and not "lazy." When the weather isn't ideal for picking needles or sewing baskets, for example, weavers take precautions not to be idle and use their time to add decorations or finish baskets previously started. Perhaps the most apparent cultural value that is underscored by basketry is a widespread avoidance of self-promotion. Basket makers collectively made the decision to put themselves in the public eye—or "take it on the chin" as frequently referenced—for the good of the tribe. Under such conditions, participating in public education activities and basket demonstrations was perceived as different from self-promotion as weavers were able to maintain privacy by working to concentrate the attention on the baskets rather than themselves. Shying away from engaging in self-promotion was reflected most clearly in the difficulty weavers encountered in setting prices for their own baskets.

This is the first book dedicated to telling the story of the Louisiana Coushatta basket makers. Existing works on Indian basket weavers primarily focus on tribes in California and the Southwest.[7] Other publications highlight the work of weavers in places like Oklahoma.[8] There is still a lot of ground to cover in the Southeast—a region of the United States that has lagged behind the rest of the nation in the public's awareness of the existence of tribal populations in general, and the maintenance of their cultural traditions in particular. Fortunately, the work of Sarah H. Hill, *Weaving New Worlds: Southeastern Cherokee Women and Their Basketry* (1997), and Daniel H. Usner Jr., *Weaving Alliances with Other Women: Chitimacha Indian Work in the New South* (2015), has already made great strides in demonstrating the significant roles of basket weavers as cultural mediators and contributors to the broader social and economic development of the South. Like the Eastern Band of Cherokees in North Carolina and the Chitimachas living further south in Louisiana, the Coushattas also worked closely with the federal Indian Arts and Crafts Board, used baskets to build alliances with collectors, academics, and politicians, and served as the linchpin of their local area's tourism industry.

This work also contributes to the growing body of scholarship on Louisiana's Indigenous populations. At the time of this publication, there are fourteen tribes or Indian groups formally acknowledged by the state, four of which also are federally recognized.[9] The Coushattas were first among them to be officially recognized by the state of Louisiana in 1972 and the second to be federally acknowledged (the

Chitimacha were recognized by the federal government in 1916). The work of anthropologists, linguists, and historians who have published on Louisiana tribes from the mid-twentieth century to the present have not only provided a foundation for this book, but their work also has served to identify where gaps persist within the Coushattas' historical narrative. Next to the *Handbook of North American Indians, Southeast,* published by the Smithsonian Institution (Fogelson, 2004), *The Historic Indian Tribes of Louisiana: From 1542 to the Present* (Kniffen, Gregory, and Stokes, 1987), continues to be the most comprehensive overview of Louisiana Indian history. In addition, Indian activism and leadership in the twentieth century, along with the evolution of the Southern Indian Movement and the challenges many Louisiana tribes faced in their attempts to become federally recognized, have received attention in recent scholarship.[10] While the Coushattas have been incorporated into these narratives—given the prominent role they played in bringing the movement to Louisiana—there are surprisingly few publications directly focused on the tribe's history outside of our own works.[11]

This book will not only fill a great need in providing a space for Coushatta basket weavers to tell their story, and in their own words, but it also contributes to the broader scholarship on the role of Indigenous women in the health and resilience of their communities. Such works as Theda Perdue's *Cherokee Women* (1998), Nancy Shoemaker's edited volume, *Negotiations of Change: Historical Perspectives on Native American Women* (1995), and Brenda J. Child's *Holding Our World Together: Ojibwe Women and the Survival of Community* (2012) have established a precedent in taking a more holistic look at tribal persistence by reaching beyond the most outwardly visible players in tribal histories to uncover the equally—if not more—significant supporters working "behind the scenes." With so much attention being devoted to the political development of the Coushattas in recent and pending publications, it is all the more critical that this scholarship be balanced with a book devoted exclusively to those women (and some men) whose skill and hard work made it possible through the baskets they produced.

There were some challenges in piecing together the early documentary record of the Coushatta basket-making tradition. Records on the colonial Indian trade typically focus on the geographic flow of goods, the politics and power dynamics between trade partners, and the actual commodities themselves. What is often overlooked, however, are the vessels, such as baskets, that were frequently used to store, carry, and process trade items and commodities. These "containers of tradition," as defined by Jason Baird Jackson, remained largely undervalued and "invisible" prior to the rise of industrialization and mass consumerism.[12] Yet, even then, Coushatta basketry did not become incorporated into the cash economy until the 1930s because the tribe lacked the early financial backers that artisans in many other tribes had. While this poses a challenge in plotting out early basket production, it also comes with a benefit because the surviving Coushatta baskets from this earlier period offer critical insight into the standards and worldviews of the makers before consumer-market demands impacted the trajectory of the craft. Furthermore, in reading ethnographic descriptions and trade records, we were able to track early uses of baskets even when the records don't directly allude to their presence. For example, we know that, in addition to serving as storage containers to carry trade items, baskets were traditionally used by the Coushattas in agricultural practices. In fact, their skill in growing and processing corn is referenced in records throughout the tribe's interactions with explorers and settlers. Where these records are silent concerning tribal basketry, we have utilized other historical sources that discuss Coushatta corn, as well as the living memories of tribal members, to better understand how baskets were used to harvest, store, and process corn. It is through this merging of sources that we have been able to cull a deeper understanding of the utilitarian—and, later, economic—role that baskets have played in the Coushattas' story.

In using a largely ethnographic approach, this book draws from a diverse array of documentary evidence, including archival materials, historical newspapers, photographs, material culture, and interviews. While some of the interviews and personal communications have been collected by the authors, the vast majority have been collected and translated by tribal members, and typically in the Koasati language.[13] The majority were conducted in the context of the community-driven Koasati Language Project, in which the weavers were generally glad to be asked questions in their own language by other tribal members, and thus were particularly forthcoming, often telling stories and adding additional comments after the interviews. Some of the particularly noteworthy interviews were conducted during group weaving sessions at someone's home where the weavers shared memories in Koasati while sewing and visiting.

Collaborating with Koasati speakers to provide and check English translations has been extremely valuable to the development of this book and in capturing the weavers' own "language of baskets." Similarly, we shared excerpts of this manuscript with featured basket makers and their families, when possible, to ensure that quotes or stories attributed to them accurately reflect their perspectives. We have done our best to note instances where Koasati concepts are not easily translated into English, or additional context is needed to understand the Koasati statements. We are grateful to members of the Coushatta Language and Cultural Committee who translated difficult concepts and reviewed the entire manuscript for accuracy and clarity. The rich photographic evidence we have been able to draw from primarily comes from the tribe's own archival collection, offering a glimpse of the weavers' lifestyles and the quantity and type of baskets produced. Tribal photographs on their own tell a story of transition, reflecting a time when weavers only produced cane baskets, then shifted to the production of a mixture of cane and pine-needle baskets, and then focused exclusively on pine-needle baskets. In recent decades, there has been a shift back to the making of both. Given that Coushatta basketry techniques and traditions are still actively practiced, we use the present tense more often here than in most historical books. Likewise, we have deliberately prioritized weavers' narratives to give this work an authentic voice, balanced with outside sources to provide context for a wider audience. Photographs and interviews related to tribal baskets that have made a full cycle to "return home" to the tribe attest to the incredible intergenerational strength of alliances formed with non-tribal families surrounding the community. We are grateful to the families whose descendants brought baskets, photographs, or related materials back to the tribe, including Hosea Hebert, Herman and Ruth Baggett, Wanda Johnson, Oscar Shuff, Joe Tupper, and Bonner Miller Cutting.

We extend a special thanks to the families of those basket makers and community members who have passed away and whose stories are integral to this work, including Ronnie Abbey, Adeline and Solomon Battise, Doris Robinson Celestine Battise, Elissa "Liz" John, Jeanette

Celestine Langley, Jamison "Jimmy" Poncho, Steven Robinson, and Rosabel Robinson Sylestine. *Komawiichito stakoyokpaahos, ahatchifa-hilkalaho maan nihta chaffaakan* (Thank you so much for helping us, we will meet up with you all again one day).

I

Naksaamit Stamahilkato
How We Began

I remember real clearly when I was small that people sewed a lot of baskets. . . . they would sell [them] and eat.

—Marion Robinson John

SOUTHWESTERN LOUISIANA IS known for its diverse cultural landscape, but it wasn't until the 1960s that curious motorists regularly traveled into Jefferson Davis and Allen parishes looking for more information on the Coushatta people. In fact, the Coushattas' story came to play a prominent role in the tourism efforts of the area. As recently as 2007, the Jefferson Davis Parish Visitor's Guide featured a commonly used characterization: "The Coushatta Tribe of Louisiana—once known as the 'Lost Tribe'—is no longer lost but thriving in the Elton community."[1] This theme of a "lost tribe" in search of a permanent home is echoed throughout the twentieth century, and was even adopted by the tribe when it incorporated this language into the Coushattas' own narrative they shared with the public about themselves. According to a 1978 source, the name "Coushatta" has two meanings:

> One is "Lost Tribe," and originated when a wandering band of tribesmen encountered a group of white men. When asked who they were, the Indians misunderstood the question and replied "Koashatt" meaning they were lost. This narrative was translated by the white men into the word "Kosati" or the present-day spelling "Coushatta." The second meaning is "white reed-brake" and was originally applied to this group of Indians whose settlement was near patches of swamp cane, which the basket weavers of the tribe utilized in weaving their fine baskets.[2]

At first glance, the Coushattas' rationale for embracing the "lost tribe" narrative appeared to compromise their agency as it related to their migration journey. However, this characterization was leveraged strategically, contributing to the mystery of their origin. In addition, by linking the tribal name to natural materials used to make baskets, the Coushatta people were able to emphasize the important place that baskets hold for them as Indigenous people in a region preoccupied with race. This assisted them in distinguishing their unique culture and history—both of which later contributed a great deal to an area they came to call home.[3]

The documentary record helps to identify the role that baskets played over the course of the Coushattas' migration history. From the Tennessee River Valley to the tribe's present settlement, cane baskets proved valuable for trade and as gifts in assisting the Coushatta people in building alliances with their non-Indian neighbors. Over time, however, river cane became increasingly difficult to get, and tribal basket makers were forced to adapt to their new environmental conditions by turning to other materials. But like other cultural practices throughout the tribe's history, the making of cane baskets was embraced time and time again through different generations, as a tradition that refuses to fully "go to sleep."[4]

Naksaamit Ontha<u>to</u> Hahchi Okchakko-f<u>a</u>
The Journey to Bayou Blue

Archaeological and historical evidence shows that the Coushatta people were far from "wandering" or "lost" after first encountering Europeans. Instead, they made a series of strategic moves to ensure their survival as a nation. The tribe lived on islands in the Tennessee River in 1540 when the Spanish explorer Hernando de Soto approached them to buy corn. That first encounter did not end well, as the de Soto chroniclers reported stealing the tribe's corn and taking the chief hostage.[5] Decades later, the Coushattas decided to move southward away from the perils of encroaching settlers and competing tribes, as documented by the seventeenth-century Spanish explorer Marcos Delgado.[6] In what became Alabama, the Coushattas settled in villages near their Muskogean-speaking cousins, affiliating themselves politically with the Creek Confederacy.[7] And, by the second half of the eighteenth century, the tribe increased their political power, culminating with the leadership of Alexander McGillivray, son of a Scottish trader and his Coushatta wife, who wielded previously unparalleled power within the Creek Confederacy.[8]

Despite the military and political strength of the Creek Confederacy, continued colonial pressures and warfare prompted the Coushattas to resume their efforts to find a permanent home. While journeying through Tennessee, Alabama, Mississippi, Louisiana, Florida, Texas, and then back to Louisiana, the tribe lived in villages along seven major river basins—each with its own unique climate and natural environment. In addition to changes in access to water and arable lands, the Coushattas had to contend with significant limitations in the availability of the natural materials they were accustomed to using for making shelters, clothing, tools for hunting, and baskets. Although there is scarce recorded evidence about the materials Coushatta weavers used to make baskets prior to the eighteenth century, museum collections, ethnographies, and archaeological data indicate that the tribe was proficient in adapting to new environments and used whatever materials were available, such as hardwoods to weave mats and a variety of available grasses to make coiled baskets. While organic basketry materials rarely survive in the archaeological record, a notable exception was found at a Tennessee River site where fragments of split-cane baskets with distinctive Coushatta rims were found. At another site in northern Alabama, fragments of a woven burial mat also were found at a former Coushatta village location.[9] In 1756, French explorer Antoine-Simon Le Page du Pratz encountered the Coushattas and concluded that they got their name from the practice of cutting cane that was as sharp as a knife.[10] Anthropologist Hiram F. Gregory reaffirmed that the Coushattas likely made frequent use of river cane throughout their migrations by pointing out its abundance from eastern Texas across the Gulf Coastal Plain, making it accessible to the tribe all along its travel route.[11] Kniffen, Gregory, and Stokes related how river cane was a significant resource to various tribes across the region:

> [T]he great curving natural levees supported the canes, the native grasses *Arunkinaria tecta* and *Arundinaria gigantica*. To the aborigines, the canebrakes were almost sacred places. They furnished blowguns, darts, arrow shafts, shields, knives, and spears. Apart from supplying

> this arsenal, the cane was used in rafts, baskets, bedding, roofing, floor and wall coverings, and as containers for everything from bones of the dead to the plant seeds to be used as food during famines. Duck calls, whistles and flutes, tubes for bubbling medicines, and even beads were of cane. The brakes of river cane, as the Indians and others called it, have been compared to a supermarket that offered something for almost every purpose.[12]

In fact, river cane was such a prominent material used in Coushatta basket production that, in the early eighteenth century, the French explorers who came into contact with the tribe expressed how impressed they were by the Coushattas' proficiency at using the material to weave large baskets and mats, both of which were commodities that had become a mainstay in colonial households.[13] The Coushattas' skill in growing and processing corn also was well documented by Europeans and Americans. Although early observers typically did not record details about the use of basketry, information provided by later generations and corroborated by known Coushatta cultural practices tell us that baskets served an important function in the harvesting, storing, and processing of corn.[14]

Whether overtly or otherwise, Coushatta baskets had a long history as major trade items, helping to sustain the tribal economy throughout the eighteenth and nineteenth centuries as the Coushattas moved between Louisiana and Texas—settling along the Red River and then onto the Calcasieu, Sabine, and Trinity rivers before finally reaching their present location along Bayou Blue in the 1880s.[15] Each move was precipitated by a new wave of encroachment from European and American settlers, and the Coushattas credit the wisdom and diplomacy of early leaders for bringing the tribe through numerous perils, including war, forced removals, and assimilation campaigns. For example, Mikko (Chief) Red Shoes is remembered for leading the tribe out of their home in Alabama and into Spanish-controlled Louisiana in 1797, over a decade before the start of the Creek Wars.[16] His intelligence and leadership were extolled by Spanish officials, as described by the Opelousas District Commandant Duralde: "The Coushatta Chief is the most distinguished chief among the Alibamons, who as [a] leader . . . has been highly recommended to me." Red Shoes served as an interpreter for Spanish officials in helping to negotiate a lasting peace between the Caddos and Choctaws in which it was noted that "His intentions are always for the pacification, the most grand concord, amity and union possible with all the nations without exception." Because of the actions of Chief Red Shoes, Spanish officials recommended that the Coushattas receive assistance to settle in the territory during a time when other tribes were denied admission or even forcibly removed.[17]

Following the Louisiana Purchase in 1803, the Coushattas moved their villages further westward. This led them into the large, irregularly patrolled neutral strip of territory between the Calcasieu and Sabine rivers, where they remained until the Adams-Onís Treaty of 1819. Although Coushattas must have used baskets daily, they were not enumerated in trade or gift exchanges when a large group of Coushattas moved westward into the piney woods of east Texas to seek sanctuary among the Spanish.[18] In Texas, the tribe became key trading partners with many non-Indians in their vicinity, including the pirate Jean Lafitte, who traded with Coushatta people for provisions when docked at Galveston Island.[19] Others, such as attorney J. Feagin of Livingston, Texas, recalled Coushatta women bartering moss rugs, reed-cane baskets, and deerskins with his mother. Another observer from that time, known as "Grandma Harrison," recalled how "no one brought more or better goods to Drew's Landing on packet days than did the (Coushatta) Indians. The women were adept at basket making, weaving, pottery, and bead work and were quite skilled in cooking, especially meats and vegetables."[20] German traveler Von Wrede was so fascinated by what he witnessed when watching Coushatta women cook in 1841 that he detailed the process of making cornmeal by "stamping corn in a mortar" and "sifting it through a number of sieves . . . until the finest meal was obtained."[21] These "sieves" are sifting baskets for processing corn and are still made by the Coushattas today.

Biographies of noted Texas historical figures provide additional information about the Coushattas in the mid-nineteenth century. For example, a biography of Benjamin Franklin Hardin, a noted Texas surveyor and legislator, discusses how he was interested "in maintaining good relationships with the [Coushatta] Indians." Hardin was particularly impressed by the Coushattas' Chief Kalita, whose strong leadership, much in line with Chief Red Shoes decades earlier, commanded the respect of his people and of their "Indian neighbors." Hardin's biographer claimed that during his visits with the Coushattas he "bought baskets and fur rugs and bowls for his cabin. He even tried to learn their language."[22] Similarly, the second president of the Republic of Texas, Mirabeau B. Lamar, was also impressed by Chief Kalita and, in spite of the fact that he ran for his position on the platform of Indian removal from Texas, Lamar supported the wishes of the Coushattas and Alabamas, another tribe that also had moved to Texas after previously being part of the Creek Confederacy, to remain. In an 1839 speech, he stated that both tribes "seem to have some equitable claims upon the country for the protection of their property and persons, [so] the hand of friendship has been extended, with a promise that they shall not be interrupted in the peaceful enjoyment of their possessions, so long as they continue the same amicable relations towards the Govt. which they have hitherto preserved."[23] Lamar's support of the two tribes staying in Texas had to do with their allegiance during the Texas Revolution, and was also likely influenced by Sam Houston, who was both his predecessor and successor as the first and third president of the Republic of Texas. Houston similarly defended both tribes against the waves of incoming non-Indians who looked to dispossess them in order to open more land for settling. By 1853, Houston attempted to offer the tribes security by facilitating the state's purchasing of nearly 1,111 acres of land in Polk County, which is approximately twenty miles from Livingston and seventy-five miles from Beaumont, for the Alabama tribe. Plans were in the works to purchase an additional 640 acres for the Coushatta people, but the purchase did not occur. During this time, the local planter, attorney, and Indian agent Alexander Hamilton Washington, allowed Kalita's village to occupy part of his plantation by the river. Travelers named the river bend near Kalita's village "Shirt-tail Bend" after the Coushatta custom of wearing long deerskin tunics.[24]

Washington had the opportunity to observe the Coushattas' year-round lifestyle, and found them to be hard-working, prosperous, and peaceable.

> Their crops are cultivated for their own use, rather than for sale. Indian corn is the principal, though many of them plant sweet potatoes, and all of them vegetables, and they usually fill their villages with fruit trees.

> During the season of cultivation they remain closely at home, working industriously, and hunting only at such leisure times as their crops allow them. . . . When their own crops are worked to a point of safety they are willing to help their white friends. At plantations where they are kindly treated, and where they find it agreeable to stay, they work for low wages. During the season of cotton picking they really give us important aid. . . . When everything is gathered and housed, and the last crevice of their granaries is closed . . . they break up into hunting-parties, taking with them their wives and children, their horses and tents, and household utensils. They seek the wild pine forests, which our settlements have not yet reached, and work their way into the dense cane-brakes on the rivers.[25]

The arrangement described by Washington changed after the Civil War, when financial hardships forced him to sell his plantation, including the land where the Coushattas had their village. After Washington's death in 1868, his lands remained in probate for two years. During this time, Kalita realized the need to move the Coushatta village, and an 1870 report filed with the Texas legislature noted that the Coushattas "have no land, or permanent place of residence, but are living around on such vacant land as they can find. . . . They are honest, industrious and peaceful, and gain a livelihood by tilling the soil, and hiring out during the cotton-picking season; they still dress in the Indian garb of their ancestors."[26]

Although some Coushatta families ultimately chose to stay on acreage initially purchased for the Alabamas, today part of the Alabama-Coushatta Tribe of Texas reservation, the majority of Coushattas decided to relocate back into Louisiana.[27] The Coushattas who moved eastward across the Calcasieu and Sabine rivers in the mid-1800s lived in small villages and hunted throughout southwestern Louisiana in the areas encompassed by present-day Calcasieu, Cameron, Jefferson Davis, Allen, Beauregard, Vermilion, Acadia, St. Landry, Vernon, and Rapides parishes. Tribal oral traditions document the role and importance of cane basketry to early tribal families. Weaver Joyce Abbey Poncho recalled a story told by her great-grandmother about gathering river cane: "Back then, they used to go to Bayou Nezpique to look for cane. They used to hunt for cane all the time. They would harvest a lot of cane, bring it home, dry it and split it, get together and weave baskets. It used to be said, 'Cane baskets are what the Indians use to fight against poverty.'"[28] The earliest photographs of Coushattas from this period also provide evidence about the types and styles of Coushatta basketry produced over the past century. For example, one image from the early 1900s shows two tribal women sitting in their yard with their daughters by their sides, weaving cane baskets. In addition to split-cane and partially finished baskets, the image shows one of the women holding the tool commonly used to pack cane tightly together.[29] Another photo from this period shows a Coushatta family, including two small children, using large cane baskets to pick cotton.[30] When Roy Nash, special commissioner of US Indian affairs, was sent to evaluate conditions in the Coushatta community in 1931, he reported that "men, women and children from six years up go into the cotton fields, sometimes from fifty to a hundred miles away, where they receive 75 cents per hundred pounds." Based on photographic evidence, Coushattas brought their own baskets into the cotton fields. Baskets also were used to supplement family wages as Nash documented that "some of the women make baskets which they trade at the stores for groceries."[31]

Indian women weaving cane, St. Peter's Congregational Church, Elton, LA. Courtesy of the Amistad Research Center, Tulane University, New Orleans.

Indian children picking cotton, St. Peter's Congregational Church, Elton, LA. Note large cane basket held by the child on the left. Courtesy of the Amistad Research Center, Tulane University, New Orleans.

Maude Reid, a lifelong resident of Lake Charles, noted that a group of Coushattas came to her community to finalize their homestead applications, bringing baskets with them to trade: "Eight of their number had come to make final proof of their homestead entries, and others accompanied them as witnesses. But for their color and strange attire, they could not have been distinguished from any other citizen in town.

They behaved quietly and manifested a high degree of intelligence. . . . [They] trade their basketry for three fingers of rice or ten fingers of whiskey, each time holding up the required number of fingers to indicate their wants."[32]

Coushatta baskets also played a prominent role in the tribe's interactions with neighboring homesteaders, and several farming families that lived near nineteenth-century Coushatta villages have extensive collections of cane baskets. Acadians, in particular, used Coushatta baskets for storing cotton.[33] Descendants of local farming families explained how their grandparents and great-grandparents left food from surplus crops, clabbered milk, or animal remains (from butchering) for the Coushattas to take after everyone had gone to bed at night. In exchange, small baskets were left where the food had been—a practice that reflected the Coushattas' value of reciprocity. Yvonne Hayes Jackson, a descendant of the Hayes family that farmed lands around the tribal community over the past century, explained:

> At night my grandmother would put her milk out on the well. . . . then during the night the Indians would come and they would drink the milk. Later on my grandfather would always put out food because he knew they were hungry. And when they butchered a calf they would save what food they could save, but they would go ahead and put the rest of the parts of the calf out for the Indians to take. And they would take that meat and they would dry it to preserve it. . . . [The] Indian population in that age was quite extensive. There were Indians at Indian Village, there were Indians at Hayes, and there were Indians near Welsh. And since these baskets are made by the Coushatta they're part of the Coushatta tribe. . . . Whenever the Indians gave the trade items, they were given as gifts for food. . . . My great, great, great grandfather told his children that the Indians never stole anything. In the summertime the milk got hot, it clabbered. To them the milk was wasted if it clabbered but the Indians loved it and they would come and drink and eat that during the night. But they always came during the night until they got used to the fact that the whites were there.[34]

Jackson shared her story in 2009 when she came into the tribal office with two small cane baskets, a sewing basket, and a cone-shaped fruit-picking basket that had been gifted to her family by the tribe in the 1880s. The time frame in which the baskets were produced was determined by Jackson's recollection of the baskets' journey through the generations of her family and corroborated by matching the stylistic elements to other baskets from that same period. She shared how her mother, who was born in 1900, was given the sewing basket by her grandmother, who said, "I've always had this sewing basket. It was made by the Indians, [so] take care of it." Upon returning the baskets to the tribe over 120 years after they were initially left for her great-great-grandparents in exchange for food, they became the oldest cane baskets in the tribe's collection.[35] The passing of baskets to the descendants of the early white settlers, as well as an increasing frequency in their return to the tribe in recent decades, reveals the longstanding friendships the Coushattas have had with their neighbors.

Clustered homesteads adjoined by lands held by non-Indian families and timber companies along Bayou Blue in what became Allen Parish is where many Coushatta families found a permanent home.[36] They continued their practices of gifting and trading baskets as a means of building social capital and establishing networks of trade partners and friends. However, with the influx of new settlers into southwest Louisiana looking for opportunities to ease the hard work of building and maintaining homesteads, Coushatta baskets increased in demand because of the many functions they served. In the first decades of the twentieth century, the tribe held a crucial place within the local economy as they transitioned from less formalized, delayed exchange networks to more direct trade and barter exchanges. The Reverend Paul Leeds, a Congregational minister who arrived in southwest Louisiana in 1893 just a few years after the Coushattas settled around Bayou Blue, and who later served as founding pastor of the first Coushatta church, noted the value placed on Coushatta baskets by their non-Indian neighbors: "Indians and white homesteaders were amicable, exchanging work and produce with mutual benefit. Indian-made baskets were of inestimable value for storing corn and other things as well as for carrying loads ranging from a dozen eggs to a part of a bale of cotton."[37] Elbow baskets, in particular, were sought after for their usefulness in harvesting crops, mixing herbs, or holding wine bottles. Wall-hanging baskets were also used to store household items away from the grasp of curious children.[38]

The selling and bartering of baskets were a responsibility shared across the Coushatta community. Tribal elder Doris Celestine Battise, who grew up at the Bayou Blue settlement in the 1920s, told of a typical basket-trading trip:

> Sometimes several cousins would get together to make baskets, then when they hitched up the wagon they would load the baskets and get on to go sell them. The group would tell us, "You go ask the people if they want baskets." I was small so I didn't know any better, so I'd knock on the door (of houses) and ask people if they wanted to buy baskets. If they said "yes," they would come to the wagon and pick out the one they wanted, and then trade for items like bacon, rice, sweet potato, and eggs. "Ask for a little bit more," they would tell me, since I was not shy. If they would bring things like rice or sugar, we had our own sack, and they would fill it up. They sewed those sacks out of pieces of clothing in those days. Then, after a while, when they saw our wagon coming, they would wave to us to stop, so my cousin said "they must really want our baskets, so ask for more!"

On the occasions when Coushattas didn't have access to a wagon or other transportation, basket-selling trips were done on foot by visiting farms and homes along major roads. Battise emphasized the importance of these efforts, stating how "the people were very glad to see we brought food home when we got back. That's how we lived and survived back then, we traded our baskets, and got rice, beans, and potatoes, and live chickens, and so we ate. We'd trade baskets for whatever we could, so we could eat."[39]

Joyce Abbey Poncho also remembered her great-grandmother's account of these trading trips:

> Back then they would go trade the baskets for food, bacon, meat, strips of cloth, clothing. They had some cane baskets that were round, with handles, and you could put eggs in it. The white people really wanted more of that kind. The white people would fill them up with eggs and send them back to the Indians, and the Indians would keep the eggs and send the baskets back. They did it the same way with dried beans, they'd put it in the woven cane baskets. When the white people gave the baskets back with rice, it was full to the brim. That's the way it was back then, there was no exchange of money.[40]

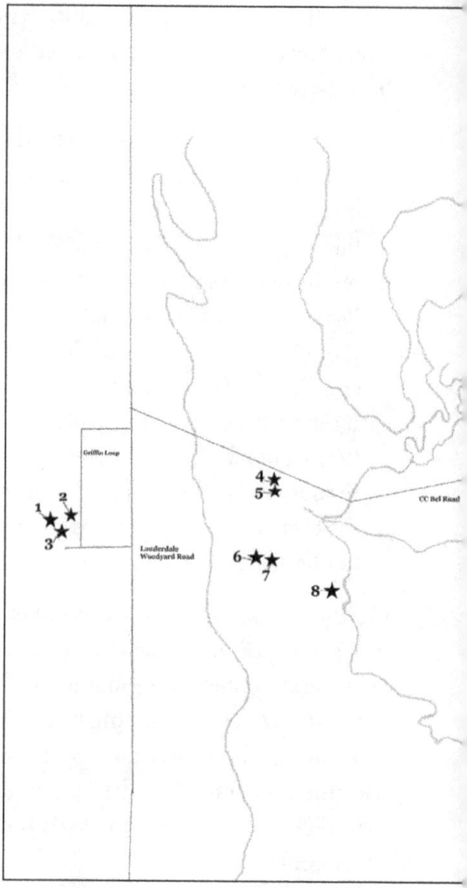

1. Wilton Langley
2. Florine Pitre
3. Elam Langley
4. Winston John
5. Marler John
6. Albert John
7. *vacant*
8. Quincy Langley
9. George Abbott
10. *vacant*
11. Bel Abbey
12. *vacant*
13. Wilfred Wilson
14. Sammy Celestine
15. Carlton Celestine
16. Gus Celestine
17. Mike Celestine
18. *same as 16*
19. *vacant*
20. Herbert John
21. Linda Loughlin
22. Wally Poncho
23. Harold John
24. Leonard Battise
25. Gideon Robinson
26. Faye Robinson
27. Solomon Battise
28. Debbie Thompson
29. Sam Thompson
30. Lovelin Poncho
31. Walter Williams
32. Newton Williams
33. *vacant*
34. *vacant*
35. Joe Langley
36. Davis Sickey
37. *vacant*
38. Ernest Sickey
39. Martin Abbey
40. *unknown*
41. *unknown*
42. Mike Thompson
43. *unknown*
44. Eula Fruge
45. Bessie John
46. Melvin Austin
47. Selma Austin
48. Rose Medford
49. Tom Battise
50. Boston Obe
51. Kent Sylestine
52. same as above
53. Chester Langley
54. *unknown*
55. Sandford Robinson
56. Clinton Robinson
57. Richard Robinson
58. unknown
59. *vacant*
60. Jamison Poncho
61. Albert Williams
62. Roy Abbey
63. Rodney Williams
64. Margaret John
65. *unknown*
66. Pauline John
67. Bobby Thompson
68. Delbert Poncho
69. Loris Langley
70. Edward Sylestine
71. Leroy Sylestine
72. Douglas John
73. Bennie Celestine
74. Woodrow John
75. Gilbert Abbey
76. Darrell Robinson
77. Eula Wilson
78. Woodrow John
79. Edmund John
80. Clamon Thompson
81. Elsie John
82. Ed John
83. Ira John
84. Lowell John
85. Coyd Langley
86. Curry Sylestine
87. Manuel John (no marker on map)

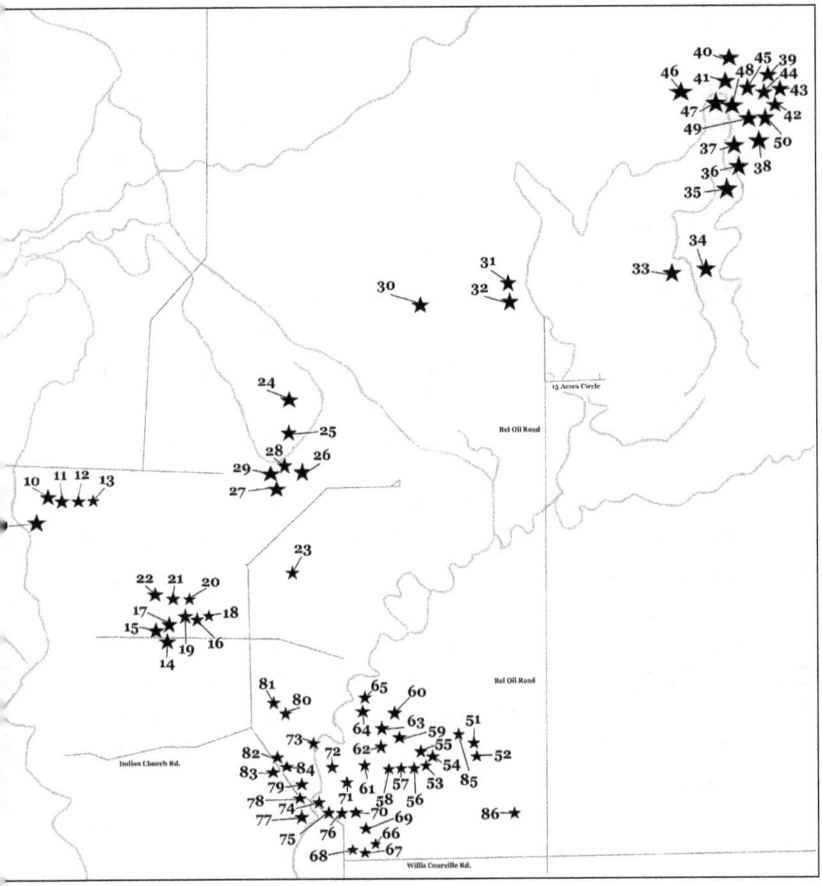

Coushatta homes along Bayou Blue, ca. 1970. Created by Arina Melkozernova, with information provided by the Coushatta Tribal Archives.

Memoirs from members of some of the first white families to settle in the area also contain descriptions of trading with Coushatta weavers: "We had plenty [of] Indians at that time and the Indian Squaws would make baskets to trade for something to eat. And they would travel on foot to trade."[41] Pat Hall, the granddaughter of a local farmer named Amos Richard, recalled that her grandfather would "trade" his rice crops and meat with tribal members for baskets, often declining to actually take baskets in exchange since his motivation was to ensure that his Indian neighbors had enough to eat during tough economic times. She recalled that her grandfather admired the Coushattas and frequently emphasized not to be scared when she saw them, assuring her that she was completely safe when they were around.[42]

Coushatta baskets played a significant function in both the Indian and the non-Indian homesteads around Bayou Blue, creating a localized economic niche that encouraged the continuation of an ancient practice. Until the late 1930s, bartering and small-cash exchanges characterized the transactional flow of baskets within the local market. For example, Maude Reid noted a Sunday afternoon drive to Elton to "purchase a reed basket from Mary Poncho, a full-blooded Louisiana Indian of the 'Quasadi' tribe."[43] In addition, the daughter of the family who operated McGee's General Mercantile in Eunice remembered local shopkeepers being eager to barter for Coushatta cane baskets because they were in high demand by area farmers: "One of the most popular baskets the Koasati made and bartered at McGee's store was a winnowing basket or *fanneaux*. . . . the baskets were shallow, the sides only about two or three inches high. The unusual shape was perfect for winnowing rice used every day in the family meal. . . . the Koasati [cane] baskets were much more popular for winnowing than the heavier split oak baskets."[44]

As more homestead patents were issued and land developed for commercial use, what had previously served as a reliable economic niche became increasingly difficult to maintain as tribal weavers had to travel further from the community to collect river cane. Kniffen, Gregory, and Stokes noted that "by 1900 most of the giant canebrakes were destroyed by burning, cattle grazing, and clearing. Further damage was done by logging."[45] This trend was reaffirmed in 1908 when an anthropologist traveling through Louisiana documented how the Chitimachas had to travel twenty to thirty miles to gather cane for their basket making.[46] In spite of the increasing scarcity of cane, ethnographers Caroline Dorman and Lyda Averill Paz Taylor observed Coushattas splitting cane for basket making in the 1930s—revealing the persistence of cane use despite its decreasing availability.[47]

While Coushatta baskets held an important place in the local trade economy, the tribe didn't have the financial investors that other tribes throughout the country had during the first decades of the twentieth century to promote their basketry within a broader consumer market.[48] As a result, this kept the market value of Coushatta baskets low and the circulation limited. This didn't deter production, however. In fact, even as river cane became increasingly scarce, Coushatta artisans demonstrated their ability to adapt as they began experimenting with new materials and styles of weaving. Solomon Battise remembered making split-oak baskets after cane became harder to find, but apparently oak never became a popular material for Coushatta weavers as only 3 of the 249 baskets presently in the Coushatta Archives are made of split oak.[49]

Ithani Asaala Tathalitǫ
Traditional Production of Cane Baskets

Coushatta baskets have long caught the attention of anthropologists and ethnographers whose field notes created a documentary record that provides a rare and valuable window into not only the construction and uses of baskets, but into the mindsets and beliefs of the basket makers themselves. For instance, when ethnographer John Swanton first visited the Bayou Blue community in 1906, he was welcomed into several tribal homes, with Jackson Langley even sharing traditional rabbit tales. Swanton also observed weavers making fifteen to twenty types of cane baskets, using a variety of techniques and resources to achieve different colors. In his field notes, he wrote:

> Black walnut [was] used for black dye. Bark of red oak down close to the roots was taken and pounded and canes were boiled in it for red dye. For yellow, roots of a grass about three feet high called in English "sawertick," sour dock, were used. Cane boiled with roots. Ishoma, tree like cherry tree that grows in swamp and sandy land, used root and bark for a red dye. Oktcaye ahesi, a grass in pine woods about 3

> feet high, a root of which were used to make fine yellow. [They] used copper bought in store for black dye. "Stink wood" growing along bayous was used for a kind of brown. Native name not known. Put blue cloth in water with canes to give it a blue color, as the old blues came off readily.[50]

Swanton made several additional trips to the tribal community over the next twenty-five years. In 1917, he purchased seven split-cane baskets for the Bureau of American Ethnology, which are now housed in the Smithsonian's Museum of Natural History.[51]

Around the same time that Swanton visited the Coushatta people, fellow anthropologist Mark Raymond Harrington also visited during a three-year trek he took to collect material cultural items from multiple tribes in the East and Midwest. His goal was to photograph and purchase objects for the New York–based Heye Museum of the American Indian.[52] Harrington described his trip as a privilege, and his visit to the Coushatta community as serendipitous:

> It was the writer's privilege to spend a month or so last spring in searching out the remnants of Indian tribes still left in the state of Louisiana, for the purpose of learning something about their location, numbers, and condition, of taking photographs, and of collecting specimens illustrating their old industries, arts, and customs. . . . While visiting the Chitimacha and Houma I heard persistent rumors of a band of Indians—what tribe nobody knew—living in Calcasieu Parish in western Louisiana. On investigation the mysterious tribe, whose name was not even known to the storekeepers who dealt with them, proved to be a band of Koasati—one of the nations of the old Creek Confederacy. More than a hundred strong, they live a peaceful life in the pine woods along Bayou Bleu, near the little village of Elton, earning their living by farming, wood cutting, and working in the sawmills. Many of them have very good houses and all dress in citizen's clothing; but the old language is still in universal use. Most of the men, especially the younger ones, have made some progress in English, however. The old dances and ceremonies are rarely practiced now, and a little new church and school show the coming of a new era.
>
> In spite of their progress along the ways of civilization I found fully as many old specimens of Indian handiwork among the Koasati as I

Jackson Langley and family on the front porch of their home, with cane baskets, 1906. Courtesy of the Coushatta Tribal Archives.

> secured from the primitive Seminoles of Florida, who still follow the ways of their ancestors. Among the most interesting things were two of the old hand-made pottery vessels, now very rare among Eastern Indians, a drum made of a cypress "knee," some very fine beaded shoulder sashes, a collection of baskets representing many weaves and forms, and some silver head-bands, brooches, and other ornaments laboriously pounded out of coins by the Indian silversmiths.[53]

Harrington visited eleven tribes from 1908 to 1911, purchasing split-cane baskets from each, representing twenty-nine different varieties of baskets.[54] He recorded descriptions and purchase prices, as well as the designs of the baskets and Indigenous names attributed to them. From the Coushattas at Bayou Blue, he purchased thirty-six baskets for the Heye Museum from thirty tribal families. All these baskets were woven out of split cane or oak splints. While a few had decorative patterns, all featured utilitarian designs that were used in carrying and processing grain. In addition to the daily uses documented by Harrington,

Coushattas used cane baskets in dances, such as the Corn Dance, in preparation of food used in ceremonies, and in the traditional collection and processing of medicines.[55] Many of the designs and colors used in Coushatta baskets also are related to these functions. Harrington's notebook contained detailed descriptions of the utilitarian baskets he acquired from the tribe, such as the one he purchased for ten cents from Winnie Thompson that he sketched and described as a tool used for "packing together the cane."[56]

The basket-making practices captured by Swanton and Harrington shifted by the mid-1930s as weavers began incorporating other natural materials. Ethnographer Lyda Averill Paz Taylor observed that, while Coushatta artisans continued to weave baskets with split cane, they also made coiled baskets of longleaf pine using the needles from the abundant *Pinus palustris* tree. "The coiled type may be of recent introduction," Paz-Taylor surmised, "as it is not reported for any other southeastern tribe." Contrary to what she concluded, however, older Coushattas shared how longleaf pine baskets were made during their childhoods, which indicated that, rather than being a new practice, it was a style of basketry that experienced a revival. In attempting to capture the trajectory by which Coushatta basketry evolved, another anthropologist claimed, "The Koasati point to baskets coiled from wire grass (*Pahi*) and tied with elm (*Silhoba*) or dogwood bark as the antecedents of their contemporary pinestraw basketry. Such baskets were also made farther east by other Muskogean speakers."[57]

The materials used for basket production were subject to the ebbs and flows of time as Coushatta artisans incorporated whatever suitable materials they had readily available over the course of their migrations. Longleaf pine needles were plentiful in the woods surrounding the Coushatta settlement at Bayou Blue, which contributed to the steadily increasing presence of pine-needle baskets alongside their river-cane counterparts. The plentiful nature of longleaf pine in the area is reflected in the Koasati language by the term for "lumberjack" (a common occupation in the tribe), which is *choiyi koiyli*—literally translated as "one who cuts pine trees." This is particularly telling given that it is a sign of how the language evolved from the more general term of *itto koiyli* or "one who cuts trees."[58] Paz-Taylor further documented the ingenuity of

Emily and Bruce Abbey selling baskets, ca. 1930. Although most baskets are woven river cane, note the two pine-needle baskets on the ground. Works Progress Administration photograph, courtesy of the State Library of Louisiana.

the weavers who also incorporated raffia that they "obtained from the Whites" as a way of reinforcing the strength of the pine-needle baskets.

Even as more Coushatta weavers began making pine-needle baskets, cane baskets maintained importance and function. These openwork baskets, where the cane is split prior to dying it, are sewn using patterns that vary from over-one-under-one to over-six-under-three.[59] While river cane was a common material used by Louisiana tribes, there are some distinct variations in technique and style. Chitimacha weavers, for example, often double-weave their baskets.[60] Coushatta and Choctaw cane baskets, on the other hand, are typically single-weave. Single-weave (also known as single-wall) baskets are often either diagonally plaited (a technique more common among the Choctaws), or made with twilled patterns with double rims, bound rims, or bound-down rims (techniques more often used by Coushatta weavers).[61] In preparing the river cane for use, Coushatta weavers typically hold the material in their hands and use a small, sharp paring knife to strip cane, while

Chitimacha weavers hold the cane in their teeth and peel once or twice to prepare for bundling and storing or dyeing.[62] In 1987, southeastern basketry artisan and scholar Claude Medford Jr., who was also married to a Coushatta weaver, noted: "I have *never* seen a single layer Cherokee diagonal weave basket, but the Choctaw and Koasati, plus the Alibamu in Texas all have this common diagonal twill single wall basket. . . . the Koasati winnowing baskets are square like the Creek, but *Florida Seminole* and *Mikasuki* make *rectangular* winnowing *and* sifter baskets, but *not* with one high side like the Choctaw."[63]

While basket-weaving techniques and styles differed among the southeastern tribes, other production aspects were remarkably similar. In fact, researchers have noted an "impressive uniformity in the split cane craft in Louisiana."[64] Common production aspects included strategies for gathering the cane, processing and dying the cane, communal sewing of baskets, and traditional methods of passing this knowledge to younger generations. More recently, weavers in each of the tribes are expanding their basket shapes and designs for the consumer market, branching out to new designs, such as bookmarks, miniature baskets, and baskets with corporate logos.[65]

Despite such similarities, tribal weavers are quick to recognize patterns and designs distinctive to their tribe. As one Chitimacha weaver noted, "When you look at the rim of a Coushatta or Choctaw basket, ours is totally different. If someone wants to know how [to make baskets], if they are Chitimacha, we'll do the same thing like what we were taught, we'll explain it to them; but they have to be Chitimacha."[66] While some distinctions between the cane baskets produced by different tribal artisans are fairly easy to spot, particularly by the colors used in dyeing and in distinctive designs, it sometimes takes a more trained eye to identify the subtle variations in the plaiting of cane baskets produced by Chitimacha, Choctaw, Coushatta, and Tunica basket makers.[67] When Harrington visited the Coushatta community in 1908, he not only documented the tribe's distinctive weaving pattern—over three, under six on the bottom, switched to over four under four on the sides—but he also sketched eight baskets and several other cultural items, such as beaded sashes, shoulder bags, and dance regalia with distinctive Coushatta diamond patterns. Over a century later, these design motifs are still universally recognized and accepted as part of traditional Coushatta symbols in the contemporary tribal community.[68]

Basket making has always been a communal endeavor. Coushatta elder Jimmy Poncho related how, when he was a child in the 1920s and early 1930s, the tribal men who worked in the timber industry often worked at job sites near cane stands. They would then bring back information about the quantity of cane they found at each site, later returning with all available tribal men and women to cut and bring as much cane as possible back home for everyone to use. He recalled:

> It was very hard to get work in those days, and the men had to go wherever the logging crews were working. Sometimes they had to walk a long way, past Basile, close to Bayou Nezpique. Grandmother would cook and pack them a lunch, and they would go camp out all night so they could be there on time to work in the morning. While they were there the men would also chop a lot of swamp cane and they would bring back the swamp cane to make baskets to sell. They used to chop as much cane as they could carry, bring it back, and then start making baskets.[69]

Similarly, Marion Robinson John remembered going into the swamp with her grandmother, Lizzie Poncho Robinson, to gather the cane. She explained how "they would take us to the swamp to help them. They would chop them down and we would gather them, carry them. They had a wagon with them to carry them. . . . they would tie the cane and bring them to the edge of the water. Then they would give us old clothes, old rags, and tell us to wash [the cane]."[70]

Contemporary Coushatta weavers remember their parents and grandparents getting together in the evenings or sitting outside with friends and relatives stripping and processing cane and weaving baskets. Similarly, tribal weavers recalled learning how to gather and strip cane by watching others and then practicing these techniques before they began weaving themselves.[71] This is how the Coushattas still maintain continuity in the production and designs of their baskets as weavers watch each other's progress, exchanging comments and ideas. Communal work and community review of work is such a pervasive pattern that, in her PhD dissertation, Stephanie Hasselbacher coined it the

Early Coushatta logging crew. Tribal logging crews were instrumental in gathering and bringing weaving materials back to the community. Courtesy of Nina Fuslier, Coushatta Tribal Archives.

Coushatta "iterative process."[72] Novice weavers still begin by sewing small mats and baskets—enduring many mistakes and critiques while becoming more proficient in making tighter and neater corners. It is through this process that they intuitively learn to recognize when a basket feels and looks "right."[73]

Asaalak Komawiichito̲
Baskets Helped Us Survive

The transient nature of basket sales was a familiar pattern among Louisiana Indians. For example, the story of Rosa Jackson Pierite, a Choctaw-Biloxi from Indian Creek, is retold in *The Historic Indian Tribes of Louisiana,* in which she relayed how, in the 1920s, "her mother and sisters put their baskets in a sheet, bundled it over a pole, and walked twelve miles from their home near Indian Creek to Alexandria" where they would spread the array of baskets on street corners to sell.[74] Coushatta basket makers did the same thing, with Loris Abbott Langley remembering how she also put baskets in a large bag and carried them on her back as a group of them walked for miles to different farms and homes to sell baskets.[75]

Coushattas also traded their baskets at general mercantile stores in the nearby towns of Jennings and Eunice, both located about eighteen miles from the tribal community. W. H. Tupper opened his General Merchandise Store in Jennings in 1910 and, when he later closed the business in 1949, the complete inventory remained on the shelves, undisturbed, effectively creating a time capsule of local history. Tupper's grandson, Joe Tupper Jr., donated the store's contents for the creation of the W. H. Tupper General Merchandise Museum, which still features a large collection of Coushatta baskets, including both split-cane and longleaf pine baskets.[76] Although the record books of individual sales did not survive, tribal members remember trading baskets at the store, and a few of the baskets in the Tupper collection still have the original price tags.[77]

Marie McGee Guillory, the daughter of the family who operated McGee's General Mercantile in Eunice, remembered tribal members trading baskets for food and cloth.

> The Indians came in by truck from Elton. . . . it was so crowded that some of the riders had to hang over the edges. The men stood together while the women chose what they wanted in the material department. . . . the women would not speak at all, [but] there was always one in the group that knew a little bit of English. He and Pawpaw dickered about the value of the merchandise and the value of the baskets they

> had brought to trade. Since they had no money, value had to be set [for everything. . . .] It was traditional to give the good customer a little lagniappe, something extra over and above what they had purchased. Pawpaw gave the Indians whatever they asked for—maybe some dinner plates, some extra cloth, or some cooking pots.[78]

Like the McGee family, other locals had stories to share about their interactions with the Coushattas. For example, Oscar Shuff, an Elton farmer with lands adjacent to the tribal community, had many encounters with the tribe during the early twentieth century. He was one of the earliest farmers living near the Bayou Blue community to get a tractor and recalled being asked to help clear land or provide rides to town. Later, he helped the tribe by pulling wagons—and later cars—out of the drainage ditches running throughout the community. He never asked for or accepted payment for these services but said that he always received gifts from the Indians, usually in the form of baskets. When Shuff passed away in 2007, his family donated the baskets he was gifted over several decades back to the tribe. His daughter recalled "It might have been the next day, or several days later, but [the Coushatta people he helped] always left a basket to say thank you."[79]

While many store owners offered what would have been considered fair value for the baskets, these transactions took place against the backdrop of southern racialized norms and attitudes. One Coushatta weaver remembered the racial tension she felt when trading baskets: "When we brought our baskets into some of the stores, you knew they didn't like or trust the Indians. You could feel it by the way they looked at us and treated us. But most of the storekeepers around here were pretty fair to us. . . . I thought the whites owned the world in those days, and that was why they had everything and we had to go to them if we wanted it."[80]

Like other towns across the region, Jim Crow defined the interactions between people. For many Indian communities in Louisiana, this meant having to contend with third-tiered school systems or complete prohibition from having access to education or local businesses altogether.[81] However, the way Indians experienced racial segregation was locally dictated, which made for a diverse set of experiences. While many Coushattas were subject to racial tensions firsthand, they didn't encounter the severity of prohibitions that other tribes may have. In fact, even before schools in Elton were forced to integrate, following a court ruling in 1965, the Coushattas had been permitted to attend white schools and occupy white public spaces.[82] There are a variety of arguments for why this was the case; however, the most likely one had to do with the tribe's careful self-identification and maintenance of its racially distinct status as full-blooded Indians. This claim distanced the Coushattas from their African American neighbors, as well as other Indian groups with documented histories of intermarriage, which proved to be a distinction that trumped the fact that the Coushattas weren't white.[83] Baskets, among other cultural items, served to reinforce the Coushattas' Indigenous identity, which was leveraged by Elton leaders who capitalized on the nearby Indian settlement as a way of distinguishing their town from other neighboring towns.[84]

While Coushatta artisans divided their time between sewing river-cane and pine-needle baskets by the 1930s, within a decade these efforts shifted to focus almost exclusively on expanding the market for pine-needle baskets. Increasing difficulty in collecting river cane factored

Minnie Williams (*second from left*), on the porch of Ellisor and Burissa Battise's home, ca. 1930. This is the first photo of a tribal weaver sewing with pine needles. Courtesy of the Coushatta Tribal Archives.

into this shift, as most of the areas where cane was collected had been destroyed as land was cleared for cattle grazing or logging.[85] However, a rising public appreciation for the ornamental beauty of pine-needle baskets also enticed weavers to refocus their efforts. Weavers became so proficient at sewing pine-needle baskets that one woman described the skill as "what we always do when we need money."[86] By the 1970s, concern over the decline in cane-basket production prompted the tribe to reinvigorate the practice by hosting community workshops taught by weavers from the Mississippi Choctaw community where cane weaving was still prevalent. These workshops were well attended and did, indeed, encourage Coushatta weavers to once again try their hands at cane basketry. The workshops also revealed how the "Coushatta way" of weaving with river cane had not been lost as the weavers remembered how previous generations had taught them distinct ways of finishing the corners, sides, and rims of cane baskets. Workshop participants recalled politely watching and practicing the weaving techniques taught by their Mississippi Choctaw guests, only to later take out and remake the basket rims because "they just looked and felt too Choctaw, not like Coushatta baskets."[87]

Cane baskets had never been entirely replaced by pine-needle baskets although most contemporary Coushatta artisans work primarily with pine needles. By 1980, there were only a few weavers who still wove split-cane baskets.[88] Today, most of the cane baskets woven in the Coushatta community are produced by Leonard Battise and tribal members who were students in the cane-basketry classes that he began holding in 2012. In his effort to remember the distinctive Coushatta weaving techniques and motifs that he learned from his father, Solomon Battise, Leonard outlined a long process of trial and error in collecting, splitting, storing, and weaving the cane—as he put it, "trying to remember what my dad used to do." Cane baskets have always held a prominent place in the Coushattas' cultural identity, and Battise's efforts to reawaken the art form demonstrate the great importance the tribe places on maintaining the link between contemporary and traditional practices.[89]

Ency Robinson Abbey Abbott, Myrna Abbey, and Bel Abbey. Bel and Myrna are holding cane baskets to be used in the sifting process once Ency finishes pounding the corn. Courtesy of Marjorie Abbey Battise, Coushatta Tribal Archives.

2

Ithani Asaala Taathatilkaak Sfaiyalok, Choiyi Hissi Asaala Achoohilitǫ

Transitioning to Pine-Needle Baskets

When I was growing up, a lot of people were doing baskets just to help them with their income. . . . I started that way too, because when I was growing up I didn't have any money. . . . if I would sell baskets, that was my spending money.

—Adrian Poncho Sylestine

LIFE ALONG BAYOU BLUE WAS tough in the early twentieth century.[1] The wages that Coushatta men and women earned as seasonal laborers on farms or in the timber industry rarely covered the needs of families. While the community worked together to share food and resources, this did little to mitigate poverty and lack of health care. By the 1930s, as the rest of the country also succumbed to the grip of an economic depression, the tribe's situation finally received attention. The Coushattas became the subject of multiple government reports that, although the preparers didn't agree on the level of assistance the federal government should extend, nonetheless documented the tribe's living conditions as "desperately poor" and "pitiable."[2] Tribal leaders who sought federal assistance to purchase farming equipment in 1938 remembered their own situation: "We were born and raised here, have our own little school, church, and cemetery, but times are so hard, and jobs are so scarce, that we can hardly live."[3] By the end of the decade, funding was finally released to the tribe for educational purposes, followed by a small budget for health care. However, it had become increasingly apparent that the Coushatta people had to find additional means of supplementing their incomes. Doing as they had always done during difficult times, they looked to their traditional knowledge and practices to sustain them. Over the course of the next several decades, the highly prized and functional Coushatta baskets transitioned from being part of a local bartering system to the focal point of an emerging cash market.

Jeff Abbey seated on his front porch, next to some cane baskets. Courtesy of the Coushatta Tribal Archives.

Tribal artisans adapted to the local environment and economy as they shifted from the making of river-cane baskets to the sewing of longleaf pine-needle baskets. Not only were the materials plentiful in the woods around Bayou Blue, but pine-needle baskets were faster, easier, and less dangerous to make.[4] Joyce Abbey Poncho recalled hearing her great-grandmother depict this transition from the weavers' perspective:

> The white people started to pay for baskets and other items with money instead of just trading. They paid a very small price for the baskets. Back then there were just cane baskets, no pine-needle baskets or grass—just cane. They had moss blankets and animal hides too. The Indians wanted to keep on trading, but the white people wanted to pay them, and . . . began paying very little for these products and felt no sympathy for the Indians. And so, it went until the Indians started naming their own prices. . . . Nowadays the moss is scarce, cane is scarce, grass is scarce, so they went to pine needles. That's how we still continue to do what we've done in the past—it's still the Indians' weapon against poverty.[5]

Lifelong Elton resident Wallace Stroud reaffirmed this point, recalling how "everybody made baskets [then]" because it was how they survived.[6] Zeline Langley Sylestine also remembered her mother, Maggie John Langley, making the transition from river-cane to pine-needle baskets along with other basket makers.[7]

There is some dispute over the influencing factors behind why Coushatta basket makers began adopting different materials and styles. Many tribal artisans attribute this shift to the encouragement offered by the religious leaders within the community, including Reverend Paul Leeds and the first Coushatta deacon and preacher, Mark Robinson, who actively looked for ways to bring additional revenue to the community. They hosted home demonstration agents who were employed by a New Deal program in the 1930s who, some claim, introduced tribal weavers to new styles and commercially dyed raffia. Claude Medford Jr. disputed this claim, however, saying that Coushatta elders remembered how they initially decided to adopt raffia after having seen it used to tie bundles of onion sets.[8] In addition to bringing the demonstration agents to the community, Leeds and Robinson circulated photographs and baskets they acquired from other tribes among Coushatta weavers, asking if they could reproduce them. Barbara Williams Langley recalled Lizzie Poncho Robinson talking about a basket from "somewhere up north" brought to her by Reverend Leeds, who asked her to make one like it. Bertney Langley, who became the director of the tribal Cultural Center in 1975, also

Lizzie Poncho Robinson starting a river-cane basket. Photographs by Robert Yellin, courtesy of the Ralph Rinzler Folklife Archives and Collections, Smithsonian Institution.

remembered hearing this story.[9] Although it is hard to imagine the level of skill and creativity required to adapt to new techniques and materials to create these baskets, tribal weavers remembered several such occurrences. For example, Leona Williams Francis recalled her mother making effigy baskets by looking at pictures of animals she had never seen, such as camels and elephants.[10] Using similar visualization skills, Margaret Williams John made a basket with Indians standing on each side of a beehive oven after seeing that scene in a picture.[11] It was a new era for basket making in which the demand for utilitarian baskets was outpaced by the popularity of woven sculptures made of pine needles that collectors were satisfied to place on a shelf to admire. Coushatta weavers embraced the challenge brought on by such shifts—working together every step of the way.

Kindah Taththa Choiyi Hissi Wihhilit

The Other Side of Kinder: Gathering and Processing the Materials for Longleaf Pine-Needle Baskets

The longleaf pine trees may have been plentiful around the Bayou Blue settlement, but weavers chose their gathering spots very carefully because the quality of the needles is paramount. As Loris Abbott Langley explained, "people think you can just pull any needle off and use them all but that's not how it works. . . . Some of the needle[s], like those where bugs have gotten into them, are not long enough. Some needles are just too short."[12] A significant part of gathering pine needles is showing respect and gratitude. Jeanette Celestine Langley remembered being taught the significance of starting the gathering process with a prayer: "When you find a stand of pine needles, my mama, she would stop in front of the pine needles where the stand was, and she would pray and thank the Lord for the trees, and then she would thank the tree for the leaves before she'd break the leaves off of the tree. Everything they did, I remember they would start with a prayer."[13]

The pine needles are plucked from the trees while still green, an arduous job that employs several techniques. The freshest, prime needles are often found at the top of trees, which necessitates either climbing the tree or bending it over to collect the needles. Weavers recall hearing that a long time ago when the Coushattas picked the pine needles, the white landowners couldn't figure out why the pine needles were disappearing from their trees and thought maybe it was due to a bug infestation.[14] Many weavers also relayed humorous adventures and mishaps experienced while gathering needles, either by themselves or their children or grandchildren brought along to assist in the gathering process. Barbara Williams Langley recalled that she was often out playing rather than sewing baskets, which caused her siblings to joke that they didn't know how she was going to eat since she preferred to play rather than make baskets to sell. Despite this, however, she was still brought to assist on pine-needle gathering trips. Younger children were especially skillful at climbing and bending trees down when the elders couldn't reach the needles.[15] Edith Sylestine Langley related one particularly memorable experience she had while gathering pine needles:

> I remember I would bring my Aunt Madeline, Aunt Lycia, my Aunt Rena and my mom, they would all get together and plan the night before. I would drive them to wherever they wanted to go look, ride around and look for the longleaf pine needle. And we'd leave like about 6:00 or 6:30 in the morning, and they would pack a lunch for us to eat. It was mostly like biscuit, bacon and egg sandwiches. After we'd find the longleaf pine needles, wherever they were, we'd go out and pick them. I would climb the little small pine trees that were bendable, that would bend, I would climb up there and jump down from it and it would bend and they would start picking it. . . . And one time, I was up there and I got up there on the limb and I was gonna hang on and it was gonna bend. And it broke, and I fell to the ground [but] they didn't worry about me. They started picking the pine needles. The whole half of the pine tree broke and fell and they started picking the pine needles and they didn't ask me how I was doing or nothing.[16]

Humorous incidents like the one depicted here were likely frequent happenings and serve to highlight the necessity of gathering in groups.

As logging practices increased and more of the forest area around Bayou Blue was cleared for farming, prime gathering areas became even harder to find and weavers had to venture deeper into the woods. Susie Sylestine Bond recalled this challenge as longleaf pine trees became scarcer in the area, stating how sometimes their travels took them nearly into Texas.[17] While Coushattas traditionally value openness and sharing within the tribal community, weavers eventually found themselves compelled to guard their favorite gathering locations. Jeanette Celestine Langley explained,

> When you went to pick the pine needles, or the grass, you didn't tell anybody where you got it. . . . I learned how to do that [after] I told somebody one time. I had went and looked, and I found a stand, and I told somebody, and they went and picked it before I got there, so I learned my lesson, and somebody told me, "You don't tell them where you find them cause they'll pick them before you do," so I learned that. They told me to say, if somebody asks you [where you found pine needles], just tell them, on the other side of Kinder, so that's what I used to tell them all the time.[18]

Edith Sylestine Langley shared how some weavers confronted the challenge of finding good gathering spots by negotiating for permission to gather on the private property of their non-Indian neighbors, or even sometimes covertly gathering needles without permission. Langley recalled,

> Sometimes, when we first started out, [good gathering spots] would be right along the road, right close to the ditch. Whenever they would hear a car coming, [someone would] say "hide, hide." So, we'd hide in the grass and when the car passed, [then] we'd get up and start picking again. And then later, my mom found this place where they had acres of long-leaf pine needles and she went and talked to the man that owned the land. He gave her a permission slip for every year [so] that she can go pick the pine needles. So, from then on, we started going over there to that man's land and she would have her [permission] letter with her that we could pick over there.[19]

These arrangements were not uncommon due to the friendships that the tribe developed among many of its neighbors. Ernest Sickey recalled approaching an heir of the Bel Estate, which was connected to a family of companies that owned much of the land around the tribal homesteads in support of interests in the timber and oil industries, to allow tribal members to gather pine needles on company lands. According to Sickey, the basket weavers were relieved to secure permission to gather pine needles without permits or escorts on Bel Estate land.[20]

Edith Sylestine Langley picking pine needles, 2008. Photo by Sarah Sawyer, courtesy of the Coushatta Tribal Archives.

Just as with the gathering of cane, the collecting of pine needles is a community effort. Gathering trips serve a social function as groups pack food and spend the day visiting and teaching the children how to identify the prime pickings. Although weavers typically gather their own needles to ensure they have the materials they need to sew their baskets, it also is common for them to sell high-quality pine needles to other weavers for use. Leona Williams Francis recalled that her mother frequently bought pine needles from another tribal member, Edward Sylestine, who gathered enough for his family's needs and sold surplus needles to others.[21] Marion Robinson John remembered her delight at being gifted a large box of pine needles. She looked so excited that her daughter-in-law joked about it later, saying the box of needles was worth more to her than a million dollars.[22]

After the pine needles are gathered, they are ready to be sorted, bundled, and dried. This is a process that must be done carefully to ensure that the materials remain pliable. Jeanette Celestine Langley detailed the process, sharing: "After we picked like a box full . . . we would bring them home and we would clean them. Sometimes there's some that are already browned, and some had spots in it. We'd throw all that away and just keep the good ones. . . . You'd get a bundle [of] all green, and . . . then we'd tie them up like this and hang them in the attic and let them dry. It takes about three months for them to dry real good."[23] Weavers designate certain areas in or around their homes for drying and storing needles, opting for cool, dark places like the eaves of their houses or in attics. Too much sunlight would dry them too quickly and cause them to become brittle, rendering them useless. As a result, basket makers check on the bundled needles periodically through the drying process, turning them carefully so they will dry evenly.[24]

Aatoiyak Ittimathaakin Asaala Stamakkahchok
The Language of Weaving: Everyone Starts a Basket Differently

In Koasati, the word *asaala* is used for both cane and pine-needle baskets, but different words are used for the process of making the different types of baskets. River-cane baskets are woven (*tathat*), while pine-needle baskets are sewn (*achoolit*). The Koasati word for "sewing" (that is, coiling) baskets is the same word used for sewing cloth, and both processes use the same type of needle (*chofa*).[25] Jeanette Celestine Langley explained that, when sewing a basket, the size of the needle used can affect the stitch size, and thus the tightness of the stitch. She speculated on the impact of store-bought needles available to modern-day artisans: "We use needles today, the larger needles. Somebody was telling me that a long time ago they'd use a fish or animal bone, and put a hole in [it for] the eye."[26] In addition , the Koasati word for raffia is *stachooka,* which translates to "something to sew or make baskets with."[27] Some of the older weavers remember hearing about plant-based dyes and weaving materials used before commercial raffia and dyes were available. They recall a time when materials were boiled with black-walnut shells to turn black or when berries were used to make red dye. Ellisa "Liz" John told of gathering plum-tree leaves to boil with cane or raffia to get a green color. She also remembered gathering a leafy plant with small red flowers that looked like tomatoes, which was also used as a red dye, but she never knew the English name of the plant.[28] Virtually all Coushatta cane and pine-needle basket makers now use commercial dyes and store-bought raffia, though a few of the older weavers still sometimes use embroidery thread to decorate their baskets.

Coushatta weavers typically start their baskets at the center and coil outward, though each artisan has a distinctive way of coiling or starting a basket center. Although other tribes sometimes use a flat piece of bark or wood as the basket center, Coushatta weavers bend the pine needles and completely wrap them with raffia to form the center.[29] In Koasati, the term for a basket's center is a *follin,* which literally means "curved" or "bent," referring to the manner in which pine needles are curled before being wrapped in raffia.[30] Marion Robinson John explained that "Everybody starts their basket differently. I take a few [pine needles], just a few to start. I wrap [with raffia] in the middle, then I fold it. Then I wrap it [again] so it will be neat. A long time ago, they never used to do it this way."[31] Young people frequently report that it is difficult to learn how to coil pine needles and stitch them tightly without letting them break or unravel, and that it takes a lot of practice to keep the stitching tight and even. Starting the basket center is the most difficult part to learn, so when the tribe holds basketry workshops and classes, teachers often help new learners by making the centers for them. Learners also are taught that it is much easier to start a basket in wet weather because the needles are more flexible, and the raffia won't unravel or break as easily. While Coushatta lands experience a subtropical climate, with frequent heavy rainfall and flooding, there are occasional dry periods that weavers must adjust for. For example, Adrian Poncho Sylestine remembered her mother, Ruth Poncho, telling her to wrap her pine needles in a damp towel overnight to keep them from getting brittle during dry spells.[32]

There are three major types of Coushatta pine-needle stitches: plain, wheat, and chain.[33] A fourth type, the closed stitch, is used when the raffia is completely covering or overlapping the pine needles, so that there is no space between the stitches. The closed stitch is much more time-consuming, so it takes weavers longer to finish these types of baskets. For example, at the time of this publication, Heather Williams is the only tribal weaver currently making closed-stitch baskets adorned with the tribal seal, and she makes only one of these baskets per year.[34] Tribal weavers like to compare their stitching techniques and baskets, and they frequently note distinctive styles and techniques, which are sometimes so pronounced that they are able to instantly identify the individual weavers whose baskets are held in museum collections. These distinctions may be in the way a stitch is made, the shape of the basket, or even right- versus left-handed stitching.[35]

The Coushatta plain stitch involves a single stitch of raffia, spread

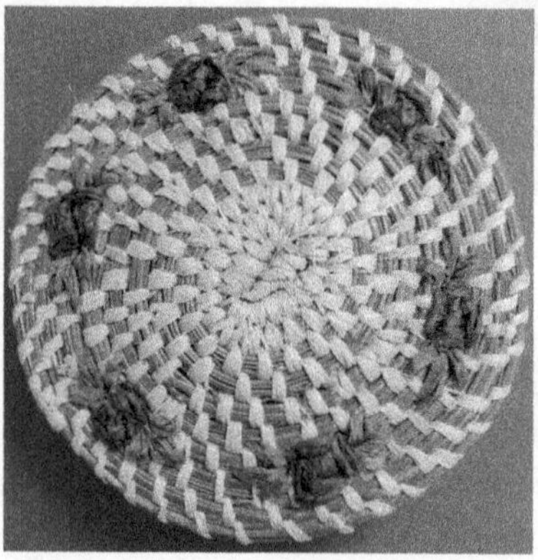

Close-up of a plain-stitch basket lid, *left,* and center of a chain-stitch basket. Photos by Marianna Luquette, courtesy of the Coushatta Tribal Archives.

out at increasing distances as the basket is built up. Some weavers make their stitches at irregular intervals, and others strategically place stitches to make a design.[36] Older weavers recalled that the earliest pine-needle baskets were made with plain stitches, and that the wheat stitch came into the community sometime in the 1960s. Marion Robinson John recalled: "Back then they used to sew only the round baskets with covers. . . . they didn't sew wheat stitch, only regular stitch."[37] The wheat stitch is made when each stitch splits part of the stitch in the row before it, making the distinctive W shape that is the mark of the wheat pattern. Finally, the chain stitch is when the raffia is pulled through the middle of the last stitch in the corresponding row to form a continuously connected chain of stitches. While each stitch is generally referenced by these names, weavers sometimes have different names for their stitches. For example, Lorenda John Poncho said she learned a "double stitch" from her grandmother, while Marion Robinson John referred to a "lazy squaw" stitch in her interview.[38]

Rena Robinson LeJeune sewing a plain-stitch basket with innovative handles inside her home, ca. 1950. She did not have electricity or running water since these utilities were not yet available in the tribal community. Courtesy of the Coushatta Tribal Archives.

Regardless of the type of stitch used, experienced Coushatta weavers are known for maintaining tightly coiled pine needles and consistent stitching patterns with even spacing. Weavers set their own high standards for well-made baskets, expecting finished pieces that are seamless, exhibiting no visible breaks in the pine needles or raffia, and no signs of loose or unraveled materials. The lids should fit into the basket so tightly and securely that they are difficult to remove. Respected weavers always take the time to be sure their baskets are finished properly and that no loose threads or frayed ends of raffia are visible. Susie Sylestine Bond remembered her mother's instruction to finish her baskets by rubbing them with a cloth and then holding them near a fire to burn off stray raffia ends. Later, she continued this practice by using the burners on her gas stove.[39]

While certain basket types are more common than others, tribal weavers enjoy innovating in their designs and use of materials. Some choose to use contrasting colors of raffia, pinecones, or other decorations to enhance the beauty and overall appearance of their finished baskets. These decorations are held to the same rigorous standards as the baskets themselves. The knobs that are found on many covered baskets today were also a recent innovation, with weavers remembering how the earliest covered baskets either had curved lids or were topped with small handles made of raffia or embroidery thread.[40] The high standards applied to finished baskets also apply to the knobs, which are expected to be perfectly rounded. When a basket doesn't meet all of these criteria, it may either be left unfinished or given away to a family member rather than sold.[41] In those rare cases when someone's basket was so terrible that it had to be restarted, raffia would be cut and stitches taken out. However, taking stitching out had to be done very carefully, since raffia was almost as valuable as the pine needles themselves. Marion Robinson John recalled just how valued it was when she first learned to sew baskets in the early 1940s, when she was about six years old, stating how "The raffia and pine needles, they used to really cherish it."[42] The Coushatta Tribal Archives have only three partially started baskets: one made to demonstrate the coiling process, one small hat ornament that was never completed, and a goblet made by Marion Robinson John with dyed pine needles and raffia left with its natural color.[43]

There is an expected level of precision involved in making baskets.

Marjorie Abbey Battise recalls learning to measure a completed basket from her mother: "She showed me how to measure it by putting a ruler across the flat part of the bottom. She'd lay it right down like this and say 'this is how big it is.' That's how I still do it."[44] Similarly, Raynella Thompson Fontenot explained that she was taught to recognize the correct order of things in everything related to making baskets, from lining up pine needles in boxes, to not rushing her stitches, and finally to measuring the finished baskets.[45] Being methodical about the basket-making process not only helps maintain the quality of the baskets made within the Coushatta community, but it ensures consistency in how young weavers are instructed in the craft.

Chokkoolit Hiichat Chaponnaak
We Learned by Watching: Traditional Koasati Ways of Teaching

Coushatta basket makers have a signature approach to teaching their techniques.[46] Gathering materials, making baskets, and then selling their work are always framed as a communal and intergenerational process. Children help parents and grandparents pick pine needles and then sort, dry, and store them. Aspiring weavers then learn to make baskets by watching their elders. Early newspaper accounts and photographs of Coushattas sewing or selling baskets typically depict at least two generations of participants. In addition, esteemed basket makers who held exhibitions or agreed to interviews often did so with children and grandchildren playing nearby. For example, one interviewer described grandchildren playing around the feet of Loris Abbey Langley during a basketry demonstration and interview.[47]

Coushatta cultural values emphasize the importance of community, the free sharing of knowledge and skills, and an emphasis on learning through observation. For most Coushatta weavers, these values are expressed during frequent communal sewing gatherings where they learn techniques by observing their elders. Loris Abbey Langley related how weavers do their best work when gathered together: "We used to sit and talk when we made baskets together. We would learn new designs from watching each other; sometimes trying to copy somebody else and sometimes thinking 'I can do that better.'"[48] Edith Sylestine Langley shared what it was like growing up with big family gatherings of basket makers: "I remember when I was little, my mom and all my aunts would gather under a big old oak tree in back of my house. And they would all get together and sit there and sew all day long." She and other weavers recalled that each basket maker would keep a "basket box" with all of their essential materials and supplies.[49] "So when we got older and learned to sew, we used to go to each other's houses at night, get together and sew, eat together and sew. . . . There was always sewing [going on] somewhere."[50]

All the Coushatta weavers interviewed recalled these intergenerational gatherings, and most remembered their earliest efforts to make baskets with the discarded pine needles of the older weavers. Rosabel Robinson Sylestine shared how she used to play with the materials: "I would constantly be by my mother's side when she was doing baskets, and I began to learn the art by beginning to feel the working of the straw."[51] Marion Robinson John had a similar start, stating, "my mom would sit and sew and I would do the same. When I turned seven, I was a little better at sewing. I only watched, she didn't teach, she didn't show me. Only by watching, I sewed."[52] Leona Williams Francis also recalled, "I saw my momma making baskets and then I watched her doing it and I started. I tried and tried, and I learned it."[53] Darlene Langley Dunnehoo remembered how, although she also learned through observation, her mother offered some guidance when she struggled with her technique: "When I used to see my mom sew, I used to try to sew. When I first started, I'd sew real pointed and couldn't make it round. 'Hold your needle this way and turn the way you want your basket to turn,' my mom would tell me over and over again. I was frustrated but I wouldn't quit. I never quit practicing."[54]

While many Coushatta children learned to make baskets, Barbara Williams Langley remembered that she never felt pressured to do so, although she was sometimes teased for not joining in. Likewise, beginning basket makers were not pressured to sew perfect stitches. In keeping with tribal cultural values, the elders encouraged their children and grandchildren rather than chastise them, saying, "they will come to learn when they are interested." Lorenda John Poncho recalled how she was supported in her effort to learn when her grandfather bought her first basket for twenty-five cents and placed it on the windowsill, a prominent place in the house. Wishing to replicate the experience, she retrieved the basket and later sold it to him a second time. However, there were limits to her grandfather's encouragement because, when Poncho tried to sell it to him a third time, he was unwilling to carry on the game, telling her: "This basket, I don't know how many times I bought it." As was likely her grandfather's hope, this experience motivated her to start sewing more baskets.[55]

Coushatta cultural traditions promote an egalitarian division of labor.[56] In fact, there is no concept of basket weaving being either "men's work" or "women's work," and Koasati does not contain gender markers (for example, verb endings) to identify the gender of a person who performs certain actions—there is no way to even express this concept in the tribal language.[57] So, Coushatta men are just as likely to weave or sew baskets as women. Yet, because of the lack of available jobs for tribal women in the early twentieth century, more of them turned to making baskets as a way to supplement their family incomes. Adrian Poncho Sylestine, Susie Sylestine Bond, and Edith Sylestine Langley all recalled examples of male weavers, sharing how many participated in sewing gatherings and also sold baskets to earn money. Susie Sylestine Bond taught both of her sons to weave at young ages, and Edith Sylestine Langley recalled her son-in-law sewing baskets with her mother, Rosabel Robinson Sylestine.[58] Adrian Poncho Sylestine shared how both her father and her son learned to make baskets: "When my dad got older and retired, he would sit around having nothing to do, so my mom taught him . . . and he started making baskets too. He made pretty good baskets. . . . my mother-in-law taught my son, Chris, because he was interested. We were all sitting around making baskets one night, and I guess he got bored watching us, and he wanted to take part in it, so my mother-in-law started him on it and taught him how to do [it] step by step." He ended up making several baskets and sold them to earn money for Christmas presents. He was "proud that he did something to earn his own money."[59]

Tribal weavers recounted learning to sew a progression of basket shapes and styles, beginning with simple shapes and graduating to more complicated ones. Jeanette Celestine Langley recalled her grandmother first showing her how to "make a little bowl, and then after that, if you learned how to go up, then she'd teach you how to make the wall basket because it doesn't have a cover. The cover is kind of difficult to do for a seven year old, so we did a lot of bowl baskets."[60] Marion Robinson John remembered first learning to sew a basic trivet or hot pad, then a wall basket, which had sides but still was uncovered.[61] Weavers started by learning to make simple baskets sewn with a plain stitch, and without decorations, such as flowers, pine petals, pine cones, or knobs. From there, they progressed to larger baskets with increasingly ornate designs and decorations.

Seasoned weavers develop their own distinctive techniques. However, they are often influenced by basket makers of previous generations whose skill and creativity are still highly valued and admired after several decades. Basket makers talk about notable basket shapes (for example, covered baskets, open trays, vases, wall or hanging baskets), animal effigy basket designs, and memorable decorative elements. While seeking to emulate the artistry of previous weavers, modern artisans try to refine their own unique styles, looking for opportunities to innovate.[62] Jeanette Celestine Langley recalled how it had always been that way and how "everybody had their own different stitches. . . . their stitches were all different and you could tell who it [the basket] belongs to by looking at the different stitches." She also explained how each weaver had a distinctive way of making the knobs for a covered basket. "Some people make it thick and other people make it thin."[63]

Coushatta basket makers are held in such high regard in the community that Susie Sylestine Bond was honored to have been named after respected weaver Susie Williams. Bond went on to make a name for herself because, even though she was known to mainly sew vase designs, she is considered the first in her generation to make a fully covered knob.[64] Outside the tribe, Coushatta artisans are best known for their coiled animal effigy baskets, which are unique among contemporary tribes and prized by collectors. A book of animal effigy baskets reflecting the collection held by the tribe has photographs of baskets representing twenty-six different animals made by fifteen different weavers.[65]

Komistilkak Immathakkito
Selling Baskets in a Changing Economy[66]

The time and effort that Coushatta basket makers put into incorporating new materials, developing new styles, refining their techniques, and teaching the next generation played a major role in economically sustaining the tribe. By the 1930s, Coushatta baskets had already begun the transition from being commodities in a bartering system to holding value within a local economy—one that was increasingly influenced by the national Indian Arts and Crafts Movement with roots in the Victorian era. The "basket craze" that was born from this movement—where it became fashionable for predominantly white middle- and upper-class collectors to acquire Indian baskets among other items identified as "curios"—impacted the Coushattas later than tribes in other parts of the country.[67] They benefited from this expanding market later than others because Coushatta weavers didn't have wealthy white sponsors or brokers to broaden the circulation of their baskets early on. Instead, they had to rely on local interest and opportunities to display their baskets for sale anywhere they could, including roadsides and at festivals.

The leadership of the Coushatta Indian Church introduced the baskets to a broader audience, helping weavers gain a wider market for their work. However, the Indian school—through its many transitions under the direction of Allen Parish, the federal Bureau of Indian Affairs, and then the Congregational Church as a charity school—also supported the effort as tribal girls were encouraged to learn "domestic arts," such as cooking, canning, and sewing. The handcrafts and garments made by Coushatta girls were a point of pride shared in a 1938 newspaper reporting on the establishment of a 4-H Club at the Indian School.[68] By 1950, teachers began doing more than just encouraging the development of Coushatta girls' domestic skills when they also actively organized and advertised basket shows held at the school. Teachers even created information cards to attach to the baskets so that whoever purchased them might learn a bit about the Coushatta people.[69] In 1952, a husband and wife were jointly employed to teach at the Indian school, with the wife expected to "work with the Indian women of the community in a general home improvement and basket weaving program."[70] The Home Demonstration Club, which was founded as a result, continued in this vein over the next several decades, with numerous photos of tribal women dressed in their Sunday best demonstrating weaving. The photos also captured the wives of non-tribal community leaders dressed in their finery buying baskets.[71] These efforts later expanded to incorporate gatherings to sew quilts.

While baskets played an important role in sustaining the tribe since initially settling around Bayou Blue, the dire economic situation of the post–World War II era increased the necessity for Coushatta families to supplement their incomes. The Coushatta people had slipped deeper into poverty during a time when much of the rest of the country enjoyed the benefits of a healthy postwar economy. They suffered high unemployment rates with little promise of relief. And, to make matters worse, the tribe was unilaterally terminated from federal Indian services in 1953, losing federal funding for health care and education—causing the Indian school to be abandoned for almost a decade before reopening as a charity-run school. The 1950s were particularly difficult years in the tribe's history, resulting in many Coushatta artisans intensely focusing their efforts on basket sales. However, market prices for baskets were still extremely low; some tribal weavers had to work at jobs outside the community during the week and make baskets late at night and on weekends.[72] Others, like Marion Robinson John, relied almost exclusively on income generated from baskets. She recalled having to leave school at the age of eleven following her mother's death, so she could raise her younger siblings. She sewed as many baskets as she could to trade for food items and continued to do so even after she got a job in Elton when she was fifteen.[73]

Fortunately for tribal weavers, the postwar years proved opportune for marketing their work. Although there had been a consistent interest in Indian arts and crafts since the late nineteenth century, by mid-century the Indian tourism market boomed across the country. In the Southeast, the Seminoles and Miccosukees of Florida, as well as the Cherokees of North Carolina, blazed the trail in establishing a foothold in the tourism industry with a number of enterprises aimed at attracting travelers through staged experiences and an assortment of crafts for purchase—all of which strategically met market demands based on popularized depictions of American Indians. The Coushattas also looked for opportunities to leverage this surge in interest; however, this proved challenging given their geographic isolation and political marginalization. Attempting to counter this, Coushattas often traveled to special events around the region. For example, Bel Abbey brought his wife and daughter to sell baskets at the Crowley Rice Festival in 1950. They also brought Jeff Abbey, who served as the tribe's traditional

Ruth Williams Poncho and daughter Adrian selling baskets, ca. 1965. Courtesy of the Coushatta Tribal Archives.

leader from 1938 to 1951, then almost ninety years old. A news article on the event noted that "the representatives speak only Indian and are expected to display cherished Indian relics along with hand woven baskets the tribe makes for sale. All will be garbed in their native costumes."[74] To increase marketing success, they also looked for local allies to assist in their efforts, such as a Boy Scout troop from Lake Charles that was led by Scoutmaster Tim Dugas. Abbey and Dugas discussed opportunities to work together, with Dugas even recruiting Coushatta boys to participate in a scouting event to make it appear more authentic.[75]

While Abbey initiated the forging of friendships with those who helped promote and support the tribe, his son, Martin Abbey, elected chief upon his father's death in 1951, continued these efforts. To do this, he embraced popularized depictions of Indians in the way he publicly presented himself. This drew attention, allowing him to build networks of friends for the tribe within the local political power structure. He dressed in Hollywood-styled costumes, marched in parades, and bestowed the honorary title of "assistant chief and advisor" to Elton Mayor C. L. Marcantel as a way of securing alliances and increasing media exposure.[76] While these actions might not have seen immediate results in addressing the Coushattas' legal status, it did help raise their profile and, as a result, presented new opportunities to market baskets.

One such opportunity came soon after Martin Abbey's election, when Dugas invited him to an event where the Boy Scouts presented the chief with a feathered headdress as a gesture of friendship. As part of the invitation, the troop also welcomed tribal artisans to sell their work on the courthouse lawn.[77] The proximity of the tribe to the troop proved ideal for an organization that had an identity shift from a militaristic persona early in the century to one that reinvented itself on the basis of romanticized Indigenous ways of life and lore.[78] Under the continued direction of Dugas, the Boy Scouts involved the Coushattas in a series of events that ranged from Indian princess contests to staged "tribal" dances and reenactments.[79] Bel Abbey helped expand the opportunities for the tribe even further by bringing tribal boys to promote rodeos and parades, and helping stage mock battles to engage audiences. Bertney Langley recalled a pretend battle staged with his cousin, Lovelin Poncho, where he pretended to die and children in the audience began to cry. Afterwards, in order to prevent the same response, the boys were instructed to show the audience they were still alive.[80] As much as Dugas was motivated to provide his troop with experiences that were fueled by fantasies and stereotypes, he exhibited a genuine concern for the welfare of the tribe and went to great lengths to assist them by sending letters to the Bureau of Indian Affairs advocating for the tribe's assistance.[81] He also helped raise the public's awareness about the Coushattas and even organized several arts-and-crafts sales over the years.[82]

In the early 1950s, tribal weavers joined others' efforts in generating attention for the tribe when they began allowing themselves to be photographed making baskets. In 1951, Lizzie Poncho Robinson and Rosabel Robinson Sylestine consented to being photographed for an article in *Rural Louisiana.* In one of these photographs Robinson wove a large cane basket, and Sylestine sewed pine-needle baskets. The caption reads: "Quasati women excel in the ancient tribal handicrafts. Lizzie Poncho Robinson is fashioning clothes baskets from strips, while pretty Mrs. Rosa bell [*sic*] Sylestine makes a sewing basket of pine needles for sale in nearby Elton."[83] A similar photo was taken of Ency Robinson Abbey Abbott making baskets for a state tourism publication, with a caption noting that she spoke "only the Koasati language as she weaves baskets and thinks of earlier days."[84] Permitting their images to be used in such a way, in spite of a reluctance to do so, was a strategic way of leveraging a growing public interest in American Indians. These efforts also expanded to the choices weavers made on the types of baskets they produced. For example, Marion Robinson John's mother found that hot pads, four-inch round baskets with lids, and wall baskets were popular among people in town, so that is what she focused her efforts on.[85] Adrian Poncho Sylestine remembered that her mother, Ruth Williams Poncho, often used to sew long, oval baskets that she called "bread baskets" because "the white people used to ask for that a lot."[86] As Coushatta baskets became increasingly stylized, they quickly found a prominent place among what was considered Louisiana folk art. In 1954, Ency Robinson Abbey Abbott made the news by winning four blue ribbons for her baskets in arts-and-crafts competitions emphasizing floral designs. The superior quality of her baskets was undeniable as they beat out the work of her non-Indian competitors.[87]

While basket shows may have earned Coushatta artisans some income, they also had a few local patrons who regularly purchased baskets. In the late 1950s, the Elton Businessmen's Club established a tourism program to boost the town's economic outlook by emphasizing their proximity to the tribe. The club invited guests to tour Elton and receive souvenirs of locally grown rice and Coushatta baskets.[88] In addition to supplying a steady stream of gifts for out-of-town guests, weavers sold to private individuals. Marjorie Abbey Battise described her mother selling baskets to a woman in Elton. "There used to be a white lady in town buying from her. . . . Her name was Mrs. Catholic. A small basket like this [two inches], she used to pay a small amount, maybe three cents. . . . The biggest one was maybe a dollar. Around that time, that seemed expensive. It was hard to make but was sold real cheap."[89] Ernest Sickey also remembered how local museum representatives visited tribal weavers at their homes to buy baskets, sometimes even encouraging the making of more by bringing raffia to replenish the weavers' supplies.[90]

The Acadian Handicraft Project also was a big supporter of Coushatta weavers. Primarily designed to promote and support French language and culture in Louisiana, the program was operated by Louisiana State University from 1942 to 1962. Louise Olivier served as the program's field representative, purchasing and marketing crafts from Acadian women throughout the state. Although the program was developed specifically to promote Acadiana crafts, Olivier strongly believed that it should support women representing all of Louisiana's cultures, including Indigenous ones.[91] As a result, the Acadian Handicraft Project played a major role in expanding the marketing opportunities for Coushatta weavers, like Rosabel Robinson Sylestine, and assisting in generating greater recognition and opportunities for other tribal weavers as well. Sylestine shared how she sold small baskets to the Acadian Handicraft Project in 1952 for about five cents each, and slightly bigger ones for "ten cents on up."[92] To continue meeting the demand, she had raffia shipped to her in bulk to ensure that she and other weavers had enough materials to work with. Her daughter explained, "she ordered it from New York. And it would come in and she would spread the word around the community, and they would go to my mom's house and buy the raffia from her. [From] whatever money she made from that, she'd reorder again. I don't know how she found the address, but she would order it from New York."[93]

With growing notoriety came increased attention, and it was no surprise that weavers were sought out by merchants from near and far who came to the Bayou Blue community to buy baskets for resale. Basket makers did not always know how buyers found out about them, nor how they got directions to their homes, but greater attention made for increased economic opportunity. In fact, some tribal people—themselves—also began purchasing baskets for resale as part of their own independent business ventures.[94] At the forefront of this initiative were

Bel and Nora Abbey and Edward and Della Sylestine, who served as intermediaries between weavers and outside buyers.

While the transition from bartering to cash sales helped basket makers bring additional income into their households, traditional cultural inhibitors against self-promotion made the process difficult. The biggest challenge was establishing prices. There is a widespread perception that there is a conflict between the traditional Coushatta cultural value of *ilaakasankohchi* (being modest) and aggressively participating in a market exchange to sell one's own baskets.[95] Marjorie Abbey Battise recalled the older weavers' struggles to get fair prices because they had a tendency to accept the prices offered rather than negotiate for higher ones: "[Buyers] would pick them [the baskets] randomly and buy them real cheap. They were hard to make but they bought it from them real cheap."[96] Many of the older weavers still sometimes demur from setting prices, even to sell to other tribal members, preferring that other people determine the prices for them.[97]

Asaala Schoolpon Hatchalichilkak
We Set Up Our Own Place to Sell Our Baskets: Creating a Tribal Enterprise

Through the mid-1960s, Coushatta basket sales were negotiated on a piecemeal basis. Tribal artisans looked for every opportunity to sell their work, providing a steady supply of baskets to regular buyers, who were either collectors or resold the baskets for a profit, and by traveling further from home to sell on the sides of roads, in towns, or at parades and festivals. Virtually no one had their own vehicle, so a continuous reliance on travel was burdensome and unsustainable. When someone set up a roadside sale, they often took baskets from multiple families to display for them, which meant that basket makers had to trust that they would receive fair prices for their work. These arrangements also promised a time lag in compensation. Eventually, the lack of a systematic process to market and sell baskets began to take its toll as more basket makers became discouraged, some altogether ceasing to continue despite an unimproved economic outlook.

By 1966, a collaboration between Solomon Battise, Ernest Sickey, and

Rosabel Robinson Sylestine changed the course of the tribe's arts-and-crafts market when they organized to open a tribally operated Trading Post. Battise, an ordained minister at the Indian Church, was well respected for his efforts to maintain the Koasati language by incorporating it into his sermons and Sunday School teachings. He also wove split-cane baskets and envisioned having a centralized meeting place near the Indian Church for tribal artisans to work, sell their arts and crafts, and teach the next generation.[98] More than a half-century later, Sickey and Solomon's son Leonard recalled Battise's admonition not to lose their cultural traditions, particularly basketry knowledge, so that they might survive as a people.[99] Sickey himself was a young emerging leader within the tribe who had only recently returned to the Bayou Blue community and got married after attending college in Houston and finishing a stint in the Air Force. With an education in broadcast communication and a penchant for writing and public speaking, Sickey was anxious to put his energy into marketing Coushatta baskets and, as a result, create a profitable market for them. Sylestine was a master basket maker whose work was greatly admired and sought-after. She also saw the value in creating a tribal enterprise within the community that would not only ease the burdens of travel, but provide an outlet for the entire tribe to sell their arts and crafts in an environment where they could all learn from one another. While Battise, Sickey, and Sylestine played a large role in getting the Trading Post off the ground, there were many others who also contributed to the plans to revive a practice that was beginning to wane. Sickey shared how many Coushatta people had begun to move away for jobs, and those who stayed found difficulty in collecting pine needles on increasingly inaccessible privately held lands. Plus, there was a notable decrease in venues for selling baskets by the mid-1960s, and artisans still were unable to get good prices for their work.[100]

The Coushatta Trading Post opened its doors on February 1, 1967, following months of hard work and a confluence of fortunate circumstances. During the initial stages of planning, concerns over the tribe's lack of legal standing after being "terminated" by the federal government prompted the Coushattas to ensure the success of their enterprise by organizing as a nonprofit 501(c)(3), a measure many other non-reservation and terminated tribes took to spur tribal development.[101]

Coushatta Trading Post, 1967. Solomon Battise, *in doorway;* Lycia Robinson John sewing a pine-needle basket, *left;* Adeline Battise weaving a river-cane basket, *right.* Courtesy of Ernest Sickey, Coushatta Tribal Archives.

Organizing under the name "The Coushatta (Koasati) Indians of Louisiana, Inc.," a governing board was established, naming Solomon Battise president and Ernest Sickey vice president. Rosabel Robinson Sylestine was named secretary and treasurer, and Deo Langley, Davis Sickey, Nora Williams Abbey, and her sister Ruth Williams Poncho were board members.[102] Soon afterward, the tribe successfully negotiated with the

Bel Estate to use a parcel of their land that was adjacent to the Indian Church within the central part of the community at no cost for ten years. With recent improvements to the road leading to the property, along with the donation of a building that was moved from the town of Basile, the tribe was able to quickly prepare for operation.[103] To demonstrate their support in what they, no doubt, saw as a turning point in the tribe's development, many of the Coushattas' neighbors attended the opening celebration for the Trading Post.[104] The Louisiana Tourist Commission also came forward with its endorsement of the enterprise, calling it the "first Indian trading post since the frontier days [run by] perhaps the last full-blooded tribe in this state."[105]

The Trading Post was a success. It attracted curious tourists from across the United States who purchased baskets as well as an assortment of other Coushatta-made jewelry, dolls, blowguns, wooden effigies, and quilts.[106] It also became a popular destination for school groups, Boy Scouts, and Camp Fire Girls whom tribal members met to carry out educational programming. Coushatta hosts took care to strike a balance between representing the Indians of popular culture and a genuine Coushatta experience shared through stories, basket demonstrations, and tribal historical accounts.[107] By selling postcards with images of Coushattas in Hollywood-like Indian costumes and headdresses, and even erecting a large tepee in front of the Trading Post, the tribe looked to satisfy the expectations of their visitors while simultaneously seizing the opportunity to share their unique story and foster an appreciation for their basketry and other artforms.[108] The Trading Post helped raise the profile of basket weavers and, by December 1968, the tribe was invited to display some of its weavers' finest pine-needle baskets at the Smithsonian Institution in Washington, DC.[109] In fact, the quality of baskets became so widely recognized that the Alabama-Coushatta Reservation gift shop in Texas placed regular orders at the Trading Post for resale—at one time even ordering a thousand small pine-needle baskets, an order that took twenty weavers three months to fill.[110]

The Trading Post also attracted several patrons and boosters from nearby towns who eagerly wished to see the enterprise a success. People like Eloise Fruge of Lake Charles publicly endorsed the Trading Post, widely encouraging people to purchase baskets.[111] One newspaper published how "the Indians are timid, but friendly," and then provided

Mona and Sheila Abbey in front of tepee outside of Trading Post, ca. 1968. Photo by Hosea Hebert, Coushatta Tribal Archives.

detailed instructions on how to get to the Trading Post. Local media outlets readily advertised the tribal enterprise, emphasizing the "local color" the Coushattas provided to the area. One anonymous letter to the *Daily World* encouraged others to venture out to the Trading Post and explained the unique role the tribe played in the area's social composition, stating how "it is very hard to get the straight story about the Indians because there is no written history of the Indians wandering in Louisiana. . . . What caused them to settle in Calcasieu Parish, later Allen Parish, is still a mystery. . . . So far as I know the Coushatta are the only Indians in Louisiana who still speak their native tongue. Many Louisianans will go out west to see some Indians when we have Indians right here in southwest Louisiana."[112]

Other allies to the tribe extended their support beyond encouraging others to visit the Trading Post. Hosea Hebert provided the funds necessary to purchase the initial inventory of baskets to stock the shelves and get the tribal enterprise started since the decision was made not to use a consignment system. He also assisted the tribe in acquiring the building that became the Trading Post and helped develop the nonprofit charter.[113] While Hebert had a history of supporting Coushatta basketry, his primary interest was in seeing "their language written and preserved," as he wrote in the *Basile Weekly* in 1968. The Trading Post, he reasoned, served as a tribal gathering point that would not only help elevate their economic status, but encourage language retention.[114] In addition, Hebert and others encouraged the weavers to continue showing their work at festivals and craft shows around the state, which helped advertise the Trading Post.

Sickey recalled how Hosea Hebert helped expand the Trading Post's marketing efforts outside the region. With his assistance, Sickey and his wife, Ena Mae, received funding in 1969 from the American Rice

Madeline Robinson Celestine, *right,* and daughter Dianna visit with the mayor of Ruston at the annual Peach Festival, 1968. Courtesy of Ernest Sickey, Coushatta Tribal Archives.

Ena Mae Sickey in front of Coushatta basketry exhibit, Smithsonian Institution, June 1969. Courtesy of Ernest Sickey, Coushatta Tribal Archives.

Growers Association to travel to the Smithsonian Institution to participate in the Cooperative Crafts Exhibition. While there, Ena Mae demonstrated pine-needle basketry while Ernest worked to "find markets and to help preserve the tribal heritage of quality crafts."[115] Sickey remembered Hebert's support in advertising the trip, going so far as to have Indian outfits made for the Sickeys and bringing a traditional corn *kihcho* and *kistapi* (log and pounder) to stage a photo shoot that ran in several local papers. Hebert even procured an outfit and headdress for Solomon Battise's son Reed, who appeared in the photographs with the Sickeys although he did not accompany them on their trip.[116]

Running the Trading Post was a Coushatta community-wide effort. While some funding was acquired to hire young tribal members to attend to the shop for a few hours a day, it was mostly run by volunteers who staffed the counter, provided basket-weaving demonstrations, and hosted guests.[117] Ernest Sickey took care of the marketing needs to attract patrons, frequently sending press releases to newspapers inviting people to come witness the making of "fine basketry work right on the premises for those who have never seen the art of pine needle craft."[118] Solomon Battise split his time between his duties as a preacher and those as the president of the tribe's nonprofit corporation charged with running the Trading Post. Just as he positioned the church as a gathering place for the tribe, he encouraged weavers and other tribal artisans to gather around the Trading Post to create items to sell while also teaching others to do the same. Bertney Langley remembered that Battise often opened the Trading Post on Sundays after church, so that members of the congregation could buy cold drinks, chips, or candy. Many older tribal members also fondly recalled the Trading Post as a place to visit weavers and use the only pay-telephone located within the community.[119]

Such an organized effort to bring basket makers to the central part of the community from both the western and eastern portions of the Bayou Blue settlement afforded weavers the opportunity to learn new techniques and styles from one another, as well as teach the younger generations. Lorenda John Poncho remembered learning to sew from her grandmother, and then, "later on seeing how the others sewed differently, I tried it and liked it."[120] These gatherings also provided the opportunity to determine what knowledge needed to be reclaimed by the tribe. As a result, Battise created a space in the Trading Post to display baskets sewn by previous generations of weavers, as well as other significant cultural items. He even engaged in repatriation efforts by negotiating with local non-Indian families who had acquired pieces of Coushatta material culture over the years, asking them to return the items to the community so they could be displayed at the Trading Post. In 1968, for example, he was able to reclaim a bow and arrow made by George Abbey in the 1920s, an exchange that received newspaper coverage and afforded Battise the opportunity to publicly request that other families holding onto historic Coushatta items come forward.[121]

The Trading Post, with its large outdoor space for teaching and mentoring, inspired the hosting of a series of workshops and classes taught by Coushattas and guests from other tribes. Of particular interest were classes on beadwork and cane weaving, which helped diversify the items sold at the Trading Post while also reinstituting traditional forms of art.[122] With the assistance of funds provided by both local private foundations and the state departments of tourism and education, the tribe

Left to right, Rosabel Robinson Sylestine, Adeline Battise, Solomon Battise, and Lycia Robinson John weaving river-cane and pine-needle baskets behind the Trading Post, ca. 1970. Courtesy of Loris Abbott Langley, Coushatta Tribal Archives.

was able to host a series of basket makers from the Mississippi Choctaw tribe to travel to the Coushatta community and hold weeklong workshops that were incredibly popular as people came from every part of the settlement to enhance existing techniques or learn new forms of sewing, weaving, and beadwork.[123] By May 1973, these opportunities were bolstered when the Jefferson Davis Parish Vocational Tech School of Jennings added four Coushatta-specific classes to its schedule: basket weaving, woodcutting, jewelry making, and beadwork. The courses were offered at the Trading Post and taught by Susan Denson, another artisan who traveled from the Mississippi Choctaw reservation. A report indicates that over seventy-five Coushatta pupils enrolled in these courses that summer—a promising turnout as the tribe positioned itself to generate even more notoriety for the community's artisans.[124] While the Coushattas' guests had their travel costs covered, the limited funding necessitated that they stay with the Sickey family, which proved ideal given that Daisy Sickey's mother was Choctaw and she spoke the language. "They were thrilled to talk in Choctaw," Sickey recalled.[125]

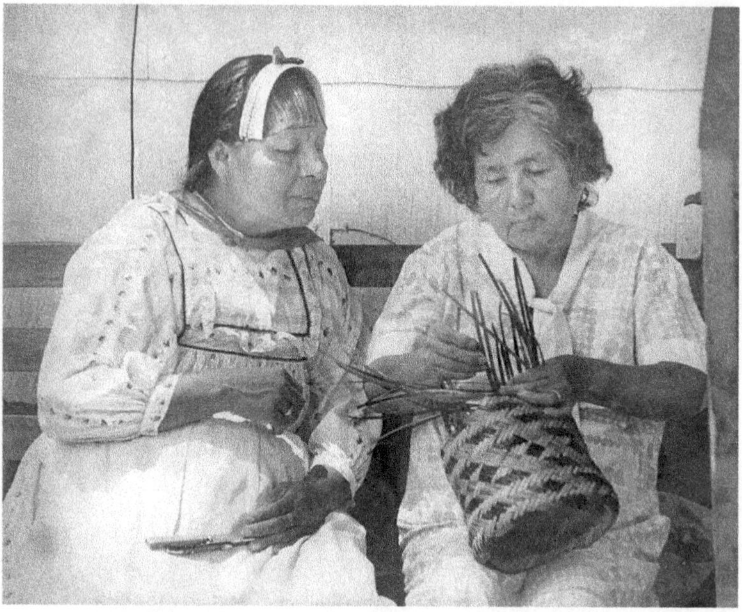

Susan Denson, instructor, and Jane Battise Poncho practicing river-cane weaving. Photo by Stephen Richmond, courtesy of Coushatta Tribal Archives.

Making it a social gathering, people pitched in and brought food to the classes and, since they didn't have enough seating in front of the Trading Post, they also brought homemade benches and chairs. Battise even supplied sawhorses and boards for makeshift tables.[126] Over the next few years, additional weavers, such as Elsie John and Maggie John Langley, who had previously conducted workshops in the community, also began teaching courses funded by the parish.[127] Langley's daughter, Zeline Langley Sylestine, remembered participating but said that it was so hard to weave river-cane baskets that she never completed any. Like many Coushatta weavers, she experienced difficulty with turning the corners on the basket base and finishing the rim correctly, only being able to make the basket "halfway" before having her mother finish it for her.[128]

Because of the opportunities that the Trading Post afforded the tribe, as well as the ability for different generations of both novice and master artisans to come together, "the spirit of the art woke up again," Sickey stated.[129] Basket makers who may have felt discouraged by the difficulty of selling their work for a fair price in the years prior to the Trading Post found that basket making had, indeed, become a viable source of income. For example, Rosabel Robinson Sylestine remembered how four-inch baskets that sold for ten cents in 1950 were sold for five dollars in 1970 after the tribe began marketing and selling their own work.[130] Leona Williams Francis also recalled that the expanded networking allowed her to bring her baskets to the Alabama-Coushatta Reservation in Texas, where she was able to sell them at higher prices: "I start taking [baskets] to the reservation in Texas. They buy it good, $20 for four inch [baskets], and I make a lot of money over there when I take it over there. Yeah, I used to make a lot of the four inch [baskets], and take them to the Texas reservation."[131] In addition to seeing an increase in the monetary value of their work, basket makers encountered an increasing freedom in the types of baskets they could make since they were no longer restricted to the few varieties that buyers once favored. A surge in collecting, as well as the growing notoriety of Coushatta baskets, afforded weavers more creative liberties as they made a broader array of basket shapes and designs, currently including over forty different varieties, sizes, and types of animal effigy baskets. The designs, colors, and other basket embellishments also became increasingly complex as each basket came to take on its own unique characteristics.

The transition of Coushatta basket making to focus primarily on the use of pine needles was an example of the tribe adapting to its environment and market demands. This shift provided an opportunity to revive some old practices while also innovating and instituting new ones—all while working collectively to ensure the success of a new tribal enterprise. The number of Coushattas who have woven cane and/or pine-needle baskets over the last century is extensive. Those who were considered master weavers, defined as those individuals recognized for both the quality and the quantity of their baskets, number approximately seventy individuals, who can be grouped into twelve major family lineages. Over time, individual basket makers established a reputation for excellence, making Coushatta pine-needle and cane baskets the highly collectable art objects they are today.

3

Asaala Schoolpak Komawiichito̲
Selling the Baskets Helped Us

> Nowadays they sell baskets very expensive. Nowadays they want the baskets that are good and tight. . . . Nowadays we would have been sewing a lot if we were able to. We would have been rich.
>
> —Margaret Williams John and Loris Abbott Langley

OPENING THE TRADING POST in 1967 was just the beginning of a larger effort to improve the tribe's economic and political outlook. Following the withdrawal of assistance from the federal Bureau of Indian Affairs in 1953, the tribe experienced difficult times as they slipped further into poverty, with astonishing rates of unemployment as well as mortality caused by preventable medical conditions. Claude H. Heyer, field secretary for the Association on American Indian Affairs (AAIA), an advocacy group based out of New York and one of the tribe's primary legal supporters through the process of federal reinstatement, visited the Bayou Blue community in 1959, describing the tribe's status as a "story of sad neglect" characterized by wage discrimination and overcrowding. Despite such a depressing outlook, however, Heyer also recognized the potential opportunity that a tribal tourism enterprise could bring, given that the Coushattas held a unique and valuable resource: their culture.[1]

The tribe's efforts to continue sharing their culture and history with the public continued to develop into the 1970s, a task the Coushattas embraced on their own terms as baskets consistently held a prominent role in this process. Ernest Sickey credited Solomon Battise for spearheading these efforts, with the Trading Post providing the tribe with a central gathering spot for weavers to convene and for workshops and classes to take place.[2] While the Trading Post may have brought new opportunities, it was also part of an ongoing effort to showcase the application of traditional knowledge in the production of baskets, wood carvings, blowguns, and a number of other forms of material culture. It offered artisans a source of income while also giving the tribe additional visibility by positioning their baskets and other forms of art as powerful symbols of their identity.

The town of Elton also benefited from the tourism that the Coushatta Trading Post brought to the area. Visitors, whether they be independent travelers or school groups, supported the local economy by patronizing Elton's gas stations, stores, and restaurants. By the early 1970s, the flow of traffic through Elton, as well as other towns along Highway 190, was under threat by plans to construct Interstate 10 across southern Louisiana—a process that started in the late 1950s but wasn't completed until 1978—that would, undoubtedly, attract motorists away from slower

Photo for postcard advertising Coushatta Trading Post, 1967. *Left to right,* Glenna Battise (later Robinson), Dianna Celestine (Shuff), Caroleen LeJeune (Fore). Courtesy of Loris Abbott Langley, Coushatta Tribal Archives.

routes like the 180-mile strip of roadway between Baton Rouge and Beaumont, Texas, that comprised Highway 190. Fear of the economic impact the new interstate might have on the towns situated along the old highway inspired the formation of the Acadiana Trail Association to promote a "scenic route" through southern Louisiana as an alternative to the new road. Each town sent business and civic leaders to join forces with locally based state legislators to compile a list of attractions each town could boast and market. Most towns focused on outdoor recreation, such as fishing and camping. Others were able to contribute museums, fairs, and festivals to the list. Elton was the only town that was able to point to a singular group of people as an attraction—the Coushatta Tribe.[3]

With this increased attention came more opportunities. For one, the tribe found new outlets for selling Coushatta baskets, beadwork, and picture cards when, in 1971, the Lake Charles Tourist Bureau began carrying these items, with the proceeds going back to the tribe.[4] The following year, representatives from the Louisiana Tourist Commission traveled to the Bayou Blue settlement to preside over a special meeting of approximately two hundred people to renew the Coushatta Trading Post's nonprofit charter because the state had a stake in the continued success and growth of the tribal enterprise. Coushatta leaders welcomed their guests in what was described as a "charter presentation ceremony." Since the initial charter was approved in 1966, the increasing role the Trading Post came to play in the region was formally acknowledged at this event, which was also attended by Wade O. Martin Jr., Louisiana secretary of state, who outlined the growing impact he anticipated the Coushattas' tourism efforts would have on the state's economy and employment prospects. In his address, Martin claimed that "tourism will eventually replace oil as the number one money maker in the state." He went on to identify the "Coushatta Indian tribe [as] a valuable asset to the state not only for the potential as [a] tourist attraction but for the heritage as well." Pleased with the interest of area and state officials in the success of the Coushattas' tourist enterprise, Ernest Sickey identified how they were about to embark on "the greatest planned development for the cultural and economic betterment of the Coushatta tribe in 200 years."[5]

Asaala Chopahak Immaiyat Ilaachito
Establishing the Coushatta Cultural Center[6]

By the mid-1970s, the Coushatta arts-and-crafts enterprise moved from its isolated location in the heart of the tribal community and directly into the town of Elton. This shift came six months after the federal Department of Interior reinstated the Coushattas' federally acknowledged status and tribal chairman Ernest Sickey joined Elton's business owners and rice farmers to discuss the town's future. The meeting came on the heels of an announcement that the Missouri Pacific Railroad Company was to eliminate its passenger service in Elton and donate the depot building to the town. Given Elton's involvement with the Acadiana Trail Association and its mission to utilize the tribe to boost tourism, it was agreed that the old depot would be turned over to the tribe to house a museum and store for Coushatta arts and crafts directly off Highway 190.[7] Congressman John Breaux, who was present at the meeting, praised Elton's leadership for turning the depot over to the tribe, declaring that Elton should be identified as the "Indian Capital of Louisiana."[8]

The new location of the tribal enterprise was in downtown Elton by the water tower, which was much more accessible to tourists than the Trading Post located several miles north of town. Once the building was turned over to the tribe, the next challenge was to determine how to pay for its relocation.[9] Fortunately, the benefit of having the tribe more centrally located within the town was quite a popular notion among Elton's business leaders and, within the month, the Calcasieu Marine National Bank agreed to donate the relocation funds. Just as the donation of the building to the tribe served as a prime public-relations opportunity, so did the bank's donation. In fact, to commemorate the event, representative Sherrill Thompson appeared in a photograph in the *Daily World* newspaper presenting the check to Sickey and Elton mayor Millie LaFleur. "The relocated home will be used in the establishment of a cultural center for the Coushatta Indians," the article explained, "the only full blooded Indian tribe in Louisiana, and will appear on maps and pamphlets soon to be circulated by the Acadiana Trailway Association."[10]

The tribe had big plans for the old train depot. The goal was to transform it into a Coushatta Cultural Center that would reach "a tremendous traveling audience . . . for the benefit of our own Indian people as well as those who are interested in the many varied aspects of Indian history." The vision was to make it a true southeastern Indian center. Similar to what Solomon Battise started with the Trading Post, the proposal for the Cultural Center demonstrated that it was to serve two purposes. First, the intent was to utilize it to sell Coushatta-made items, with an emphasis on baskets. The tribal newspaper pointed out how baskets demonstrate that "the traditional values of the Coushatta people still exist and [are] carried on by the young people."[11] The second part of the plan was to carve out a space for a museum "displaying past historical events of the Coushatta Tribe, and other Southeastern tribes that once roamed southwest Louisiana."[12] The objectives also included the creation of brochures, books, and other printed material about the Coushatta Tribe, and the production of informational films about the tribe's history and culture. In addition, the plan included the organizing of a small Coushatta dance group to perform at the Cultural Center or special events throughout the state and nation, a training program for Coushatta people on how to manage the center, a lecturing unit of one to three Coushattas who could be called upon for public speaking events, and a formal public relations program to promote the center and its activities.[13] The Cultural Center was to continue in the role of the Trading Post as a place where Coushatta artisans could sell their work either on-site or through mail orders.[14]

Once the building was relocated, the inventory of the old Trading Post was moved to the new site. The tribe, then, turned to refurbishing the structure—an effort that required both knowledge and additional funding. To learn more about how to go about preparing the building, Sickey attended a workshop in Indianapolis, Indiana, focused on the renovation of old railway stations.[15] He also spoke to elders in the community who suggested that he incorporate cedar into the interior of the building to keep the materials fresh and to repel bugs.[16] To fund the renovation, he pursued grants, which proved successful when, in 1975, the tribe was awarded $30,000 from the Economic Development Administration, as well as a small seed grant from the "America the Beautiful Fund" aimed at supporting community-based projects.[17] The tribe was even featured in one of the organization's flyers alongside a picture of Solomon Battise talking with two children about some cane baskets.[18] At the local level, the tribe was able to tap into the substantial resources offered by the Imperial Calcasieu Regional Planning and Development Commission in preparation for the Bicentennial celebration. While grants were distributed among various parish committees, the Coushatta Bicentennial Committee was included among those funded.[19] Collectively, each funding source allowed the tribe to make substantial changes to the building, which was officially completed in 1977. The refurbished Cultural Center gave the tribe much to be proud of. "We had it [looking] really nice, with cedar walls, and cedar interior so it would smell good," Sickey recalled.[20] It wasn't long before the shelves were stocked with both pine-needle and river-cane baskets and a case was dedicated to displaying beadwork and other handmade items. To mark the occasion, the tribe even created new sales tags. While the Trading Post tags had a simple design of an arrow pointing to the east and the words "Indian Craft, Koasati also Known as Coushatta Indians, Elton LA," with a blank line for the weaver's name, the Cultural Center's tags reflected the tribe's new political status.

Following the federal reinstatement of the Coushatta Tribe, tribal leaders seized the opportunity to develop an official tribal seal donning a *nitobi* (garfish), which became synonymous with their political identity. The symbol appeared on the new sales tags, becoming a verification of authenticity and stating that the items were "certified Coushatta Handicrafts, made in Elton, LA."[21] The information that was provided about the baskets, in particular, was also much more detailed, including the weavers' names, descriptions of the baskets, and the materials used. At the time of its opening, the Cultural Center displayed over one thousand objects.[22] One photograph from this time shows a display of five small river-cane baskets, all different shapes, several small covered baskets and trivets, fifteen effigy baskets, and several beadwork baskets displayed among photographs of basket weavers.[23] Other images show display cases full of coiled pine-needle baskets of various shapes and sizes, and shelves full of pine-needle baskets lining the walls of the building.[24]

Just like the Trading Post previously, the opening of the Coushatta Cultural Center was a success. "We brought tourism into the town," Sickey shared. "[Many] people came to buy baskets, so we brought a lot of traffic into Elton."[25] Within the first several months, school groups from Abbeville and Lake Charles visited and were presented with demonstrations on the process of weaving.[26] Hosea Hebert, who was a basket buyer in the years before the Trading Post opened, noted how Coushatta women continued to supplement their family incomes by selling "beautiful baskets of all shapes and sizes" at the Cultural Center in Elton and that "several enterprising craftsmen have out-of-state outlets for their baskets."[27] The tribe instantly saw the benefit of moving the tribal enterprise to town. For one, tribal weavers got relief from buyers unexpectedly showing up at their homes. Lorenda John Poncho shared how "the basket buyers used to go around and they would go to houses and ask [for baskets]. If they [the weavers] had baskets already made, they would sell it to them. . . . I don't know how they found out to go to the people's house."[28]

As a result of the opening of the Coushatta Cultural Center, weavers also saw a much-needed increase in the prices they received for their baskets. Jeanette Celestine Langley recalled the frustration of being underpaid for her work in sewing baskets prior to the transition. She figured that she was compensated about fifty cents per hour based on the time it took to pick the pine needles. Then, she continued, "it takes me two, three days to clean them, and then tie them up, and then I hang them up, and I'm not counting the waiting for the pine needles to dry or the grass to dry. Then you start working on it from there. . . . It takes a long time. We slowly started getting the price that we want for our baskets."[29] Marion Robinson John shared how critical higher prices and recognition were to her ability to provide for her family: "He [Hosea Hebert] would ask one dozen of them from me and I would make one dozen within a week. . . . I'd sell all the time even if they bought it cheap." Eventually, John increased her asking prices.[30] According to one source, tribal artisans sold approximately $42,000 worth of baskets and other craft items the first year of the Cultural Center being in operation.[31] Although the center opened after the tribe's federal status was reinstated, it was organized under the nonprofit Coushatta Alliance, Inc., because it was an operational structure that worked well for the Trading Post, and the profits from the sales went directly back to the weavers and other tribal artisans. With assistance from the Comprehensive Employment and Training Act (CETA) funding, and a few other sources, tribal

Interior of Cultural Center, 1977. Darlene Langley Dunnehoo is waiting on customers. Note tag with tribal seal on cane elbow baskets (on the wall) and wheat-stitch open baskets on the counter. Courtesy of Bertney Langley, Coushatta Tribal Archives.

members also comprised most of the workforce that kept the center running.[32]

By the late 1970s, Bertney Langley, son of weaver Loris Abbott Langley, became manager of the Cultural Center and focused on continuing the educational programs that had initially been part of the Trading Post. Langley remembered one of his primary goals was to grade the baskets, so the highest-quality baskets had higher price tags. He developed new brochures and mailed out advertisements and information about the basket makers throughout the Southeast. He was also instrumental in securing a grant from the Louisiana Arts Council in 1977 to run programs that served to educate the public while also promoting enthusiasm within the tribe to continue teaching the next generation the craft of weaving.[33] He hosted basket-weaving contests for tribal members, actively promoting them via local television and newspapers, and then encouraged nearby businesses to purchase the winning baskets.[34] He recalled how these efforts enabled the Cultural Center to be self-sufficient, and helped the community by making the

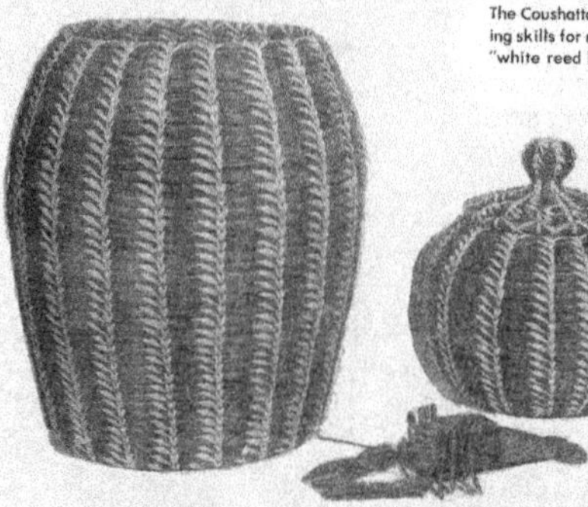

The Coushatta Indians have been recognized for their basketweaving skills for many generations. The name "COUSHATTA" means "white reed brake" and was originally applied to this group of Indians whose settlement was near the patches of swampcane that was utilized to weave plaited baskets.

Gradually the availability of swampcane became scarce as the farmers began to cultivate land which had been abundant in this basketweaving material. This is when the basketweavers of the tribe enlarged upon a second basketry media they had developed, that of the pine needles in a coiling technique, bound together with raffia, creating numerous decorative and utilitarian basketry forms as well as unique effigy creations.

Today, the Coushatta tribal leaders are giving special emphasis to the arts and crafts of its members in order to promote and retain this rich heritage.

COUSHATTA INDIAN CRAFT SHOP
P. O. BOX 248
ELTON, LOUISIANA 70532

To:
Name____________________
Street____________________
City____________ State________
Zip Code______________

Coushatta Indian Craft Shop
ARTS & CRAFTS

PHONE (318) 584-2148
P.O. BOX 248
ELTON, LOUISIANA 70532

Basket brochure with wholesale and retail pricing, ca. 1975.
Courtesy of Bertney Langley, Coushatta Tribal Archives.

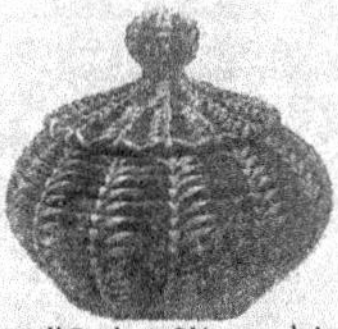

TO BUY AT WHOLESALE PRICES

MINIMUM ORDERS MUST BE $150.00

	WHOLESALE	RETAIL
Wall Basket, 3½ cup plain	11.90	14.00
Wall Basket, 3½ cup decorated	12.75	15.00
3"-Basket with lid, plain	5.95	7.00
3"-Basket, wheat stitch	5.95	7.00
3"-Basket with decorations	6.40	7.50
4"-Basket with lid, plain	8.50	10.50
~~4"-Basket with lid, wheat stitch~~	~~8.50~~	~~10.50~~
4"-Basket with lid, decorated	8.90	11.00
5"-Basket with lid, plain	11.05	13.00
5"-Basket with lid, wheat stitch	11.05	13.00
5"-Basket with lid, decorated	11.50	13.50
6"-Basket with lid, plain (knob on lid)	13.60	16.00
6"-Basket with lid, wheat (knob on lid)	13.60	16.00
6"-Basket with lid, decorated (knob on lid)	14.05	16.50
8"-Basket with lid, plain (knob on lid)	21.25	25.00
8"-Basket with lid, wheat (knob on lid)	21.25	25.00
8"-Basket with lid, decorated (knob on lid)	21.70	25.50
10"-Basket with lid, plain (knob on lid)	38.25	45.00
10"-Basket with lid, wheat (knob on lid)	38.25	45.00
10"-Basket with lid, decorated (knob on lid)	38.70	47.00
12"-Basket with lid, plain (knob on lid)	63.75	75.00
12"-Basket with lid, wheat (knob on lid)	63.75	75.00
12"-Basket with lid, decorated (knob on lid)	64.20	77.00
12"-Basket with lid, Geometric (knob on lid)	85.00	100.00
Oval Cracker Basket-12" from handle to handle	25.50	30.00
Vase-6" tall x 6" wide, plain stitch	17.00	22.00
B. Vase-6" tall x 6" wide, wheat stitch	17.00	22.00
Vase 10" tall x 8" wide, plain stitch	34.00	40.00
b. Vase 10" tall x 8" wide, wheat stitch	34.00	40.00
ANIMAL, BIRD, REPTILE BASKETS - Small sizes (4" - All Shapes)		
a. Chicken effigy basket	12.75	15.00
b. Duck effigy basket	12.75	15.00
c. Swan effigy basket	14.45	17.00
d. Frog effigy basket	12.75	15.00
e. Owl effigy basket	12.75	15.00
f. Turkey effigy basket (pine cone petals)	21.25	25.00
g. Alligator	21.25	25.00
h. Crawfish	19.15	22.50
Medium sizes (8" - All Shapes)		
a. Turkey effigy basket (pine cone petals)	42.50	50.00
b. Alligator (pine cone petals)	42.50	50.00
c. Armidillo (pine cone petals)	42.50	50.00
d. Ducks	34.00	40.00
Hot Plate Mats - 6", 7", 8" set	15.30	18.00
Waste Basket, 11" wide x 11" tall	85.00	100.00

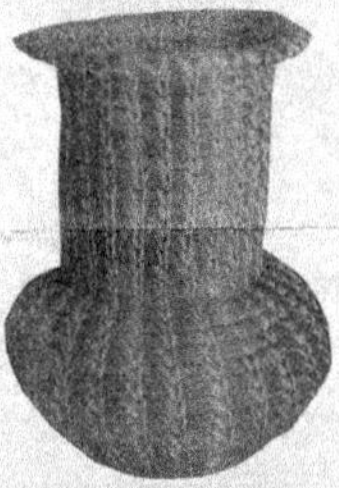

It is difficult to picture crafts accurately in a brochure, as the Indian craftsman seldom makes two identical items. Therefore, sizes, shapes, coloring, designs and prices will vary from item to item.

COD orders accepted. A 50% deposit is required on all orders, plus 7% charge on the total order for postage, insurance, and handling. Prices are subject to change without notice.

baskets more visible and selling them for higher prices. Traders from other states began making annual trips to the Cultural Center, buying as much as $5,000 worth of baskets during a single trip.[35] Langley also built a portable exhibit for displaying the baskets when traveling to news stations, museums, or wherever a display was needed. He established a protocol for numbering the baskets, hooks, pictures, and labels so they could be packed, shipped, and then re-assembled quickly and accurately. He recalled packing the display to fly to Las Vegas, where he and other tribal members sold enough to pay for all their trip expenses; plus they received first place in the exhibition category at the event.[36]

The success in sales and increased exposure had an impact on Coushatta basketry. To start, it encouraged many basket makers to expand their skill set and diversify the techniques they used, creating different styles, shapes, designs, and decorations. Many embraced the challenge of further refining their craft and took pride in trying new approaches. Coushatta weavers strategically focused on making baskets that met market demands. For example, Adrian Sylestine recalled a customer asking her to make a tiny, miniature pine-needle basket. Once she overcame the logistical difficulties of gathering and drying younger, smaller pine needles that were particularly tender, she was able to sew miniature covered baskets that were less than an inch in size. This experience led to Sylestine specializing in sewing and decorating miniature baskets. She recalled how "Then another lady from Tennessee that used to order a lot of baskets from me found out that I was making these miniature baskets, and she called up one day and said, 'Well, could you try to make a pair of earrings from those baskets?' So, I started making pairs of earrings."[37] Similarly, Loris Abbott Langley made a "man in the maze" basket inspired by a design often used by southwestern tribes. She recalled one of the basket buyers bringing a picture of the design when he came to the Cultural Center, and her desire to "try to see if she could make a basket like that."[38]

While expanding styles provided a diverse array of options for patrons, it also fostered misunderstandings by those outside the tribe who were concerned about the impact this might have on Coushatta traditional aesthetics and styles, sometimes even mistakenly claiming to see forms of religious diffusion appear in the baskets. What these claims failed to acknowledge, however, was that artistic innovation and adap-

Top: Southwestern-motif baskets: Pueblo Family with Beehive Oven; Man in the Maze. *Bottom:* Interior of Cultural Center, ca. 1977, with Myrna Abbey Wilson, *left,* and Gloria Battise Cernek, *right.* Note Pueblo pottery-style open basket, *top shelf, far left;* and thunderbird design, *second row, center.* Photos courtesy of Linda Langley, NMAI, Ernest Sickey, and the Coushatta Tribal Archives.

tation is part of the Coushatta basket-making tradition that, like culture, is fluid. And, as is often the case, certain practices and uses of materials sometimes outpace other ones, and popular designs are incorporated to meet market expectations. This was the case when the increasing demand for pine-needle baskets at the Cultural Center contributed to a growing decline in cane weaving following a temporary surge of interest generated by workshops held at the Trading Post just a few years prior.[39]

Asaala Achoolihak Achoolik Hoimponnafookon Hasaikahchok Inchopahiik Ilaachito
Raising the National Profile of Coushatta Basket Makers[40]

By the early 1970s, Coushatta baskets attracted the attention of the Department of Interior's Indian Arts and Crafts Division. It wasn't long before the southeastern field representative, Stephen M. Richmond, began making regular trips to southwest Louisiana from his headquarters in North Carolina. Ernest Sickey explained how Richmond, who had been working with tribes as a field representative since 1963 yet had limited exposure to Louisiana tribes, was astonished at the level of quality his trained eye observed in the Coushatta basketry. Following this revelation, he committed to working with the Coushattas to ensure they received national recognition. Richmond began making trips to the Bayou Blue community, frequently staying at a hotel in Jennings for a week at a time while documenting the basket-making process through photographs and interviews. "I think he even learned some of the language," Sickey recalled. "He was a great man."[41] Over the course of his many visits, Richmond regularly purchased baskets for the Indian Arts and Crafts Board collection.[42] It is uncertain exactly how many he acquired for either this collection or his private one, but in 2000 nine baskets from the Bayou Blue community (including an owl-effigy basket woven by Rosabel Robinson Sylestine and three basket trivets) were transferred to the National Museum of the American Indian in Washington, DC.[43]

Since Richmond's initial interactions with the community coincided with the tribe's acquisition of the old train-depot building, he was able to lend his expertise to the renovation project and help the tribe make design decisions. He even met with the architect hired for the job to provide input on how best to use the space for displays.[44] Richmond also assisted the tribe in reassessing their pricing structure for baskets and other handcrafts. He was particularly concerned about setting high standards for the quality of items sold, remaining firm in his position that tribal artisans and weavers shouldn't undervalue their own work by also selling generic Indian souvenirs—even if they appealed to eager tourists.[45] Richmond's greatest contribution to the tribe, perhaps, was in his marketing abilities that further expanded their exposure. By 1976, the Indian Arts and Crafts Board directory began listing items sold by the Coushatta Cultural Center, including "long-leaf pine needle basketry in forms of round baskets to effigies, stone-polished pottery, cane and white oak baskets, [and] woodcarving."[46]

The Coushattas' relationship with Richmond created renewed opportunities for weavers to develop exhibitions around their work to be showcased across the state and beyond. Allowing themselves to be spotlighted or having their work be set apart from that of others in the community was not something Coushatta basket makers were accustomed to doing, nor was it something they were comfortable with. Bertney Langley explained how weavers consciously worked to overcome their shyness and culturally based aversion to putting themselves into the public eye. As Ernest Sickey phrased it, "They were too shy to speak or demonstrate in public, but they took it on the chin by agreeing to do basket-making exhibitions in order to educate the public about the tribe and attract potential tourists and customers to the community. They made a personal sacrifice because they knew it was helping our people."[47]

In 1973, Rosabel Robinson Sylestine agreed to be the first basket maker to work with Richmond who was eager to display her pine-needle baskets, which he considered representative of work that "has been developed to new dimensions of proficiency and artistic achievement." In all, twenty-eight styles of Sylestine's coiled baskets were prepared for display, including a series of effigy baskets shaped like a turkey, armadillo, turtle, lizard, swan, skunk, cat, duck, chicken, crawfish, and owl.[48] Sylestine's daughter, Edith Sylestine Langley, recalled how hard her mom worked. "She was always sewing, every day. Whenever she had time, every chance she got she was on the porch sewing. Or at night, she had it [her materials] in the living room with her box. And she would sew and watch TV."[49] To launch her exhibit, Richmond contacted venues throughout the state and received immediate interest from the Louisiana State Historical Museum in New Orleans. The museum reserved six weeks at the end of the summer to dedicate to the event. The museum staff also issued a special request that Sylestine demonstrate her skill at the opening on July 16, 1973. "I have a feeling this is going to be a big attraction," Richmond eagerly wrote Sickey as he began putting the wheels in motion for additional exhibitions.[50] With the exhibition space secured, Sickey reached out to Dallas Johnson, the director of the American Indian Program within the Save the Children Foundation, for funding for marketing materials, special invitations, and travel expenses. The foundation had a history of working with the Cherokees in North Carolina and had been generous to the Coushattas in the past, providing supplies for the various workshops held at the Trading Post years earlier. Sickey positioned them as a partner in the Coushattas' development program—a successful strategy that yielded the foundation's support for many years.[51] With proper funding in place, invitations donning an impressive pencil drawing in the likeness of Sylestine's crawfish effigy basket were extended to state politicians and local public figures.[52]

The timing of Sylestine's exhibit was fortuitous. It came right as the tribe had gained momentum in mobilizing their political allies within the state legislature to assert pressure on the Department of the Interior to recognize the tribe. On June 27, 1973, the years of work that had been devoted to this end came to fruition when the decision was issued to fully reinstate services to the Coushattas administered by the Bureau of Indian Affairs on behalf of federally recognized tribes.[53] The opening of the basket exhibit, which happened just weeks later, provided an opportunity to celebrate the occasion as the tribe's friends and allies gathered to marvel at Sylestine's work. The museum staff reported that the exhibit exceeded their expectations, garnering a great deal of press coverage in both newspapers and television and selling over $1,000 worth of baskets.[54] Plans were promptly underway to bring Sylestine back to New Orleans within a few months following the next show that had already been lined up for her at the Louisiana Arts and Science Center in Baton Rouge.[55]

Following the launching of Sylestine's exhibit, Richmond returned to the tribe to enlist another basket maker. This time, Edna "Lorena" Abbott Langley agreed to work with him and show her work in what became marketed as an "educational opportunity" that allowed others to view a "way of life, much of which remains hidden from mainstream

Rosabel Robinson Sylestine with granddaughters Tana and Kathy (in bassinet). Image from Princeton University, William Byler Papers. Photo by Sam Guillory.

America."[56] Langley's baskets were first shown at the Cabildo in New Orleans, followed by a series of other venues throughout the state.[57] While her work received much praise, she was uncomfortable with being the sole focus of the exhibits. As a result, she soon transformed the events to also incorporate the work of her husband, Joe, and children Evelyn, Rosaline, Ronald, Marilyn, Clement Joe, Paul Steven, and Trudy Joan. Like many other Coushattas, Joe mostly made his living in the timber industry, but the opening of the Trading Post allowed him to supplement this income by making gourd utensils, stickball rackets, bows and arrows, blowguns, and an assortment of items made of tanned buckskin. The Langleys passed their knowledge onto their children, who followed in their footsteps into the craft-production industry.

The family's work was exhibited throughout Louisiana, but also became part of a special exhibition at the Southern Plains Indian Museum and Crafts Center in Anadarko, Oklahoma. As Lorena Abbott Langley was quoted in the promotional materials: "We continue to make these items, along with the everyday speaking of our Koasati language, to carry on the traditions of the Koasati Tribe. . . . We feel that if we make our crafts, we are following the advice of our Mother and Grandmother who told us that if we kept our Koasati crafts, spoke our language every day, did not cut our hair, and followed the rules and medicine of our people, we would continue as a tribe forever."[58] While the family honored traditional designs and approaches in their work, Langley, like other tribal artisans, enjoyed challenging herself. Identified as one of the "most versatile members" of the tribe in her artistry, she began experimenting with different creative mediums and, in an effort to demonstrate the relevance of traditional Coushatta designs within a modern aesthetic, she created a collection of clothing that was exhibited in Texas and Louisiana in 1977.[59] She explained her perspective, stating: "I was thinking that knowledge of our designs go back many hundreds of years. . . . I have used our pine needle and cane basket designs, varied beadwork designs, and have recorded them on these shirts, dresses, capes, and shawls of mostly modern design and cut in the same way that a historian records words on paper so that they will be seen, and others will remember that some of our ancient ways are living still."[60] Her designs were recognized by the National Endowment for the Arts, and she was awarded a Craftsman's Fellowship grant to continue her work with the assistance of her daughters, who previously worked in the garment industry.[61]

Langley's son-in-law, Claude Medford Jr., also earned notoriety for his basket-making skills that not only incorporated Coushatta techniques, but additionally drew from other styles borrowed from a variety of Louisiana tribes. Of Choctaw descent, Medford originally came from east Texas before marrying Rosaline Langley and settling in Elton. Prior to his time with the Coushattas, Medford earned a bachelor's degree in anthropology and art history from the University of New Mexico

Lorena Abbott Langley and son Ronald, a skilled weaver himself, selling baskets at the 1978 New Orleans Jazz & Heritage Festival. Photo by Michael P. Smith, © The Historic New Orleans Collection.

before moving between Indian communities, living with the Alabama, Tunica-Biloxi, Pamunkey, Caddo, Delaware, and Yuchi people at different times. During his travels, he learned different styles of basketry, pottery, as well as an assortment of other handcrafting techniques. He also was interested in Native languages and worked in tribal cultural program development. Over time, Medford focused on developing his own weaving skills, particularly with the split river-cane baskets, which earned him wide acclaim as he was invited to display his work in numerous private collections, as well as museums that ranged from the Smithsonian to the Louisiana State University Museum. In 1983, Medford was inducted into the Louisiana Folklife Center's Hall of Master Folk Artists at Northwestern State University. He published works on Louisiana's Indigenous material cultures, served as a consultant, and taught basket-weaving workshops around the state.[62] Medford briefly managed the Coushatta Cultural Center in the early 1970s, assisting the tribe in writing grants and marketing their baskets.[63]

Marion Robinson John was another talented weaver who worked

with Richmond to showcase her baskets. First learning to weave at the age of seven, John was confronted with the responsibility of helping to care for her younger siblings after her mother died, which resulted in her leaving school at sixth grade to begin taking jobs as a domestic in the surrounding area. She supplemented her income by joining other weavers in selling pine-needle baskets, at first on the roadside and at various venues, and then at the Trading Post and Cultural Center. Earning a reputation for the quality of her work, John taught her children how to sew baskets because, as she shared: "I love doing my basket weaving and would like very much to continue and encourage others in the tribe and especially young people."[64] Her initial exhibit of forty-eight baskets was received well by the Louisiana State Museum in New Orleans, giving it momentum to continue touring the state, and then onto Houston, Texas, in the summer of 1974.

Houston's Contemporary Art Museum had recently opened its doors, and Richmond found the site to be the "most encouraging" venue for Coushatta artistry yet.[65] Ernest Sickey expressed his enthusiasm for the Houston location, calling it a "culturally-minded community."[66] His instincts proved to be accurate as the exhibition was met with great success, featuring John's fine work and a special visit by her once a week for nine weeks during the course of the exhibit to hold demonstrations.[67] Sickey identified this as "one of the finest shows on Indian arts in the Southeast."[68] Like Langley before her, John also received a grant from the National Endowment for the Arts. She recalled Sickey telling her that this would bring great exposure for her work: "'You will be the best basket maker [that] ever lived,' they told me and I was happy, but when I say that I don't mean to brag about myself. They said that and then they . . . fixed the money and then I sewed all the baskets that were on the list."[69]

Later, expressing her appreciation for the funding, John wrote: "For the first time in my life, I was given the opportunity to spend the time necessary to design and produce a series of special Coushatta Indian long-leaf pine needle baskets. In the past, I have had to weave baskets that sold as souvenirs at a very low price. . . . From all this activity, I have been able to increase the prices that I received for my basketry creations significantly, and I am receiving much recognition along with an abundance of new orders."[70] In addition to earning a competitive grant,

John's work was honored in several ways. She was specially selected by the Renwick Gallery of the Smithsonian American Art Museum to display her baskets, and then she was able to launch a two-year traveling exhibition with the Louisiana Council for Music and Performing Arts throughout Louisiana and Texas, offering demonstrations.[71] She was able to take her children with her on one-day visits to nearby cities as crowds of onlookers marveled as her expert fingers shaped longleaf pine needles into tightly bound baskets.[72] They were also drawn to what one photographer called "the whimsy and humor of the effigy baskets."[73]

Reflecting on this time of her life several decades later, John expressed gratitude for the recognition and financial benefits: "I traveled almost everywhere by airplane, to Washington, even Virginia. They would tell me that's where you're going to bring it [your baskets] to. . . . They were waiting for me and buy all the baskets the same day. . . . 'Demonstrate,' is what they call it, so that's all I did the three days. It went on and on like that. We bought an old house by me helping, by making baskets. Basket making really helped me out."[74] John received invitations to show her work all over the country as Coushatta basketry became increasingly representative of the material culture from the Southeast. In 1983, she was even invited to Ganado, Arizona, to show her work alongside a potter from Santa Clara Pueblo and a Navajo rug weaver.[75] By 1985, she was a featured artisan at the Louisiana Folklife Festival.[76]

Just as Coushatta baskets helped raise awareness of the contributions of southeastern tribes to American Indian art, they also raised the profile of Louisiana's folk art. It seemed that the weavers had an eager audience, as indicated by their frequent invitations to conferences and exhibitions. By the late 1970s, Coushatta baskets found prominence alongside the work of other craftspeople whose work came to embody what was considered Louisiana's unique and multicultural aesthetic. In 1976, the Louisiana State Arts Council awarded the tribe a $1,750 grant to help supplement multimedia costs for additional showings. Governor Edwin Edwards wrote to Sickey, directly, to share the news that the state was issuing a grant to the tribe. "I congratulate you and your group for your fine work and dedication to the art world," Edwards wrote. "The programs you sponsor provide much to the overall well-being of Louisiana and give additional credence to the era of excellence my administration is promoting for our great State."[77] This was a long

Marion Robinson John sewing pine-needle basket for the Renwick Gallery, 1975. Courtesy of Ernest Sickey, Coushatta Tribal Archives.

time coming, according to Richmond, who clearly felt that Louisiana should have been doing more to fund the Coushattas' efforts for some time, adding, "this grant is the result of my work with the Coushattas."[78]

Richmond's success with showcasing the Coushattas' work prompted him to expand his efforts to work with other Louisiana tribes, such as the Chitimacha and Houma.[79] He began with a basket exhibition featuring a Chitimacha weaver, Ada Thomas, who also received a National Endowment for the Arts grant, and like in the Coushatta community, began organizing workshops that focused on basket weaving and wood carving.[80] With the increased attention that Indian artisans and weavers received, it is no surprise that they were prominently featured in a 1980 publication, *Louisiana Traditional Crafts.* Alongside the introductions to All Saints' Day wreaths, corn-shuck mats, quilts, and lacework, Louisiana's Chitimacha, Coushatta, Houma, and Choctaw basket weavers were acknowledged for their ingenuity in adapting to changing environmental conditions and incorporating new materials and techniques into their work. Identifying the "most famous contemporary Indian basket makers," the book highlighted the "creative development" of Coushatta baskets with the introduction of effigy baskets and other decorative details brought on using raffia, dyes, pinecones, and feathers.[81]

While the short-term goal was to raise the profile of Coushatta basket weavers within Louisiana and Texas, Richmond aimed to push things further by connecting the tribe's work with that of other well-known southeastern tribal artisans. In 1975, for example, he arranged for the Coushattas to be featured in *Applied Photography* magazine with a full photographic spread. The magazine's senior editor, William A. Reedy, was interested in expanding the magazine's coverage to include profiles of Native artisans and had previously published an issue featuring Cherokee carvers. Sadly, while plans were underway to shoot a feature on Coushatta basket makers, Reedy suffered serious health issues and died before even visiting southwest Louisiana. As a result, the project was never implemented.[82] These unfortunate circumstances didn't deter Richmond, however. By 1980, he organized a "Southeastern Indian Basketry" exhibit that included work from the Choctaws of Mississippi, the Cherokees of North Carolina, the Seminoles of Florida, the Catawbas of South Carolina, and the Coushattas and Chitimachas of Louisiana. This combined exhibition was intended to "provide far-reaching benefits for the Indian Tribes of the Southeast" and ended up being the final exhibition the Coushattas did with Richmond prior to his retirement in 1983.[83] The show displayed work by Sylestine, Langley, and John and traveled to different states across the region. According to Richmond's own account, the Coushatta baskets were the "highlights of this show [and] people have been eager to find out where these baskets might be purchased."[84]

The Coushattas' association with Stephen M. Richmond and the Indian Arts and Crafts Board proved valuable in helping the tribe elevate their efforts to generate more visibility. Each exhibition was expertly executed with attractive marketing materials exhibiting professional photographs of the weavers and artisans, as well as samples of their work. The press releases and brochures included quotes from the basket makers themselves, providing insight into their lives and motivations for continuing their work. By incorporating the weavers' personal stories and perspectives, the exhibits took on a personal dimension and compelled patrons not only to come to appreciate the baskets but to learn directly from the weavers who were often on-site demonstrating their craft. Richmond regularly provided the Coushattas with examples of marketing materials from other tribes, such as the Cherokee of North Carolina, to help in the process of developing their own materials.[85] Sickey claimed that, collectively, the exhibitions offered the tribe international attention and that "the current program provides more outlets [and] more income through better pricing structure. And as a result of all of this, we see better quality."[86] As early as 1975, Sickey claimed that "all of our crafts people are involved full speed ahead in their projects and things are getting better for them every day."[87]

Asaalak Hasaikahchon Okhiicha̠ Komintiwwito̠
Our Baskets Opened Doors for Us: The Role of Baskets in the Campaign for Tribal Self-Determination

Baskets are powerful symbols of Coushatta identity that have been strategically incorporated into the practice of gift giving, which initiated and fostered economic and political alliances at both the local and the national levels. This became a particularly effective approach in the years following the tribe's termination from federal Indian services as the baskets served as reminders of the traditional knowledge that prevailed in a community that had been marginalized and legally neglected. In 1964, for example, the tribe enlisted the assistance of local attorney Paul C. Tate to travel to Washington, DC, to meet with the director of the federal anti-poverty programs, R. Sargent Shriver Jr., to deliver a petition for assistance that had been drafted by Coushatta leaders. Along with the petition, Tate was sent with a pine-needle basket and a blowgun to gift to Shriver on behalf of the Coushatta people. Although this meeting didn't have the immediate impact that was hoped for, accounts indicate that the gifts left an impression on Shriver, who took notice of the tribe and promised to investigate their situation.[88]

A few years later, the practice of gifting baskets evolved into what Ernest Sickey coined "basket diplomacy"—a strategy he embraced at the suggestion of a tribal elder who gave him some of her baskets to use as part of his efforts to seek support in getting the tribe's federal status reinstated.[89] Soon other weavers joined in the effort by putting aside a few baskets from the inventory they sold to the Trading Post.

Solomon Battise contributed cane baskets while others supplied Sickey with pine-needle baskets to carry along with him as he met with lawyers, politicians, or other potential tribal allies. He recalled that the first basket he gifted was to Louisiana Senator Russell Long, which was followed by dozens of others that made their way onto office shelves or private collections of Louisiana's political elite.[90] "I didn't have a business card," Sickey stated. "I would leave a little miniature, maybe four inch, basket on a Congressman's desk. . . . Then, sometimes their wives would call and say, 'We'd like to order some.'"[91] These efforts served the dual purpose of boosting the tribe's economic outlook while also securing loyal friends and advocates. Reflecting on this practice nearly a half-century later, Sickey noted that he was following the example of earlier Coushatta leaders in making strategic alliances: "We used to sit around and brainstorm, thinking how do we get around these [obstacles]? So, we did the same thing Red Shoes did [in the late eighteenth century], and we were successful."[92]

Among some of the tribe's most significant and impactful allies were Judge Minos D. Miller and his attorney wife, Ruth Means Lloyd Miller. The Millers were influential political and economic players in the area, with connections in the oil and gas industry. Judge Miller served on the Judicial District Court for both Allen and Jefferson Davis parishes, and Ruth Miller was among the first wave of female attorneys in Louisiana. The couple had a long history of assisting the tribe with local matters that dated back to the 1950s. Yet, by the early 1970s, they began dedicating a lot of their time to working directly with Ernest Sickey on getting the Coushattas' federal status reinstated by first lobbying the state legislature to formally acknowledge and stand by the tribe. Without having the means to pay them for their assistance, Sickey regularly gifted the Millers with pine-needle baskets until they had quite a private collection of their own. According to the Millers' daughter, Bonner, they cherished them and appreciated the skill and artistry that went into their creation.[93]

The Millers were so impressed by the skill of Coushatta basket makers that they even introduced them to Lucille Blume, a New Orleans socialite and president of the Louisiana Council for Music and Performing Arts. Together, the Millers and Blume made regular trips to the Trading Post in the early 1970s to purchase baskets so that Blume could share them with her circle of art-collecting friends.[94] She expressed her enthusiasm about the artistry of the baskets with a reporter, stating that "there is something in American Indian art which is viable, exciting and relevant to Americans today."[95] Blume's interest in Coushatta baskets also prompted her to join the Millers' advocacy efforts in discussing the tribe's situation with politicians. Sickey remembered how "she would harass them and get right in their faces about how the state has mistreated Indians."[96]

The Coushattas' connection to the Millers also initiated a relationship with David Garrison Jr., the great grandson of J. A. Bel, who was a businessman involved in the timber and oil industries with vast landholdings that both surrounded and divided Coushatta-held properties. The tribe had a historically strained relationship with the Bel Estate, which rapidly acquired large tracts of property once held by Coushatta families who were either unable to keep up on the taxes or who were victims of unethical practices.[97] Over the years, the Bel Estate did donate several acres to the tribe to operate a school and a church.[98] Yet, as the longleaf pine needles became more difficult to find, and as the tribe looked to acquire land to place into federal trust as a reservation, there was a renewed pressure to negotiate with the Bel Estate. The budding friendship between Garrison and Sickey, as initiated by the Millers, benefited the tribe on this front. Garrison's enthusiasm to lend his assistance to the tribe prompted him to join forces with the Millers and Sickey in establishing a Louisiana Office of Indian Affairs (LOIA), the first of its kind in the state and one of the first in the region. Expressing to a reporter how the "economic and sociological advancement" of Indians was of "deep concern" to him, Garrison accepted the position as the LOIA's first commissioner.[99] Sickey was appointed as deputy commissioner and consultant, making him the first Indian to be hired by the state to oversee Indian affairs.[100]

While Garrison's advocacy efforts contributed to the successful outcome of the Coushattas' federal reinstatement, he also played a critical role in helping further advance tribal development. Among other things, he met with the Louisiana Economic Development Office and the Louisiana Tourist Commission to encourage them to play an even bigger role in promoting the Coushatta arts-and-crafts enterprise.[101] He also assisted Stephen Richmond in locating and securing venues around

Louisiana and Texas for Coushatta basket exhibitions.[102] As one of the heirs to the Bel Estate, in 1975, Garrison even secured a donation of over twenty acres of land in the central part of the Coushatta community to be placed into federal trust for the tribe as a reservation following their reinstatement.[103] According to Sickey, Garrison was disappointed that he couldn't get more land donated to the tribe from the Bel Estate; however, he did arrange for basket makers to have greater access to his family's property to collect pine needles.[104]

Sickey's efforts, combined with the tribal basket makers' skill and generosity, came together right as the tribe gained momentum in mobilizing their political allies. These allies helped the Coushattas establish a foothold within the state government, reinstate their status as federally recognized, acquire a reservation land base, and continue to expand their craft enterprise. Though Sickey has been identified as the driving force behind tribal re-recognition, he actually credits the contributions of tribal weavers: "It is the power of the baskets that got us re-recognition. The baskets are our culture, our traditions, our language all woven together."[105]

When interviewed in 2019, Sickey expressed how deeply touched he was by the role that basket makers played in contributing to the tribe's development nearly a half-century ago: "When I got discouraged about politics or our economic struggles, I would go to visit the basketmakers. They were so gracious and hospitable, they offered me coffee and food, we would visit while they worked on their baskets. Solomon and Adeline [Battise], Florence Robinson, Jane Poncho, Rosabel [Sylestine], Lorena [Langley]—I tried to order from all of them so nobody would be left out." Sickey says he especially remembered his frequent visits with Maggie John Langley: "I remember her bare feet—she didn't even have money for shoes. But I told her that what I was doing would help people get better housing and health care, and when I didn't have money to buy baskets, people would give them to me." Thinking about their sacrifices, and how they survived, gave Sickey the inspiration to keep moving forward with his efforts to improve the tribe's political and economic outlook. "People all pitched in and helped each other. They gave everything they had."[106] While everyone played their part, Bertney Langley particularly credited the women for being "the backbone of our tribe."[107]

Ernest Sickey also credited the weavers, who were mostly the community's women, for much of the tribe's success. It was clear that the appreciation was mutual because the basket makers conspired to do something nice for Sickey. They had firsthand knowledge of his efforts, including all the traveling he did, how many meetings he attended on behalf of the tribe, and the quantity of baskets he distributed. Bertney Langley recalled Rosabel Robinson Sylestine telling him that she wanted to do something to thank Sickey for all his work: "She said the basketmakers knew that he and [his wife] Ena Mae didn't have a washer and dryer. They had all those boys, and so much laundry, but no washing machine or dryer. So Rosabel went door to door to get donations so they could buy them for Ernest. She even got a donation from Ernest so he wouldn't get suspicious—we laughed about that for a long time, that he donated to himself. Ernest was so surprised, he cried when they gave it to him."[108] This touching story demonstrates the interdependency of the tribe's efforts and an acknowledgment of how they had to work together to promote their shared interests.

Ernest Sickey receiving weavers' gift of washing machine and dryer, with Rosabel Robinson Sylestine, 1982. Courtesy of Ernest Sickey, Coushatta Tribal Archives.

In the years following the tribe's federal reinstatement, baskets continued to be used as powerful symbols of Coushatta identity and strength in traditional knowledge. The exhibits and demonstrations organized by Stephen Richmond and the Indian Arts and Crafts Board provided one outlet to this end. However, tribal basket makers found additional opportunities to showcase their work. For example, in 1974, the tribal nonprofit organization that ran the Trading Post and organized into a co-op of about one hundred members, raised funds to send Ernest and Ena Mae Sickey to Washington, DC, where Ena Mae demonstrated her pine-needle baskets at the Cooperative Craft Exhibition at the Smithsonian Institution.[109] The following year, Marion Robinson John also traveled to Washington, DC, to show her baskets. Because of the popularity of her work, particularly after her successful showing in Houston, John explained to one newspaper reporter how she traveled with her baskets about once a month to various locations with her five children in tow.[110]

Coushatta baskets gained such acclaim in the 1970s that they even made an appearance in the American home-fashion industry. William Byler, executive director of the AAIA, took a personal interest in the Coushattas' development efforts. As one of the recipients of a basket gifted to him by Sickey, Byler instantly recognized the broader potential and versatility that the art form held. It wasn't long before he contacted his brother, James H. Byler, president of consumer products and the corporate vice president of the Bibb Company, a manufacturer of home furnishings with textile mills in Georgia and a corporate office in New York.[111] The Bibb Company was a massive operation, with a great portion of its business dedicated to developing exclusive patterns and designs that appeared on bedspreads, draperies, blankets, and sheets that were sold to major department stores like Sears, Roebuck and Company. In 1973, the company began developing a collection of tribal designs, called the "First Americans Collection," for home fashions. James Byler made admirable attempts to ensure the authenticity of the designs that were, at that point, inspired by designs from the Kiowa, Pueblo, Miccosukee, and Northern Cheyenne.[112] Within a few months of William Byler submitting a proposal to his brother to consider including Coushatta designs in the collection, Sickey received a letter indicating that Sears had approved the request and the tribe was to be compensated

$1,000.[113] In addition to the compensation for use of Coushatta designs in their housewares, the Bibb Company also agreed to work with the tribe to design an official tribal seal.[114] The design not only assisted the Coushattas in their marketing efforts as the seal appeared on sales tags for items sold at the Cultural Center, but it became synonymous with their political identity as Louisianans were just learning about the implications of tribal sovereignty.[115]

To increase the emblem's visibility further, a large wooden sign was made and installed on the front of the Coushatta Cultural Center to get the immediate attention of motorists traveling on Highway 190 through Elton. Then, as a result of the Bibb Company's continued efforts, merchandise with the tribal logo printed on it, such as T-shirts and blankets, were available for sale at both the Cultural Center and in Sears and Roebuck catalogs.[116] In keeping the momentum, weavers were asked to make pine-needle baskets with reproductions of the tribal seal. However, reproducing the colors, the interlocking semicircles, and the shape of the garfish is particularly difficult. To date few tribal basket makers have successfully sewn tribal seal baskets.[117] Loretta Robinson Williams recalled Bertney Langley asking her mother, Florence Robinson, to make a tribal seal basket for display at the Cultural Center. "I remember watching her work on it—I know which one was hers because it's the only logo basket where the garfish comes up above the basket."[118]

The 1970s marked a time when the Coushattas were at the height of their popularity as baskets were used not only to supplement the incomes of tribal families, but to serve political purposes in impressing upon the public what made the Coushattas unique as they made significant contributions to Louisiana's cultural heritage. The town of Elton had leveraged its proximity to the tribe for some time, but with the tribe's growing relationships with the federal Indian Arts and Crafts Board and the AAIA, they entered the 1980s with a new level of recognition that not only identified the tribe as having some of the country's most skilled basket makers but positioned the Coushattas to take on the new challenges they would soon face.

4

Ittoiyat Ittillokoolit Intoliino Maththit
We Had to All Stand Together and Work Together

People always pitched in and helped each other. The greatest part of our story is the way that people helped each other—a small tribe working together that never gave up. To revitalize a tradition, an art form, a language—it takes a whole tribe working together, with the same vision.

—Ernest Sickey

BY 1980 COUSHATTA BASKET makers had been widely acclaimed as world-class artists. Their skill and innovative designs earned them permanent invitations to Louisiana folk art events and American Indian exhibitions across the country at the same time that their generosity in gifting baskets played a pivotal role in the tribe's political and economic stability and development. Since first settling near Bayou Blue, the Coushatta people worked together to make a home for themselves by using the resources they had available: their traditional knowledge to transform the natural materials that surrounded them. It was a remarkable demonstration of resilience that carried them into a new period of development in the years following federal reinstatement, one focused on building the infrastructure of a tribal nation.[1]

The decades following federal reinstatement saw tribal development efforts unfolding at a rapid pace, generating a lot of discussion within the community over how best to proceed. Successes in economic growth, health care, and community development led to a desire for even greater and more rapid expansion. While the Coushatta Cultural Center in Elton continued to attract loyal patrons and play a significant role in maintaining the tribe's visibility, the Coushattas' earlier success in linking their identity with their basketry proved difficult to sustain. Some critics believed that the tribal leadership wasn't doing enough to generate economic prosperity, and others thought they no longer focused enough attention on promoting basketry. Stephen Richmond of the federal Indian Arts and Crafts Board was particularly disappointed about how much the tribe's community development efforts began to outpace its tourism enterprise, claiming in 1983 that Coushatta "arts and crafts are being neglected."[2]

The tribe didn't, in fact, lose interest in continuing to foster its arts-and-crafts business, yet it became clear that the community's needs were far greater than what could be met by a singular effort. The federal Indian funding that the Coushattas received following reinstatement was scarcely enough to cover their basic expenses. Tribal leadership had to actively pursue grant funding and private donations to acquire reservation land and erect administrative buildings. There also never seemed to be enough funding to cover the tribe's basic health care and dental needs.[3] In an effort to mitigate this, on January 18, 1984, the tribal council unanimously authorized the establishment of a gaming operation on the reservation. Tribal ordinance no. 84-1 permitted "Bingo, Keno, and related games of chance for amusement purposes on Reservation property in Allen Parish."[4] Tensions about the tribal bingo enterprise, and related issues of how best to lead the tribe into the future, generated political divisions that shifted the trajectory of the tribe's development efforts. These conflicting perspectives were further exacerbated by outside government agencies, each with its own motivations, intervening in internal Coushatta affairs.[5] Within two years, the Coushatta people had elected a series of three new chairmen (Edwin Poncho, Leroy Sylestine, and Lovelin Poncho), dealt with the Bureau of Indian Affairs intervening in their elections, and endured the repeated freezing of tribal bank accounts and other assets.[6] These abrupt transitions and lack of access to resources generated divisions within the tribal community that resulted in a general decline in tribal programs by the mid-1980s. This also proved to be the beginning of the end of the Cultural Center, which closed early in the decade after going through several managers and slowly decreasing its hours of operation and marketing pursuits. This was the first time in two decades that tribal artisans lacked a viable outlet for sales—leaving them to revert to independently brokering the selling of their work.[7]

Maan, Stamahilkato̲ Asaala̲ Scholpaak
A New Beginning for Tribal Tourism and Public Education Efforts[8]

The Coushatta historical record reflects a series of recurring themes and patterns. Among them are the rising and waning of their traditions as a result of both internal political and social conflicts, as well as external pressures shaped by land encroachment, environmental problems, and other adversities. This was a pattern they experienced over the course of their migrations, and it was one that continued into the twentieth century as the tribe experienced periods when certain traditions appeared to decline only to then reappear seemingly overnight.[9] Tribal members phrase this as a process of safeguarding their traditions underground by keeping them closely held within families, with an awareness that it is their responsibility to bring these traditions back and showcase them again when the time is right. Curtis Sylestine reflected on the apparent "overnight emergence" of tribal dance traditions:

> It's funny the way things happen. After the influence of the church people and the way the old people seemed to almost lose our songs and dances, I just couldn't get anyone interested in learning or reviving the traditions. I used to sing, and I talked to my uncle Bel [Abbey] as often as I could, but there just wasn't anyone enthusiastic about joining me in those efforts. Then overnight, about seven years ago, it just seemed to happen that our traditions re-emerged full blown. People keep asking me how it happened, and to be honest I'm really not sure. It literally happened overnight.[10]

The revitalization of cane-basket weaving was another example of cultural reemergence, after Solomon Battise organized weaving classes at the Trading Post in the 1960s. Because of such enduring practices as safeguarding and revitalizing, the closing of the Coushatta Cultural Center may have had an adverse economic impact on tribal artisans, but it didn't pose a real threat to the endurance of basket making.

In fact, dedicated weavers proved undeterred as they went back to finding their own avenues for marketing and selling their work. Many of them had established personal markets for their baskets over the previous two decades, through contacts established at the Trading Post and Cultural Center. So, without a tribal enterprise to assist them, they resorted to conducting business through those other outlets. Louisiana festivals also provided tribal artisans an important opportunity for sales during this time, particularly the annual Louisiana Folklife Festival, held at Northwestern State University in Natchitoches, and the New Orleans Jazz Festival.[11] Bel Abbey and his family, Rosabel Robinson Sylestine, and Lorena Abbott Langley were annual demonstrators at one or both of these festivals, as well as other smaller events.[12] They were among the tribal artisans who kept Coushatta basketry in the public eye during a period when the tribe was no longer able to manage their own arts-and-crafts enterprise. In 1982, Bel Abbey and two of his daughters, Marjorie and Myrna, were honored when they were inducted into the Northwestern State Folklife Festival Hall of Master Folk Artists. More than a decade later, Bel's sister, Lorena Abbott Langley, was similarly honored, followed by Doris Robinson Celestine Battise nearly two decades after that. To date, they remain among the five Coushattas to have received this recognition.[13]

While Coushatta weavers continued to nurture informal sales networks in the years following the closing of the Cultural Center, the restabilizing of the tribal government by the late 1980s brought renewed interest in pursuing opportunities to promote arts and crafts. When Lovelin Poncho was elected tribal chairman in March 1988, he was vocal about his objective of bringing equanimity and economic development to the tribal community.[14] Poncho had served as the Coushatta community housing director during the Sickey administration; like many of the tribal members, his parents, grandparents, siblings, and spouse were all active basket weavers. As a result, one of Poncho's first actions as tribal chairman was to resume the tribe's efforts to secure funding for cultural maintenance and revitalization projects, as well as to increase employment opportunities for tribal members. Inspired by the federal Indian Self-Determination and Education Assistance Act of 1975, which promoted "the full participation of Indian tribes in programs and services" and encouraged "the development of human resources of the

Indian people," Poncho implemented policies intended to reclaim the tribe's developmental momentum of previous years.[15]

He attended national conferences looking to leverage new opportunities and network with other tribal leaders who were also looking to bolster the economic outlook of their communities. In 1989, for example, he attended a Public Law 93-638 training conference hosted by the Narragansett Tribe in Rhode Island,[16] where he met Linda Parker (later Langley), a doctoral student gaining attention for successfully procuring grant funds for Indian organizations.[17] Agreeing to work with Poncho to apply for funding on behalf of the Coushattas, Parker submitted a social and economic development grant proposal to the Administration for Native Americans. By November, the tribe was notified that they had received the funding and immediately set about improving upon a small gas station and convenience store that had previously been built on the reservation, expanding it to also include a café and gift shop.

Several years had lapsed since the Coushattas had a centralized location to market and sell their arts and crafts, so artisans were glad that the tribe had once again embarked on a tourism enterprise. As Jeanette Celestine Langley explained, "We needed a place to bring our baskets, to sell them. . . . when we used to have a Cultural Center in town, we didn't just wait for people to come buy our baskets." She recalled how, in the absence of a local shop to sell baskets, "we took a lot to the Indian Fair in Choctaw, Mississippi and we sold most of them there. . . . We got a van and we would put all of that stuff in the van and put a display out and we would sell. I would sit there and make baskets—like for advertising, and they would come and buy a basket from us. We would sell it all."[18]

As with previous ventures, baskets were the focal point of the new gift shop. The *Lake Charles American Press*'s coverage of the shop's grand opening in 1991 emphasized how the Coushatta people "are nationally famous for their handmade, long-leaf pine needle basketry."[19] Perhaps in recognition of such acclaim, nearly one thousand visitors were present at the ribbon-cutting event, which featured a full day of craft demonstrations, singing and dancing, and historical presentations. The event served as an occasion to recognize the contributions that elders like Bel Abbey made to continuing to pass traditions onto the tribal youth despite the difficult years. He responded by sharing how "these are my neighbors and my relatives, and I like to teach those things from our heritage. . . . it's good for me to do these things, and show the young people anything they want to learn."[20] Lovelin Poncho was also interviewed, providing him the opportunity to reflect on how it took approximately three years to get the tribe back on a path toward economic stability and growth.[21] This was news that many of the Coushattas' neighbors were eager to hear, given a particularly dismal depiction published a year earlier of the tribe's living conditions as being like "a time machine gone haywire" where evidence of previous development seemed to have abruptly stopped "under towering pines and blue sky."[22]

Just months before the opening of the tribal gift shop, Bertney Langley opened his own shop in the old train-depot building that once housed the Coushatta Cultural Center in Elton. He named the company and store "Bayou Indian Enterprises" as a way of differentiating it from the tribal enterprise. Yet, the name still let people know it was run by "Indians from the Bayou State."[23] Much like with the tribal gift shop, the grand opening of Bayou Indian Enterprises drew crowds as it featured longleaf pine-needle basketry demonstrations because, as Langley explained, "Basket weaving is the art most associated with the Coushatta Indians" and it is "known the world over."[24] One of Langley's first products was a proprietary seasoning blend he called "At-homma Hooma" (Indian Seasoning Spices), with a label which featured a picture of a twelve-inch pine-needle covered basket made by his mother, Loris Abbott Langley. The caption read "*Asaala* (Basket): The Koasati people are famous for their long-leaf pine-needle baskets, which were once a means of survival and are now highly prized collectibles exhibited in museums worldwide."

In continuing the Coushatta practice of building strategic partnerships and alliances, Langley invited Louisiana lieutenant governor Paul Hardy to the shop's grand opening to participate in a peace-pipe ceremony. Hardy issued a commendation to "the Coushatta Indian Tribe and Bayou Indian Enterprises for their efforts to preserve a cultural and historical part of our state."[25] Langley also worked with state tourism commission offices to receive technical assistance for promotion and advertising, as well as to attract more tourists to both gift shops. As he explained to one reporter, "We are trying to combine resources and efforts so we can share our culture with outsiders."[26] His efforts were recognized, and in 1992, Langley received the Louisiana Travel Promotion Association "Attraction Employee of the Year Award" for "diligently promot[ing] the artwork and handicrafts of the Coushatta Indian Tribe." This was followed by the Louisiana State Art Council's 1999 "Folk Artist of the Year" award.[27]

As the tribe rebuilt its arts-and-crafts enterprise, former allies demonstrated an eagerness to rekindle their previous roles in promoting tourism in the area. Local newspapers advertised both the reservation gift shop and the Bayou Indian Enterprises store, encouraging visitors to patronize both. Reflecting the endurance of the craft and variety of styles that weavers had developed over the years, one reporter stated, "Neither the long-leaf pine needle baskets nor the art of weaving has changed. . . . baskets are of every conceivable size, shape and function. . . . with or without lids, they are available with interwoven decorations. There are effigy baskets shaped in the form of ducks, turtles, swans, turkeys and alligators."[28] The town of Elton also demonstrated a willingness to resume a partnership with the tribe to nurture its mutually beneficial economic interest in tourism. This was clear in 1994 when the town's council voted unanimously to authorize the mayor to renew the lease with Bayou Indian Enterprises to continue operating out of the town-owned train-depot building.[29] Throughout the decade, Elton leaders continued to rely on the Coushattas for what one reporter explained was a joint effort "to promote improvements to the Elton community" by engaging in such practices as inviting Bertney Langley to give presentations in City Hall as part of a tour held in Elton for the Chamber of Commerce of Jefferson Davis and Acadia parishes.[30]

Such invitations to promote Coushatta culture provided tribal weavers with new opportunities. As Langley was on the front lines of getting the tribe's tourism enterprises back on course, one of his goals was to raise the prices weavers received for their baskets—much like he had done when he was manager of the Cultural Center years earlier. He realized that, during the period when weavers didn't have a tribal enterprise to help promote sales, they had developed their own networks of personal contacts and customers, resulting in the reemergence of unregulated pricing practices. As a result, many weavers were considerably underpaid for their work. While his mother, Loris Abbott Langley, was one of the weavers he wished to ensure received the appropriate compensation for her work, she found the conversation uncomfortable and the transition difficult:

> The first time my son [Bertney] wanted to raise the prices on my baskets I was embarrassed. He kept insisting because he knew how much I was selling them for and he wanted me to get a fair price. When he packed the box [to send off to a buyer], I tried to put more baskets in when he wasn't looking! My daughter-in-law, who's an anthropologist, finally convinced me to raise my prices by telling me how much these dealers I sell my baskets to are marking them up for sale to other people.[31]

Traditional Coushatta values promoting modesty and humility made it difficult for Loris and other basket makers to negotiate prices for their work for fear of appearing boastful. In fact, photographs of tribal basket makers participating in weaving demonstrations or selling their baskets almost always show the weavers looking down at their hands or away from the camera to draw attention away from themselves. With the closing of the Coushatta Cultural Center in the early 1980s and an increased need to independently promote their own work, weavers were confronted with the necessity of putting themselves forward in ways they never had to previously. Without someone brokering sales or marketing their work for them, they had to promote their own artistry to secure a market. The opening of the reservation gift shop and the Bayou Indian Enterprises store came as welcome signs that the tribe had not only reinvested in supporting its basket makers but was once again on course to engage the public by telling its story and generating interest in the tribe.

This was just the beginning of these efforts, however. In fact, tribal members soon organized more opportunities to interact with the public. For example, in 1992, the first Coushatta Powwow was held at Lambert Park in Kinder. The event advertised Native American song, dance and drum groups from across the country, as well as Native arts, crafts, and food booths. According to Florine Pitre, the powwow chairman, this was "the first event of its size ever sponsored by a Native American tribe in Louisiana."[32] In addition to the exposure the powwow brought the tribe, McNeese State University began offering a leisure learning course taught by Barry Langley on Native American culture and history, even featuring tribal dancers to demonstrate powwow-style dancing.[33] Tribal elders, such as Bel Abbey, also continued to actively participate in events around the state as part of a strategic process of promoting the tribe and its artisans. Abbey organized parades, worked with scholars and community organizations, and coordinated basket-weaving demonstrations.[34]

In 1990, Abbey's picture appeared in the *Eunice News* when he served as a guest in a fifth-grade class at Central Middle School to demonstrate the use of a blow gun.[35] That same year, he received an apprenticeship grant from the Louisiana Division of the Arts to teach traditional storytelling to his nephew Timothy Langley.[36] Abbey's storytelling was a featured event at an antique car show on the reservation in 1990, which was emceed by Bertney Langley and also included basketry demonstrations by Rosabel Robinson Sylestine and other weavers.[37] Building upon his uncle's efforts to organize events, in 1992 Bertney Langley began an annual Bayou Indian Festival. He promoted the festival throughout southwest Louisiana utilizing television, news, and other media outlets, which also brought a lot of publicity and exposure to the tribe and the weavers. Some of the notable instances of publicity came when news anchor Peter Jennings filmed a segment of ABC's *World News Tonight* on location at the festival.[38] The following year, the festival featured James Billie, chairman of the Seminole Tribe of Florida and renowned musician, who flew his airplane onto a nearby airstrip for a musical performance.[39]

Throughout the 1990s, opportunities to promote Coushatta culture continued to increase as the tribe received additional exposure in television and film. For example, in 1991, the Louisiana Tourism Commission (LTC), which operated out of the Department of Tourism, sent a camera crew to the reservation to film Coushatta dancers and artisans offering demonstrations that were produced for national distribution. A spokesperson for the LTC explained how the "purpose of the videos is to demonstrate the many reasons tourists should visit the State of Louisiana, and to show them the variety of interesting sights and events the state has to offer." It was clear that members of the LTC recognized the contributions the Coushattas made to the state's tourism industry, with the films focusing on basketry and the perseverance of the Koasati language. They also noted the "exquisite Coushatta handicrafts" sold at the shop on the reservation, including "the intricate pine needle baskets that are hallmarks of the Coushatta nation."[40] The LTC films—as well as a few others that were produced years prior—were widely distributed and used as educational resources in elementary schools, particularly around Thanksgiving time. The tribe also leveraged the opportunity to use these films in their own public education efforts as Jeanette Celestine Langley, the Coushatta public relations director, incorporated them into presentations she gave to local organizations and social clubs.[41]

In addition to the state-sponsored films, the tribe had a hand in producing its own film, called *Coushatta Heritage: Louisiana's Hidden Treasure*, to advertise the reservation gift shop, profile basket makers, and highlight other tribal traditions.[42] Bertney Langley even made a video featuring tribal dancers and, along with his mother, Loris, made guest appearances on a nationally syndicated cooking show hosted by Cajun chef John Folse.[43] While films and media coverage provided a new and effective platform for the Coushattas to educate the public and bolster their economic enterprises, not everyone was at ease with being filmed. Even Jeanette Celestine Langley, who frequently spoke in public on behalf of the tribe, was captured during the shooting of a tribally made film joking in Koasati that she hoped her nail polish wasn't faded during the cameraman's close-ups of her basket weaving.[44]

Before his death in January 1992, Bel Abbey appeared with his nephew Bertney on a few television shows and at events around the area. The two men appeared on the local television show *Parlez Vous*, produced in Opelousas. Abbey told tribal stories and demonstrated the making and use of cane baskets, blowguns, and whistles. Langley then shared the process of sewing pine-needle baskets, taking the audience through the steps from gathering and drying the needles to sewing and decorating the baskets. Emphasizing the artistry of basket making, he shared how tribal weavers are able to customize baskets into almost any shape or design.[45] During one notable instance, Abbey and Langley worked together with the Louisiana Division of Folklife on a publication, film, and accompanying statewide folklife curriculum, entitled "Swapping Stories: Folktales from Louisiana." The film that was produced for this larger project eventually premiered in 1998.[46] Langley recalled his uncle as a kindhearted person who always had a story to share, telling one reporter: "He was the last link of the past that we are ever going to remember. He knew all of the stories. . . . now that he is gone, it is up to us to keep the Coushatta traditions alive."[47] After Abbey's death, Langley continued the work of his uncle in telling stories and doing demonstrations of tribal history and culture, sometimes traveling with a small group of basket weavers and dancers. He organized these performances on the campus of Louisiana State University in Eunice in 1996 and 1997. Langley was also invited by the town of Jennings to be part of the ceremony to greet the Olympic Torch as it made its way to Atlanta in May 1996. He was invited again in 2002 to a ceremony honoring some visiting Navajo Code Talkers.[48]

Tanihilka Toknaawa̲ Stiltoliinoto̲
Investing in Culture and Language Programs during the Gaming Era[49]

The passage of the Indian Gaming Regulatory Act (IGRA) in 1988 established a precedent for legalized gaming on Indian lands in the United States. Louisiana officials had long been discussing gaming to address the state's economic woes; however, this new legislation offered an opportunity for the Coushatta Tribal Council to actively pursue casino gaming as a means of bringing prosperity to the tribe.[50] After several years of planning and addressing legal and legislative challenges, the Grand Casino Coushatta finally opened its doors to customers on January 16, 1995, becoming the largest casino in Louisiana. At the ribbon-cutting event, a crowd of approximately two thousand customers were waiting to enter, and so many others were en route to the new casino that traffic was backed up on the interstate for twenty miles. Casino officials estimated that twenty thousand visitors entered the casino on opening day, and thousands more were denied entry when the facility reached its legal capacity. After only eighteen months, the tribe added a twenty-seven-thousand-square-foot expansion to the original building, featuring 740 additional slot machines and a poker room, and increased the reservation land base from 156 acres to over 1,000. In 2000, the tribe spent $100 million to build two hotels, a convention center, an eighteen-hole golf course, and a swimming complex adjacent to the casino. By January 16, 2002, the Coushattas took over management of the casino from Lakes Gaming, Inc., a company the tribe partnered with to get the enterprise off the ground. The tribal casino was successful, and the Coushattas began investing gaming revenues into cultural and language revitalization programs, health care, and housing initiatives for the tribal community. Casino revenues allowed the tribe to hire more staff, increase departmental budgets, build additional facilities, and allocate resources to projects long discussed.

The opening of the Grand Casino Coushatta also ensured that the tribe had a broader audience when sharing their story, educating the public about the implications of tribal sovereignty, and—of course—promoting the work of tribal artisans. The headline in one local newspaper advertised how "Allen Parish Has Hit the Jackpot" with the opening of the tribal casino, which boosted the area's economic outlook. The article also went on to highlight how the tribe is "known nationally for the beautiful longleaf pine needle baskets" and encouraged people to visit the reservation gift shop "full of handmade wares."[51] Even the tribal police department, who now had the responsibility to police both the casino and the reservation, had a new badge that was partially created by Kevin Sickey, featuring a longleaf pine-needle basket as the center.[52] While the advertising of the casino also doubled as a way to educate the public about the tribe, the casino itself showcased baskets in a variety of ways. For one, the decor was heavily influenced by the baskets, providing an aesthetic that was uniquely Coushatta as weavers sold their baskets directly to the casino. Also, the gift shop in the casino lobby provided a new opportunity for sales. Both venues paid higher prices, and some of the earliest baskets made and sold for the casino opening were large, impressive examples of the art form.[53]

In addition to providing a new avenue to promote basketry, the casino affected the tribal community through demographic shifts as the tribal population in the area steadily grew. Prior to opening the casino, there had been a steady outflow of tribal members leaving the area to find better opportunities elsewhere. A 1981 report noted:

> Indian populations have begun to diffuse much more in southwestern Louisiana. In 1970, there were 317 Indians in the five parishes, with 162 located very close to the reservation. There are now (1981) 565, with 240 living in the area near the reservation. . . . the general vicinity near the Coushatta Alliance has increased at 48% during the last decade,

> the remainder of the five-parish area has increased even more rapidly (110%). Even though this increase is not all related to diffusion, it is certain that many Coushattas have left the reservation for employment opportunities.[54]

After the casino opened, Bertney Langley recalled an old Coushatta prophecy that "someday everyone would want to be an Indian." At a presentation to the Southwest Louisiana Historical Association two weeks after the casino opened, Langley remarked, "Now this prophecy appears to be coming true," noting that those who had left the area were returning to their Indian heritage after tribal re-recognition and the advent of casino gambling.[55]

By the turn of the new century, the increased resources that gaming brought in went a long way in bolstering the types of programs the tribe was able to offer; however, rapid economic shifts also ushered in a series of concerns expressed by tribal elders on the impact such changes had on younger tribal members.[56] In particular, there were grounds for concern over the long-term sustainability of the tribe's language and culture, as well as the preservation of its history. Bertney Langley, who served as secretary-treasurer of the tribal council from 1999 to 2003, proposed a new effort he initially called the "Koasati Historical Project" to gather photographs, historical documents, and other materials about the tribe. This effort culminated in the tribe hosting a gathering to present information about plans for the historical project, partially to gauge the level of community interest for this endeavor. Langley and his wife, Linda Parker Langley, now a professor of anthropology at Louisiana State University, Eunice, distributed a book on tribal history as well as sign-up cards for volunteers.[57] Linda later recalled this process of seeking input and volunteers:

> At the first meeting I had this western, academic division of everything. So, we had books on one table, asking "would you be interested in where your tribe is written about?" Then we had another table for original documents, like treaties, and asked, "Would you be interested in that?" Or, "would you be interested in language?" I had it all divided with sign-up sheets on each table thinking how some people will be interested in language, while others will be interested in photographs. In my mind, this was all separate. Delson "Dan" and Janice Sylestine

> were the first ones to sign up. They went to each table and signed up [for everything] because I was so dumb not to realize that in their minds it's all connected. They went and made sure they signed up at each table.[58]

The meeting generated several insights. For one, it was abundantly clear that there was an intense interest among the community to be involved in the preservation of the tribe's language, history, and culture. Also, it was discovered that these efforts were to be handled in a comprehensive fashion, rather than through the efforts of divided committees.

In 2006, the tribe decided to further extend its efforts and pursued funding to document and revitalize the Koasati language. Following traditions of earlier generations, they made strategic alliances and partnerships, in this case with the University of Arizona's American Indian Language Development Institute (AILDI), where the Langleys, working with the Coushatta Tribal Council, began developing a comprehensive Koasati language documentation and revitalization plan.[59] Soon after, they drafted a formal language plan and submitted a grant application to the National Science Foundation's Documenting Endangered Languages Program. The following year, after being awarded the grant, the tribe entered a partnership with McNeese State University to administer it. In April 2007, the tribal council held a community meeting to present the plan and solicit volunteers. In all, over thirty volunteers signed up to work on the Koasati Language Project at that first meeting, and thus the tribe's first community-based language documentation and revitalization project was born.

To support these efforts, tribal revenue was directed toward funding a new tribal Heritage Department to house this program. Over a decade later, the Langleys recalled the early days of getting the program off the ground when they realized that it wasn't going to just be about preserving the language because "it's all connected" to the tribe's history and culture as well. For example, in working on Koasati words about cane basketry, they realized that without anyone making cane baskets—which was the case at the time—it was difficult to capture the words surrounding this process. "You have got to get started making them again to be able to talk about the process of making them," Linda Langley shared. "Even though we started with language, it evolved into the preservation of a more holistic heritage. The language doesn't exist in a vacuum." Before long, what started out as an effort to record and maintain the language evolved into also refocusing the tribe's efforts on promoting basket making within the community, as well as documenting and preserving the work of artisans from previous generations.

The Coushatta Heritage Department provided a new arena for not just the Koasati language, but for basket making, to thrive. The staff organized potlucks and offered classes. They also conducted interviews with basket weavers and collected baskets and historical archives to store as part of a tribal collection. It was a daunting task, and the Langleys quickly realized that they needed more assistance to collect, organize, and archive the information. Linda explained:

> When you work on a tribal community driven project, it's a whole different approach. Bertney would tell me that he had his eye on certain young people in the tribe. I've heard this from many other tribes too. It's like you get tapped on the shoulder and told, "hey, we want you to work with us on this." But Bertney would notice which ones [we] should talk to and run it past the older people. Then he would tell me who to go talk to and ask for help. Heather [Williams] was the first one. ... I actually went to [her mother] Loretta's house because Heather was still in high school. This was a way of recognizing that you can't do all this without the young people being trained as you do it. So, Heather was right there with us. Jacob [LaBuff], Marion's grandson was another young person we worked with.

Heather and Jacob both came from a long line of respected tribal weavers. They, among others who also worked with the Heritage Department, represented the next generation of tribal youth who were tasked with carrying Coushatta traditions and history forward. Their training with the Heritage Department included learning how to take pictures, catalog historical materials, and inventory baskets. They were also trained in how to interview, translate, and transcribe.[60]

With all the new exposure the tribe received through the casino, gift shops, marketing efforts, and language documentation projects, there was a marked increase in requests for tribal members to demonstrate their cultural traditions to an interested public. As in previous generations, weavers and other tribal members often had to overcome their natural hesitation to being photographed or recorded—an echo of their elders "taking it on the chin" to benefit the tribe. For example, when weaver Rosabel Robinson Sylestine was interviewed in 1995, the interviewer asked her to tell stories about weaving her baskets "in her own language." The recording contains several minutes of her expressing confusion to her daughter Edith about what she was being asked to say, followed by instances of Rosabel repeating the interviewers' questions in Koasati rather than answering them. After Sylestine was finished sharing all that she felt was necessary, she ended the interview by saying in Koasati, "That's all I'm going to say. I'm done now."[61]

Similarly, Steven Robinson overcame his reluctance to being recorded when he agreed to be videotaped in 2007 demonstrating the process of making *chawahka* (a traditional corn soup), utilizing his grandfather Solomon Battise's cane baskets.[62] Not only is some of the traditional knowledge related to *chawahka*-making closely held within families, it is also difficult to demonstrate the process in one shot, so camera operators had to take multiple shots from different angles in order to capture it. Although he was uncomfortable being recorded, Robinson agreed to being featured in this film project because of the benefits it held for the tribe in preserving this knowledge. He did feel much more at ease, however, that fellow tribal member Ernest Sickey was there to ask him questions in Koasati, rather than an outsider talking to him in English."[63] A major aspect of maintaining the traditional knowledge of cane basketry involves maintaining knowledge of the traditional uses of the baskets. During the filming, Robinson expressed his gratitude to his grandparents both for teaching him how to make *chawahka*, as well as for gifting him all the baskets used to process the corn into soup. "I'm glad I was taught to do this—everybody should know how."[64]

Robinson recalled that as a child he spent numerous hours watching his grandfather pound the corn, then sift it through the sequence of cane baskets with increasingly fine diameter weaves. He learned the importance of taking his time with each step of the process by watching Solomon and observing all that he did. Years later, he was careful to demonstrate the process of transferring the corn from the pounding log to the cane baskets by hand. He arranged his baskets in order of the diameter and size of the holes in the bottom, starting with the largest-size holes to those with the finest, most tightly knit bottoms, being sure to look at the bottom of each basket to be sure he had the right "gauge" before he transferred the corn into it. Throughout this process, Robinson only used cane baskets that were made and handed down to him by his grandfather. He explained that the amount of *chawahka* desired determined the amount of corn to be used, which in turn determined the number of times he had to go through the entire process of sifting the corn to an increasingly fine consistency so it would cook correctly. The process cannot be rushed, and the baskets should not be overloaded or "you got to start over again."[65] Over a decade after conducting the interview with Robinson, Ernest Sickey reflected on that recording, and the amazing efficiency of the cane-basket technology used in processing corn:

Steven Robinson processing corn for *chawahka*, 2007. Courtesy of the Coushatta Tribal Archives.

> I remember watching the elders hold the basket they were using to sift the corn over another basket, so that the finer, smaller grains that fell through one basket could be caught in another. The larger grains that stayed [in the first basket] were made into *chawahka,* and the ones that fell through to the second basket were used to make bread. Then they did that again, and the waste [that fell through to the third basket] were fed to the chickens or hogs. . . . It's not the size of the basket, it's the weave that defines the end product.

Calling this manufacturing process "ingenious," Sickey explained how the Coushattas found a "way to process food, to make tools and utensils out of cane, things that we needed, that would last us for hundreds of years."[66] In 2013, the call to educate others about Coushatta traditional knowledge was passed onto Jonas John, who was invited to demonstrate the making of *chawahka,* as well as traditional Coushatta crafts like the making of stickball racquets and balls, for a nationally circulated issue of *Indian Country Today.*[67]

Asaala Achooka Stinfaihilaahis Komatlaawista̲
We Are Leaving Our Basket Industry to Our Children

Ensuring that Coushatta basketry and other traditions endure relies on a commitment to collaboration between the tribe, the weavers, and their children and grandchildren. In addition, securing access to the natural resources needed for basket making has required the tribe to enter into agreements with the US Forest Service to secure continued access to land. As a result of this agreement, pine-needle gathering day trips for all weavers, which has grown to approximately sixty people—as well as their children and grandchildren—are conducted annually. As they have done for generations, tribal children are shown how to climb the trees or bend them down so elders can pick the needles. Efforts also have been made to ensure that tribal lands offered the materials artisans needed when the tribe collaborated with the US Fish and Wildlife Service to complete three "Partners for Fish and Wildlife" projects on different tracts of tribal lands since 2009. Those projects resulted in approximately 350 acres of habitat restoration and improvement, including longleaf pine and bottomland hardwood reforestation, wetland rehabilitation, invasive species control, and soft mast plantings. In 2013, the program gave the tribe a Regional Landowner's Stewardship Award for its habitat restoration efforts, noting that tribal elders utilized pine needles from the restored longleaf pine trees to weave intricate baskets, helping to preserve an important part of their tribal heritage.[68]

Teaching the next generation of Coushattas how to sew baskets continued to be a priority. Although the number of tribal weavers shrank for several years as the tribe underwent some political and economic transitions, a major revitalization effort emerged in the 1990s and into the new century. The first pine-needle basketry classes for children were taught by Heather Williams, one of the first young tribal members to work with the Heritage Department, and who is a proficient fifth-generation weaver herself.[69] Bertney Langley recalled watching Williams learn to make baskets before she even reached her teen years. He was particularly intrigued to see her develop a method for sewing a closed-stitch basket with the tribal seal, like the one he asked her grandmother to sew for the Coushatta Cultural Center back in the 1970s.

Langley asked Heather's mother, Loretta Robinson Williams, if she knew why Heather was so interested in learning to sew. Williams replied: "Since she was small, she has always been interested in anything Indian. . . . She said, 'I want to sew baskets; teach me.' And I gave it to her and said, 'here, just watch me or watch others and you can do it.' She would sit there and ask, 'am I doing it right?' And I would say, 'yes,' and didn't really show her. And she would watch and watch and sometimes I would tell her to pull harder and she would do that, and eventually she finished. She is getting good now."[70] Heather's enthusiasm and natural talent for basket making have been shared with many tribal youths as her classes grew in popularity, resulting in standing-room-only classes and waiting lists. Heather also began serving in the role of cultural ambassador as she and her mother gave public presentations about the art of Coushatta basketry around the area to such groups as the Rotary Club in Kinder.[71]

While tribal weavers—both seasoned and new to the art—committed to the perseverance of the practice of sewing pine-needle baskets, tribal members were also eager to revitalize the tradition of cane basketry.

Top left, Heather Williams teaching Haley John how to start a basket, 2008. *Top right,* Tribal seal basket woven by Heather Williams. *Bottom,* collection of tribal baskets. Note the large tribal seal basket made by Florence Robinson, Heather's grandmother, with garfish rising above the top of the basket. Courtesy of the Coushatta Tribal Archives.

When anthropologist M. Raymond Harrington visited the community in 1908, all of the tribal families had cane-basket weavers, and he was able to purchase thirty-six baskets representing thirteen different basket forms. A century later, cane basketry was no longer dominant, with the last master weaver, Solomon Battise, still weaving cane baskets well into his nineties.[72] However, when Battise passed away in 2003, the community hoped that this form of traditional knowledge had not died with him. More than a decade later, Battise's son Leonard made the decision to revive the art form so that it "won't be lost."[73] He depicted a process of resurrecting his own muscle memory and reconstructing his father's teachings, sometimes resorting to taking apart one of his father's baskets to see how the corners and rims were constructed: "When I picked it up again in 2012, everything was really hard for me—the stripping, everything. There wasn't anybody to ask because there wasn't anybody who made cane baskets anymore. One day I picked up one of my dad's baskets. I was talking with my wife while I was looking at it, thinking about how my dad always said he didn't want us to lose that art, and I said 'I believe I can make that.'"[74]

Battise said that, once he started, he began to recall what his father taught him, but "it was really hard." In addition to taking his father's old baskets apart to recount the steps, Battise also began working out designs in his head and then attempting to make them. Like his father, he opted not to draw designs out on paper, preferring to work tactilely. Sometimes he works on a basket for a few hours and then sets it down and walks away so that he can look at it with fresh eyes later. This helps him see, upon returning to it, if he made any mistakes. Leonard Battise kept the first cane basket he made for himself because it had numerous mistakes and was loosely woven and uneven. It serves as a reminder to him of how far he has come in revitalizing a traditional art form, which motivates him to keep going and teach others.

Locating and cutting river cane proved more difficult than Battise anticipated. He recalled that his father was able to tell the best cane for making baskets just by looking at it. "He used to tell us that the ones that grow by the bayou are the best; to choose cane that is straight and thin, with joints that are a little bit further apart." Battise later explained that, when he got used to cutting the cane, he could tell by the sound of the knife whether it was a good stalk of cane or not. "You can tell by 'thunking' the cane if it makes the right sound."[75] Like other tribal members, Battise explained that weavers also had to be in the right mindset in order to find the right cane to cut: "My ancestors used to say that if you go looking for cane, you go in there quietly or reverently. . . . if the wind is not blowing, you'll spot a cane brake. . . . you find it and go up to it gently, and look on top of the leaf right here, and if there is a leaf twirling, they said that was a sign from the spirits that you could cut that group of cane. That's the old saying."[76]

Like most of the older tribal members, Battise recalled watching the elders split the cane to make baskets. Although the older people did all the cutting and splitting by hand without using gloves, Battise opted to use gloves to protect his hands. He also remembered that some of the elders held the cane in their mouths and sometimes split it with their teeth, but he didn't use that technique, either. Adhering to other aspects of the process that he was taught, Battise begins by splitting the cane into four equal parts "right in the middle," continuing the splits straight down the entire length of the cane. He soon learned, however, that splitting the cane is a difficult, time-consuming process that cannot be rushed. "You can't push the knife, you have to find the middle and just work the knife gently, swing it, then go back and forth, pulling one side, then pulling the other. You can't rush [the splitting process]; you have to take your time and be really careful or the cane will split unevenly and be ruined."[77]

Like his ancestors before him, Battise improved the cane-splitting process by integrating traditional knowledge with his own innovations. To facilitate the splitting process, he made himself a small tool of two crosspieces of metal welded together and then embedded this tool in a block of wood. He uses this tool to split the cane into four even parts after he notches the top of the stalk. He works the full length of the cane down the tool to ensure that he splits it into four equal splints and sets the splints out flat to dry. This wasn't the only modern innovation he created to facilitate the weaving process, however. Although his father and other basket makers from previous generations typically wove baskets in their laps, Battise makes a square board with gridlines to start his baskets. He also lays out the long pieces of canes and then uses bricks and books to hold the edges down; in addition to gloves, he sometimes uses pliers to make the weaving easier. One of his weaving students, Clifford Poncho, uses a power sander to smooth out bumps on the cane.

Although outsiders sometimes see a conflict between innovation and tradition, tribal weavers encourage such inventions, viewing innovation itself as a part of Coushatta culture. Like Battise taking apart his father's basket to relearn the weaving process, people understand that baskets and other cultural items are not just saved and put away, but used and reconceptualized. Coushattas maintain that every generation is expected to develop its own innovations to keep traditions fresh and vibrant.[78] Lorenda John Poncho, who was a student both in the first cane-basket workshop organized by Battise's father and also the current cane-basketry class, commented on weaving innovations she observed over a forty-year period.[79] Cane baskets in the Coushatta Tribal Archives have examples that span decades, such as unique closures on large cane "picnic baskets" and woven "scrapbook covers."[80] In addition to reviewing new tools and techniques, contemporary weavers discuss innovations in methods of dyeing cane and raffia.[81]

Battise says he came a long way in the years since he started weaving again, even being able to distinguish the quality of baskets by looking at them. After getting to a point where he felt comfortable with his own skill level in weaving cane baskets, he finally gave in to repeated requests from other tribal members to start teaching classes. "I like teaching [basket weaving to] students, but they have to be serious about learning. They have to really want to learn how to do it. I teach students the basics, but I tell them it's up to each one of them to find little shortcuts, to learn and make it their own."[82] Battise started with a group of dedicated students that included Clifford Poncho, Loretta Robinson Williams, and Lorenda John Poncho, as well as one of his daughters.[83] He started by taking the students into the woods to cut their own cane, warning, "To get to the cane you have to face snakes, spiders, alligators and mosquitoes—but all that is nothing compared to the landowners who might be mad and shoot at you." Battise says that he later learned that not all students were as dedicated as this first group: "Some people come for classes, but then they see how hard it is to find the cane, to cut and strip it, how time consuming it all is, [so] they quit and don't come back."[84] Unlike the tribal pine-needle basketry classes that enroll both children and adults, Battise limits his classes to adults for safety reasons.

Loretta Robinson Williams, the mother of Heather Williams, was one of Battise's first cane-basketry students and expressed her appreciation for how challenging it was to work with river cane. She reported that one of the hardest things about it was making the basket edges and turning the corners. Battise taught his method of making small baskets, which involves measuring the length of the cane before starting, so that

Cane-basketry class, March 2016. Note innovations: gloves and modern tools. *Left to right,* Loretta Robinson Williams, Kassie Battise Dawsey, Leonard Battise, Lorenda John Poncho, Clifford Poncho. Photo by Cameron Poncho, Coushatta Tribal Archives.

all the cane splints are equal. He also soaks the cane used for the corners for at least an hour, so the materials will be pliable enough. If the cane breaks during this process, it takes a lot of work to splice a new piece in so that the break won't be noticeable. It is also hard to hide the joints in the cane so as not to ruin the design or pattern. Bertney Langley recalled once, when he was young, he watched his grandmother Ency Robinson Abbey Abbott split her cane. After he told her that it looked easy, he remembers her saying "'you try it then,' so I did, and right away I split the cane wrong and it broke. I never thought it looked easy or said anything to her after that."[85]

A resurging interest in basket weaving in recent years has not only resulted in ongoing classes and workshops, but it has situated basketry—once again—as an anchor in bringing the community together. In addition to the annual community pine-needle gathering trips, the tribe began organizing events where basket makers were invited to sew together. As always, weavers appreciate opportunities to get together; without these gatherings, some expressed a lack of motivation to work on their baskets. Lorenda John Poncho underscored this point, explaining, "I get lazy by myself."[86] This is quite a commentary given that laziness is traditionally considered one of the worst possible conditions one could have. Leveraging the community's collective creative energy, the Coushatta Education Department initiated an annual Christmas ornament contest for tribal elders. Although participants can use any materials to make their ornaments, there is a category dedicated to basketry ornaments. In the years since its inception, tribal elders have produced an amazing variety of pine-needle and cane basketry Christmas ornaments representing numerous new designs and ideas. Particularly innovative ornaments have included a longleaf pine basket shaped and decorated like Santa Claus, a Frosty the Snowman basket, a lighted Christmas tree basket, a cardinal with holly in its beak, and a cross woven of river cane.[87]

The teaching and marketing of basketry has always been a multigenerational practice within the Coushatta community, and recent happenings have proven to be no exception. Basketry demonstrations and presentations are offered at the tribal immersion schools, as well as area schools and museums. Children are typically included in these presentations, so they learn how to continue the tradition of conducting family basketry demonstrations and educating the public.[88] Other recent intergenerational outreach activities involved a November 2017 trip to the Northwestern State University Basketry exhibit. Approximately thirty tribal weavers attended the event, representing several generations of basket makers. Reflecting on the visit, younger tribal members were struck by how happy the weavers were to see baskets made by their parents and grandparents in the exhibit, and by how intensely they studied and discussed each basket.[89] The younger weavers also reflected on their own motivations for maintaining the basket-making tradition, which was fueled by a desire to maintain Coushatta culture and identity rather than primarily responding to the economic pressures that previous generations of weavers faced.

While experienced basket makers demonstrated their commitment to teaching other tribal members the art of pine-needle and cane bas-

Christmas ornament contest winners and entries. *Left to right,* Heather Williams (2018), Zeline Langley Sylestine (2019), Lorenda John Poncho (top, 2012), Jeanette Celestine Langley (2007), Marion Robinson John (2008). *Bottom left,* Coushatta Tribal Police and Fire Department badge, with large covered basket behind tribal seal. *Bottom right,* Darlene Langley Dunnehoo and Chester Langley at Williamson Museum exhibit (2017). All photos courtesy of the Coushatta Tribal Archives.

ketry, younger weavers embraced their responsibility to maintain cultural continuity. Assisting in this effort, the tribal council ensured that baskets continued to be used as prominent symbols of tribal identity throughout the gaming facility and hotels, as well as by having baskets sold at the casino gift shop. Basketry is also used more subtly in mar-

Top, Adrian Poncho Sylestine teaching Clarissa Wier how to start a basket, July 2014. *Bottom left,* wheat-stitch basket by Clarissa Wier, 2019. *Bottom right,* Landon Daigle with his decorated wheat-stitch basket, 2020. Courtesy of the Coushatta Tribal Archives.

keting themes and presentations, such as the border or background on tribal clothing, mugs, and even mouse pads. In continuing the practice of basket diplomacy used a half-century earlier by Ernest Sickey, the tribal council also continues the practice of presenting baskets to political allies, leaders, and diplomats. Recent examples include gifting baskets to a United Nations ambassador, the consul general of Israel, and a White House tribal liaison. In addition, the tribe had a bundle of longleaf pine needles placed at Arizona Senator John McCain's gravesite.[90]

The practice of gifting baskets is also used for more personalized gestures of gratitude and friendship. Individual weavers, for example, regularly give baskets to visiting scholars, linguists, and other professionals who help the tribe. Jeanette Celestine Langley explained that she gifted a large pine-needle basket to landowners who let her pick pine needles on their land.[91] In addition to giving baskets as a form of appreciation, value is also placed on the time that Coushattas give to others outside of the tribe—particularly researchers or others interested in learning about the tribe's culture and history. While there was a period when many Coushattas felt their generosity was taken advantage of by researchers whose motivations and approaches were exploitative in nature, changes in how academic fieldwork is conducted, along with shifting mindsets that embrace Indigenous-driven research initiatives, have significantly reshaped modes of academic inquiry. As a result, during one Koasati language committee meeting, Barbara Williams Langley suggested that non-tribal students be allowed to observe the proceedings, stating, "If we don't let them come in, how will they ever learn to actually work with Indians?"[92]

Having gift shops located at both the reservation and the casino initially resulted in different price scales and options for tribal weavers. Although basket makers appreciated the opportunity to receive higher prices, they also wanted some consistency in appraisal and pricing standards. Accordingly, Loretta Robinson Williams developed basket-pricing guidelines based on internal tribal standards of appraisal that remained consistent since the height of the industry several decades earlier. These standards included the tightness and evenness of stitching, orientation and spacing of stitches, quality of decoration and finish work on the basket, size of the basket and originality of the design, and the overall quality of the basket. While there is a consistent understanding of what constitutes a high-quality basket, it wasn't until weavers came together and began discussing how best to value their work that a standard price schema was developed.

Himaayaamiip, Yaamosin Stonth
At Present, This Is How Far We Have Come

The traditional knowledge of Coushatta basket making—along with the way this knowledge is transmitted across generations—continues to the present day. Weavers show youth how and when to pick needles, where and when to cut cane, how to process these materials, and how to sew and weave different styles of baskets. The tribe facilitates the continuity of this tradition in a variety of ways, including the hosting of basketry classes and the sponsoring of annual pine-needle gathering trips. Older weavers continue to demonstrate approaches to weaving to the younger generations by encouraging them to join intergenerational sewing circles, as well as modeling the importance of maintaining a modest disposition. Ernest Sickey recalled a continued aversion to boastfulness despite repeated accolades that basket weavers had received for their work from tourists over the years, in which they consistently reply: "I'm still learning."[93] Leonard Battise epitomized this mindset when he received recognition for his efforts in revitalizing cane weaving, insisting that "I'm sure they got people out there that know more than I do."[94]

Coushatta youth today share similar childhood memories with the generations who came before them. Young weavers recently interviewed remembered growing up watching their elders sew baskets, practicing with raffia and pine needles on the floor, then asking their grandparents, parents, aunts, and uncles for advice and suggestions.[95] Weavers are still taught that everyone starts a basket differently, to make their stitches in a way that feels right to them, and to begin with easy shapes, like the hot plate, before trying to make covered baskets or animal effigies. Even in situations where tribal youth have taken basketry classes sponsored by the tribe, they still go to family members for assistance. Clarissa Wier recalled the support she received from her grandmother, Jeanette Celestine Langley, explaining:

> I was really scared when I first started [learning to sew baskets], and I remember that after my first day I went to go visit my *aapo* [grandmother] and she gave me a bunch of tips, like ways to keep my hand from hurting, different stitches I could use, how many pine needles to

> use when I'm sewing, and what thickness of raffia was best, so I would go to her house almost every day after those classes to pick up tips like that. Those tips really helped me, in addition to what I was learning in the class. . . . I remember that in the class, I wanted to mimic the older women's styles and stitch patterns, but . . . the older women told me that everyone has their own style, that imperfection was okay in making baskets.[96]

Upon losing her grandmother, Wier further reflected on the importance of basket weaving to their relationship, stating how "this story makes me kind of emotional, but I remember my *aapo* always wanted a basket from me, because I was one of her only grandchildren that sewed actively, so she really wanted a basket from me. The last Christmas that she was with us, before she passed away, I was finally able to make her a basket and give it to her, and I remember seeing how happy she was, and how proud of me she was. I was really glad I was able to give that to her before she left us."[97]

Similarly, Landon Daigle recalled learning to sew baskets as a child in a family sewing session, then again as a teenager in a tribal basketry class.[98] As a nineteen-year-old returning to the community, Daigle had a strong desire to start sewing again and complete a basket. He recalled being motivated by finding a big bundle of raffia and some bundled pine needles in an old house.[99] He wanted to try a large covered wheat-stitch basket, usually considered too difficult for a younger weaver. He initially got advice about starting the basket and measuring it from his cousin, Lorenda John Poncho.[100] Despite knowing the basic technique, Daigle still wasn't certain about details like needle placement to make the wheat-stitch pattern, so he called her on the phone for advice. Poncho recalled telling him where to place his needle, thinking that he would only be starting or working on a small section of the basket, but to her amazement he next called with a question about finishing the basket lid! Poncho was so impressed by the quality of Daigle's basket that she invited him to the weekly quilters' club meeting to show it to other weavers, and to get advice in sewing pine cones on the finished basket.[101] Daigle's basket was deemed so well-made that he was encouraged to bring it to a recent Language and Cultural Committee meeting, where it was enthusiastically passed from hand to hand among the fifty elders present.

In situations where younger weavers no longer have a grandparent to teach them, they learn basketry from other older relatives. Ronnie Abbey recalled that his son Elliott was interested in basket weaving as a child but didn't have the opportunity to learn from his grandmother, Irene Abbey, because she had passed away before Elliott was born. Abbey remembered a group of elders that used to gather at his grandmother Phoebe Celestine's house in the mornings to sew baskets. "They would all get up and cook their husbands' lunches for the day, then come to grandma's house and make baskets, gossip, laugh, share news and go back around noon or so to get supper started." Abbey said his son Elliott was "the little 'gofer' for the group."[102] Elliott recalled that, as a young child, he thought of these basket-making gatherings as work and preferred playing outside.

> I always thought it was a chore to go and do these things, but little did I know that they were incorporating all these different [basket-making] processes within me, you know, [making sure] I learned step-by-step what to do. You know, the hardest part of the basket is starting it off and them ladies would always let me start the basket off, but never let me finish them. They would take the starters. What they were doing is just having me do the hard part and then they would take those starters from me and make baskets from it. That way they didn't have to start the baskets off. That was kind of my job back then, but, you know, little did I know that all these different steps were being put into my mind and put into my memory to keep things within me. And I didn't know back then that I would carry this thing on.[103]

Young tribal basket makers often relate the significance of participating in this time-honored tradition of sewing in an intergenerational setting where they learn different techniques from seasoned weavers and savor the opportunity to practice speaking Koasati. An example is when Gwyneth Thompson recalled the help she received from Marjorie Abbey Battise:

> My dad [Leland Thompson] and I went to a grocery store to pick her up [a] gift just to thank her. Then my *aapo* [Deretha Sylestine Thompson] and I had gone over and we ended up sitting outside under the porch. [When we first started] it was confusing trying to follow along with her because she was left-handed, and so am I, but eventually I started

to pick it up. And we were talking back and forth. . . . She spoke to me in Koasati the whole time that she was doing the process—it was very surprising to me, but I understood all of it. And it was really awesome, it was exciting.

Similarly, Gwyneth Thompson remembered another special time spent with her grandmother: "One of my favorite memories when I was sewing baskets, was me and my *aapo* were at her house and we were sewing and we were just talking and talking away sewing and we were like 'Oh God, our thumbs are hurting,' and she's like 'yeah, my neck is hurting' and then we looked at the clock and we [realized that we had been] sewing until five o'clock in the morning."[104]

Tribal weavers of the emerging generation are passionate and articulate about their commitment to the continuation of the art form. For example, Clarissa Wier explains the impact of learning to weave on her own cultural identity:

> One thing that I've really gotten spiritually and emotionally from making baskets is that—because I'm mixed, I'm both white and Native—there's always been this kind of pull between both worlds. Either I'm too white to be Native, or I'm too Native to be white. . . . When I started making baskets, that's what brought me closer to my culture. . . . Making baskets isn't just about the art because it inspired me to one day, hopefully, become a political advocate for Native American civil rights, [which is] still a problem today. I think it's important to emphasize the fact that art, in our culture, isn't just art. It's a movement to recognize that Native people are still here, our culture is still here, and it matters. . . . My identity isn't my race, but it's what I do with the culture that comes along with that.[105]

Elliot Abbey similarly pointed out a healing motivation for returning to basketry in his twenties:

> I fell into a bad lifestyle and I just couldn't let it go. . . . And that's when I turned to the baskets. The baskets were kind of like a medicine for me. . . . once I got into the baskets, the whole culture aspect started coming back to me. When I got into class and started making the baskets, something just clicked in me. My family has been known for these baskets and they always tell me that travels through families, and these gifts pass on to the younger generations if you're thankful for it and

use it wisely and don't take it for granted. I'm just thankful that I was blessed to be able to spend all that time with them [my aunts] to sit on that porch. Yeah, at the time I thought it was work, it was a chore and a hassle to do all that. Now, being older, I realize they weren't just giving me chores and work, they were teaching me, blessing me, and giving me a gift. It's important for me to carry on those things.[106]

In describing the powerful motivations for continuing these weaving traditions, another young weaver shared: "I tell my sisters 'you should take pride in basket weaving because there's nothing like that in the world. That's the one thing you'll have as a Coushatta person. This art is dying and if it dies, who are you to say that you are Coushatta? It's kind of like part of your identity is dying. It's a practice that I think is integral to being Coushatta."[107]

While scholars have noted that river-cane weaving represents the oldest living basketry tradition in the Southeast, the Coushattas have also embraced pine-needle basketry as integral to their tribal history and cultural identity.[108] The survival of basket-making traditions using both types of materials has been possible because of the efforts of weavers like Leonard Battise and Heather Williams, who work to teach and pass these traditions on to the next generation. Likewise, the continuation of this art form wouldn't have been possible without the hard work and dedication of students who had committed to learning.

The younger generation of basket makers have a great deal to share about what the art form means to them; however, the reflection of older weavers also offers an essential perspective on how the practice has endured. In 2007, weavers gathered at the tribal museum to sew baskets and reminisce about changes they had observed in basketry traditions over the course of their lifetimes. Marion Robinson John noted how "Things are different now. It's hard to find good pine needles, because the trees are scarce, and they're all fenced in. We used to find them everywhere a long time ago, even alongside the roads, but not anymore."[109] Jeanette Celestine Langley commented that new materials were available, but even though she could buy colored raffia, she still liked to buy it plain and dye it herself. Loris Abbott Langley observed that, despite the challenges in acquiring materials, the skill of the weavers had increased over time: "The ones making baskets now have gotten a lot better."[110]

There are many contemporary examples of the continuity of Cous-

Weavers gathering at tribal museum, 2007. *Left to right,* Geraldine Sylestine Reed, Marion Robinson John, Marjorie Abbey Battise, Loris Abbott Langley, Elizabeth Marie Abbott Thompson. Courtesy of the Coushatta Tribal Archives.

hatta basketry traditions and how they are being incorporated into innovative tribal projects. Yet, the one that best reflects the arc of recent efforts is a collaborative project, the "Long Swamp: Life in the Etowah River Valley," a traveling exhibit on southeastern archaeology and Indigenous cultures. This is the outcome of a partnership between the Coushatta Tribe, the Waring Archaeological Laboratory, the Georgia Department of Transportation, and the Sowela Technical Institute in Lake Charles. The exhibit brochure emphasizes that "the Coushatta people work hard to preserve their Koasati language and their traditional crafts, such as their longleaf pine needle and river cane basketry, which is renowned worldwide." Loretta Robinson Williams contributed a longleaf pine-needle basket for the exhibit, which is also pictured in the brochure. At the exhibit opening, Leonard Battise and three of his tribal students demonstrated cane-basket weaving. The cane weavers were accompanied by six experienced Coushatta weavers and students demonstrating pine-needle basketry.[111] The exhibit opening, as well as other tribal events, demonstrated that the art of Coushatta basketry is alive and well. While this is reassuring, tribal weavers continue to warn against letting their guard down, resulting in the potential of not keeping the children engaged in the art. As Lorenda John Poncho explained, "When I was small, I would watch my *aapo* sitting there sewing baskets. I was interested, so I learned. I think we need to do the same so when the little kids see us, they will go on being interested. So, we shouldn't give up."[112]

Epilogue

Atchakki
Following

Raynella Thompson Fontenot and Heather Williams

My children and the children of the Tribe were taught to be receptive to the old ways and to respect the tribal elders. . . . I think this is why we are able to continue.

—Edward Sylestine

IN 2019, ALMOST 150 YEARS after the first Coushatta families settled along Bayou Blue, our tribal basketry traditions are still thriving. It's relatively easy to take for granted how rare and valuable a gift it is to grow up in a tribal community and be taught how to make baskets in traditional ways. Through age, we've come to cherish those moments of having had the opportunity to learn and sew with our mothers, grandmothers, great-grandmothers, and extended family members. Continuing the practices of our ancestors remains a strong priority today because part of our identity is upheld through our basket traditions. Conducting research for this book in our tribal archives, translating interviews with elder basket makers, cataloging baskets, reviewing old photographs, and speaking about these topics with basket makers have made us keenly aware of these gifts, and we are honored to write this epilogue.

As children, we grew up hearing of our great-grandmother, Maggie John Langley, and her skill at weaving river-cane baskets. Listening to the stories of times when basket making was a necessary survival skill for our elders is very humbling. As children, we learned from many in our tribal community who participated in the laborious efforts of gathering, splitting, drying, sewing, weaving, and selling baskets that would help our families and our tribe survive. Despite having grown up with these truths, we did not fully understand the amount of work involved until we began teaching these traditions to younger tribal members and to our own children and relatives. Watching the desire and interest of this next generation of basket makers grow and seeing them share in the experience and knowledge of carrying on basketry traditions in the same way afforded to us by our mothers, grandmothers, and great-aunts have richly inspired us all. Without the elders, our existence and story as Coushatta people would likely be much different today, and without the youth, we would see no hope for an unbroken line of Coushatta weavers stretching far into the future.

Like most Coushatta traditions, basketry is a time of sharing, storytelling, teaching, learning, reminiscing about favorite memories, and encouragement. Losing track of time while sewing is a common occurrence and is usually described as an enjoyable experience. We can recall many stories of family members sewing into the early hours of the morning, despite having a full workload the very next day. This behavior is never viewed as reckless, but as hardworking and supportive of the family's well-being. As fourth-generation basket makers, we are proud to uphold these time-honored traditions. However, it is not enough for our children to learn the techniques of basketry; they must learn to live with the quiet dignity and respect that has allowed generations of our people to survive and thrive against all odds.

This book depicts the role of Coushatta basket makers in guaranteeing our tribe's continued existence—gifting, bartering, and selling baskets to forge key alliances and ensure economic survival. The vision and determination of our elders, many of whom played a less visible public role, comes through clearly in every photograph, story and quote. The timing of this publication coincides with the twenty-fifth anniversary of the opening of our tribal casino, which has brought significant growth and prosperity to our tribal nation. From an initial reservation base of fifteen acres in 1973, the Coushatta Tribe now owns over seven thousand acres in trust and fee-simple lands, including almost six thousand acres in Allen Parish, Louisiana. Our tribe now has over nine hundred enrolled members and operates over twenty departments to provide services to members, including a Health Department and Health Clinic, an Education Department, a Social Services Department, a Fitness and Wellness Center, a Tribal Pre-School, and much more. We also maintain our own Tribal Court and Department of Public Safety, which includes Fire, Emergency Medical Services, and Tribal Police departments.

We now have a generation of tribal youth who have been raised with this economic prosperity; significantly, one of their most frequent requests is for programs to teach and revitalize our Koasati language, basket making, and other cultural traditions. Their expressed interests provide parents and elders a hopeful outlook for our tribe's future in maintaining the values and ways of Coushatta people. We believe this written work will resonate well with our youth and community, developing a greater appreciation of our history and basket traditions, and how, as the elders say, "the struggle has made us stronger."

From our perspective as both the children of our elders and the parents of future tribal leaders, we can hope for no greater legacy to leave future generations than that they continue to maintain our Koasati traditions. With the blessings of *Aba Chokkooli* (the One Who Sits on High) and the guidance from elders, future tribal members will continue to weave and sew our traditional baskets and thereby thrive for generations to come.

Appendix 1

Koasati Asaala Achooliiha
Louisiana Coushatta Weavers

IT IS VIRTUALLY IMPOSSIBLE to compile a definitive list of Coushatta weavers over the past two centuries, particularly because so few records were kept before the 1960s. This alphabetical list includes Coushatta basket makers who are either actively engaged in the craft or who have been identified as weavers in historical records or tribal oral histories. One resource used was *Members of the Koasati Ayiksa* (12th ed., 2002), compiled by Geoffrey Kimball, on loan by Bertney Langley to the Coushatta Tribal Archives. However, this list is primarily the result of assistance provided by contemporary weavers and reviewed by the tribal Language and Cultural Committee. Names of additional weavers were still being brought to us at the time of publication, so the list will continue to grow. For more information about the family relationships between basket makers, visit the Coushatta Tribal Archives or the Koasati Heritage website.

Abbey, Bel
Abbey, Elliot Rain
Abbey, Emily
Abbey, Fern Williams
Abbey, Irene Annette Celestine
Abbey, Jeff
Abbey, Nora
Abbott, Ency Robinson Abbey
Alabama, Sissy Robinson
Austin, Dorothy
Battise, Adeline
Battise, Burrissa
Battise, Doris Celestine
Battise, Elisor
Battise, Leila Obe
Battise, Leonard
Battise, Lorraine
Battise, Marjorie Abbey
Battise, Solomon
Bond, Susie Sylestine
Boudreaux, Hannah Nichols
Celestine, Madeline Robinson

Celestine, Phoebe
Courville, Kaitlynn Nichols
Crosby, Sharon Robinson
Daigle, Landon
Daigle, Sophia John
Dirt, Lilian
Dunnehoo, Darlene Langley
Fontenot, Raynella Thompson
Fore, Caroleen
Francis, Leona
Hasting, Claudine Celestine
John, Elsie
John, Liz
John, Lycia Robinson
John, Margaret
John, Marion Robinson
King, Virginia Poncho
Landry, Eleyna Langley
Langley, Delia
Langley, Edith Sylestine
Langley, Edna Lorena Abbott
Langley, Elizabeth Abbott Thompson
Langley, Jeanette Celestine
Langley, Lora John Poncho
Langley, Loris Abbott
Langley, Maggie John
Langley, Ronald
LeJeune, Rena
LeJeune, Sabrina
Lester, Kiana
Lowe, Julia Robinson
Noack, Ida Mae Poncho
Obe, Minnie
Obe, Sequoia
Polite, Weaver
Poncho, Clifford
Poncho, Jamison
Poncho, Jane
Poncho, Joyce Abbey
Poncho, Lorenda John
Poncho, Ruth
Poncho, Tracy
Reed, Geraldine Sylestine
Robinson, Florence Langley
Robinson, Glenna Battise
Robinson, Isabel Celestine
Robinson, Lizzy
Robinson, Louisa Williams
Robinson, Steven
Shuff, Dianna Celestine
Shutt, Gladys Celestine
Sickey, Ena Mae Robinson
Sylestine, Adrian Poncho
Sylestine, Calvin
Sylestine, Chris
Sylestine, Della
Sylestine, Rosabel Robinson
Sylestine, Shirley
Sylestine, Tana
Sylestine, Wanda
Sylestine, Zeline Langley
Thomas, Ada
Thompson, Derethea Sylestine

Thompson, Gwyneth
Wier, Clarissa
Williams, Adele
Williams, Ethel
Williams, Fannie
Williams, Heather
Williams, Loretta
Williams, Marcie
Williams, Minnie
Williams, Necy
Williams, Nissie
Williams, Susie
Williams, Wynema
Wilson, Myrna

Appendix 2

Naksofon Komasaala̲ Hochikkilooli? Where Are Our Baskets Stored?

FOR MORE THAN ONE HUNDRED years, Louisiana Coushatta baskets have been acquired by private collectors and museum acquisitions staff on a global scale. In 2019, we began the long process of identifying and documenting the locations of these holdings. The following is the result of these efforts to date, with an emphasis on collections held in Louisiana. This list will continue to grow as more locations are identified. Basket acquisition details can be found in the Coushatta Tribal Archives.

ARIZONA

Heard Museum, Phoenix

COLORADO

Denver Art Museum

LOUISIANA

1850 House, New Orleans

Cabildo Museum, New Orleans

Capitol Park Museum, Baton Rouge

Hiram "Pete" and Jeanette Gregory (private collection)

Historic New Orleans Collection

Dayna Lee (private collection)

Louisiana Office of Cultural Development, Division of the Arts, Louisiana Folklife Program, Louisiana State Capitol and Capitol Park State Museum, Baton Rouge

Louisiana State Exhibit Museum, Shreveport

Louisiana State Museum, New Orleans

Museum of Natural Science, Louisiana State University, Baton Rouge

New Orleans Museum of Art

Vermilionville Living History Museum, Lafayette

Williamson Museum, Northwestern State University, Natchitoches

MISSISSIPPI

Lauren Rogers Museum of Art, Laurel

OKLAHOMA

Museum of the Red River, Idabel

Sam Noble Museum, University of Oklahoma, Norman

WASHINGTON, DC

Smithsonian Institution

US Department of the Interior Museum, Stewart Lee Udall Building

Notes

Introduction

1. Throughout this book, the word *Koasati* is used to refer to the tribal language, and *Coushatta* is used to refer to the people. In some of the sources, particularly the personal narratives, the words are used interchangeably in reference to both the language and the people.

2. This basket is discussed further in chapter 2 and shown in chapter 3.

3. This expression even served as the title of a tribally produced publication. See Coushatta Tribe of Louisiana, "The Struggle Has Made Us Stronger."

4. Kniffen, Gregory, and Stokes, *The Historic Indian Tribes of Louisiana*, 157.

5. For a detailed political history of the tribe and its practice of "Basket Diplomacy," see Bates, *Basket Diplomacy.*

6. *Malmaamin* literally means "to be the same." See Coushatta Tribe of Louisiana, *Koasati Dictionary*, 149.

7. For example, in 1996, the Grace Hudson Museum published *Remember Your Relations: The Elsie Allen Baskets, Family and Friends*, utilizing the stories of twenty-six California Indian basket makers to construct a broader narrative of cultural perseverance and cross-tribal relationships in the nineteenth and twentieth centuries. The museum also published *Pomo Indian Basketry*, by Samuel A. Barrett, with an introduction by Pomo and Miwok museum curator Sherrie Smith-Ferri. Also, see Cathleen D. Cahill, "Making and Marketing Baskets in California"; and Sherrie Smith-Ferri, "The Development of the Commercial Market for Pomo Indian Baskets"; and Mason, *American Indian Basketry.*

8. For example, see Cooper, *Oklahoma Cherokee Baskets;* Fariello, *Cherokee Basketry;* James, *Indian Basketry;* Turnbaugh and Turnbaugh, *American Indian Baskets;* and Bernstein, *The Language of Native American Baskets.*

9. The federally recognized tribes in Louisiana include: the Chitimacha Tribe, the Coushatta Tribe, the Jena Band of Choctaw Indians, and the Tunica-Biloxi Indian Tribe. Additional communities recognized by the state of Louisiana include: the Addai Caddo Tribe, the Biloxi-Chitimacha Confederation of Muskogee, the Choctaw-Apache Community of Ebarb, the Clifton Choctaw, the Four Winds Tribe Louisiana Cherokee Confederacy, the Grand Caillou/Dulac Band, the Isle de Jean Charles Band, the Louisiana Choctaw Tribe, the Pointe-Au-Chien Indian Tribe, and the United Houma Nation. "National Conference of State Legislatures: Federal and State Recognized Tribes," accessed April 4, 2019.

10. See Bates, *The Other Movement,* and "Reshaping Southern Identity and Politics"; Gregory, "The Louisiana Tribes"; Klopotek, *Recognition Odysseys;* Miller, *Forgotten Tribes,* and *Claiming Tribal Identity;* and Mueller, Goldsmith, and Mueller, *Nations Within.*

11. Following the publication of historian Denise Bates's *Basket Diplomacy* in 2020, this will be the second book-length work published on the history of the Coushatta Tribe of Louisiana since 1976, when *The Coushatta People* by Bobby Johnson was released as part of a series. Most publications in circulation focus on the Coushatta language and traditional tales. Historical accounts are limited to book chapters, articles, and broader collections covering tribes across the region. Much of the scholarship focused on the Coushattas, specifically, has been by Daniel Jacobson during the mid-twentieth century. See "Koasati Cultural Changes" and "The Origin of the Koasati Community of Louisiana." The more recent scholarship is by coauthor and anthropologist Linda Langley, the Coushatta tribal historic preservation officer, who has published articles and book chapters on the Coushatta language, basket weaving, and homesteading, as well as historian Jay Precht, who has published articles on the Coushatta gaming enterprise, the role of baskets in their identity politics, and homesteading. See Langley, Oubre, and Precht, "Louisa Williams Robinson, Her Daughters, and Her Granddaughters"; Langley, LeJeune, and Oubre, eds., *Les Artistes;* Langley, Langley, Martin, and Hasselbacher, "The Koasati Language Project"; Langley, "Koasati (Coushatta) Literature," and "The Tribal Identity of Alexander McGillivray"; Precht, "'The Lost Tribe Wanders No More,'" "The Nine from the Pines," "Coushatta Basketry and Identity Politics," and "Coushatta Homesteading in Southwest Louisiana and the Development of the Community at Bayou Blue."

12. Jackson, "Containers of Tradition." For a historiography of American food production and consumption, see Bentley and Hobart, "Food in Recent U.S. History."

13. Citations of these community-collected interviews are referenced throughout this book.

1. *Naksaamit Stamahilkato̱*
How We Began

1. *Jeff Davis Parish Visitors Guide,* Coushatta Tribe of Louisiana Archives (hereafter CTLA), DC.321, 26.

2. US Department of the Interior Indian Arts and Crafts Board, "Contemporary Coushatta Fashions by The Langleys," May 1978, CTLA, DC.06.148.

3. A similar argument regarding the role of baskets in reaffirming Indigenous identity is used to explain the emphasis of the Chitimacha Tribe on their basketry, which became "tightly interwoven with their racial identity." See Usner, "'They Don't Like Indians around Here,'" 96; and "From Bayou Teche to Fifth Avenue," 339. Also, acclaimed Coushatta storyteller Bel Abbey's rendition of the "Lost Tribe" story was captured in a 1997 collection of "Folktales from Louisiana" and should be noted that it is uncertain whether he actually believed this version of the story as much as he acknowledged the

significant role it played in promoting the tribe. See Harvison and Owens, "Bel Abbey: Koasati Stories," 81–82.

4. Indigenous groups often prefer to describe their languages and customs as sleeping, rather than "dead" or "extinct." For a discussion of the implications of using this metaphor, see ABC News, "NAIDOC Week." The Coushattas typically say that a practice or tradition went "underground" rather than "died out."

5. Reprinted in Jacobson, "Koasati Culture Changes" (1954); Jacobson's testimony found in "Fulton Battise, Chief of the Tribal Council of the Alabama Coushatta Tribes and Ernest Sickey, Chairman of the Tribal Council of the Coushatta Tribe of Louisiana, and All Other Enrolled Members of the Alabama Coushatta Tribes of Texas and the Coushatta Tribe of Louisiana Respectively: Report" (to Accompany H. Res. 69). Report / 98th Congress, 1st Session, House of Representatives, No. 98-412. Washington D.C.: G.P.O., 1983, CTLA.

6. The relevant sections of Marcos Delgado's report read: "On leaving here there is another place at one league distance called Qusate [Coushatta] of an unknown nation which came a great distance from the north, fleeing from the English and the Chichumeco people which are the greatest conquerors (*politica*) among all the nations of Florida. This village has more than 500 warriors and is on the very bank of the river which goes to Mobila. . . . Going from this village to the northwest bend, about 3 good leagues, is a place called Tubani also of the Qusate nation which came from the north because of persecution from the English and Chichumecos and another nation called chalaque [Cherokee] which obliged them to flee from their lands in search of a place to settle, finally arriving at the margins of the river of Mobila. They have more than 200 warriors. . . . Dated in the village of Tuave province of Cosate, Oct. 30, 1686," rpt. in Boyd, "Expedition of Marcos Delgado, 1686," 30.

7. To better understand the political complexity of the Creek Confederacy, see Ethridge, *Creek Country*, and Hahn's *The Invention of the Creek Nation, 1670–1763*.

8. Coushatta women, as well as those of other southeastern tribes, were so skilled at bartering with Europeans that the Indian agent Benjamin Hawkins instructed his officers not to intermarry with Indian women. The relevant text of Hawkins's Act, issued January 14, 1799, shows that women of the Creek Confederacy were exerting too strong an influence over their husbands and children to further the American goals: "Having obtained from my own observation this degrading fact, that a white man by marrying an Indian woman of the Creek nation so far from bettering his condition becomes a slave of her family, I have deemed it proper in furtherance of the plan of civilization to order that no assistant in the Creek department shall be suffered to commit himself with a Creek woman as a wife. And if any assistant shall act in violation of this regulation he is to consider himself as free from his public engagements and no longer in the department." Grant, ed., *Letters, Journals and Writings of Benjamin Hawkins*, 239. For more on Alexander McGillivray, see Langley, "The Tribal Identity of Alexander McGillivray."

9. Outside of Louisiana, evidence for basketry dates back to 10,000 BP, with the earliest calibrated dates on three types of basketry from the Great Basin of western North

America. The oldest twined basketry dates to 10,380–10,918 BP, reed duck decoys to 2355–2773 BP, and wooden sandals of sagebrush bark or twined tule to 9247–10,375 BP and 9242–9836 BP, respectively. See Berger, Bendat, and Parker, "America's Oldest Basketry." Outside of North America, research indicates that basket-making technology existed more than 27,000 years ago (Brenda Fowler, "Find Suggests Weaving Preceded Settled Life," *New York Times*, May 9, 1995, C1). Within North America, coiled basketry techniques are typically seen after twined and plaited weaving techniques. Once developed, the coiled basketry industry typically increased in quantity, technical sophistication, and economic importance. See Geib and Jolie, "The Role of Basketry in Early Holocene Small Seed Exploitation," 96. In his comprehensive categorization of precontact North American basketry techniques, Weltfish identified ten "basketry areas" based on weaving techniques and materials used. He identified eight of these ten areas in the western third of North America. The remaining two were Algonquin and Southeastern. The Southeastern area includes baskets made by Cherokee, Chickasaw, Choctaw, Alibamu, Koasati, and Chitimacha weavers, primarily made of cane woven in the twilled-plaiting technique. See "Prehistoric North American Basketry Techniques and Modern Distributions."

10. Le Page du Pratz, *The History of Louisiana*, 293.

11. Gregory, "Asá:la Koasati Cane Basketry," 116. Gregory also noted that the Coushattas used river cane to make other commonly used items such as blowguns, darts, whistles, bird calls, and awls. Contemporary tribal crafters use river cane to make flutes. Bertney Langley, personal communication, April 1, 2019.

12. Kniffen, Gregory, and Stokes, *The Historic Indian Tribes of Louisiana*, 146. In General Teran's 1828 journey through Texas, he noted large stands of "pasturage" near Coushatta villages on the Trinity River, likely comprised of this type of cane and swamp grasses. He did not describe any Native basketry, though he did describe some native homes with "thatched" roofs. See Jackson, "Containers of Tradition," 130 and 255, and Mier y Terán et al., *Texas by Terán*.

13. In exchange for aid in subsistence, a critical factor for the poorly supplied French colony, and for military alliance, the French offered the Gulf tribes protection from larger, more powerful neighboring tribes, which they were careful to identify. On May 28, 1701, the French expedition noted: "On the banks of the River there are 36 nations of Savages in different villages, including Alebamons and Conchaque"—a common French spelling for Koasati/Coushatta. Upon his return to France, Iberville later wrote about this encounter, stating, "The Conchaques and Alibamons . . . villages may consist of four hundred families; the greater part have guns, are friends of the English and will shortly be ours." In 1703 the explorers noted the statement of other tribes that the "Conchaques" had a great amount of corn to trade, which would typically have been carried and stored in baskets. See Conrad, ed., *The Historical Journal of the Establishment of the French in Louisiana, 1698–1723*, 60 and 71. Also, Dayna Bowker Lee and others noted that Indian baskets were common items in colonial households by the early eighteenth century. See Lee, "The Ties That Bind," 43; Estes and Thompson, "Cane," 44–57; and Gregory, "Pieces and Patches," 9–11.

14. American surveyor Thomas Freeman visited the Coushattas living in what is now North Louisiana and recorded: "We visited the Chief of the Coashutta [*sic*] Village, who resides a few miles below it, and has a large corn field." Flores, *Southern Counterpart to Lewis & Clark*, 149–50. For more recent references to the significance of corn to Coushatta culture, see Jacobson, "Koasati Culture Changes."

15. See Neuman, "Split-Cane Items in Louisiana," for a discussion of archaeological evidence for split river-cane mats and baskets constructed in Louisiana circa 2000–2500 BC. In addition to the traditional concept of using cane baskets for storage, transport, and food processing, basket impressions indicate that baskets and mats were used in mound construction, to line burials, and to hold grave goods. The Coushatta settlement along Bayou Blue in what came to be Allen Parish is not to be confused with the Bayou Blue of Lafourche and Terrebonne parishes.

16. Albert J. Pickett, interview with Abram Mordecai, September 30, 1847. According to Mordecai, Chief Red Shoes came to his store and shared how he saw the coming destruction in a dream and encouraged everyone, tribes and non-Indians alike, to leave the area while they could. Approximately half of the Coushattas followed their chief in "seventy large canoes," which is a testament to their high regard for him. Pickett Family Papers, LPR185. For additional historical background on the Coushatta diaspora, see Shuck-Hall, "Alabama and Coushatta Diaspora and Coalescence in the Mississippian Shatter Zone," and *Journey to the West*.

17. The Spanish referred to Chief Red Shoes as "Soulous Mestabe." The chief told the Spanish officials that he and his people did not want to live under the American government and wanted to move into Spanish-controlled territories. Carondelet to Intendant Juan Ventura Morales, AGI, Audencia de Santo Domingo, legajo 2614, folio 130; Duralde to Valentine Layssard, December 29, 1797, AGI, Cuba, legajo 214, folios 672–73, both cited in Donald G. Hunter, "The Alibamons: Notes on the Occhanya, Pacana, and Coushatta in Louisiana During the Spanish Colonial and Early American Periods," unpublished manuscript, May 10, 2000, 12–15. CTLA, DC.019.

18. The most detailed list of exchanges and gifts to the Coushattas and neighboring tribes is found in Indian agent John Sibley's "A Report from Natchitoches in 1807." Sibley detailed his exchanges and gifts to the various tribes in great detail, noting trade in buffalo robes, bear oil, deerskins, seeds, brass kettles, axes, cloth, flour, gun flints, and even items he designated as gifts for wives such as cooking utensils, shawls, combs, looking glasses, thread, and needles. However, he did not ever mention gifting or receiving baskets from any tribe. Likewise, he described the various tribal women's work as dressing buffalo skins, painting and ornamenting them; making clothing; making and repairing leather halters, ropes and tents; and cooking, but did not mention basketry. Presumably this was also a part of everyday life, but not one Sibley observed directly. Similarly, the 1843 Texas Republic's "Ledger Sheet of Gifts to Indians" included $9.25 of gifts to the Coushattas, including blue flaps, sheeting, a bucket, hoe, beads, and tobacco but also did not mention baskets used to store or carry any of these gifts. See Winfrey and Day, eds., *The Indian Papers of Texas and the Southwest, 1825–1916*, 283.

19. Lafitte told of trading with the Coushattas for provisions. Although he did not specifically describe Coushatta baskets, these provisions would logically have been transported and stored in baskets. Davis, *The Pirates Lafitte,* 358.

20. J. Feagin to Cato Sells, June 19, 1917, CTLA, Bureau of Indian Affairs files. See also Abernethy, *Tales from the Big Thicket,* 73.

21. Wrede, "Sketches of Life in the United States of North America and Texas," 7, 11.

22. Trammell, *Seven Pines: Its Occupants and Their Letters, 1825–1872,* 6–7. Several Texas legislators had a history of maintaining good relationships with the Alabamas and the Coushattas. See also Martin, "Coushatta Indians," and Franco, "The Alabama-Coushatta and Their Texas Friends."

23. Speech of Governor Lamar, November 12, 1839, cited in Binkley, "Journals of the Fourth Congress of the Republic of Texas," 11–12.

24. Martin, "Alexander Hamilton Washington."

25. Washington, "Friendly Indians on Trinity River," 127–28.

26. Report of Capt. Samuel M. Whiteside to Colonel H. Clay Wood, Fifth Military District, Austin, TX. February 6, 1870, CTLA and National Museum of the American Indian (hereafter NMAI), MS 4166, 4.

27. See Johnson, *The Coushatta People,* 34–46; Smither, "Alabama Indians of Texas," 85; and Winfrey and Bryant, *Indian Tribes of Texas,* 5–14. The "Act for the Relief of the Coshattee [*sic*] Indians" was presented to the Texas legislature on February 6, 1854. See General Sam Houston to Ashbel Smith, December 8, 1855, box 2G224, Ashbel Smith Papers. Some Alabamas joined the Coushatta families who moved to Louisiana, and both groups appear in records compiled by Rev. Paul Leeds in St. Peters Congregational Church Records, Bayou Blue, Elton, LA (1901–58) and St. Luke Congregational Church on the West Side of Bayou Blue (1913–21), CTLA.

28. Joyce Abbey Poncho, "Ithani (Cane)," recorded by Jack Martin, November 18, 2009, trans. Bertney Langley, courtesy of Dr. Jack Martin and CTLA, CKU05019-20. Poncho used the expression "*baalisi stitihapka,*" which literally translates to "the weapon against being poor."

29. Image 10b, American Missionary Association Photographs, 1887–1952. These photographs must have been taken after September 1901, when the tribal church was named. This tool is called *stittatihkachi* (literally, "what one weaves with," Kimball, *Koasati Dictionary,* 215) and was sketched by Harrington in 1908. Leonard Battise still uses a similar tool to pack the cane tightly together.

30. Image 10a, American Missionary Association Photographs, 1887–1952. This photo must have been taken at the same time as the image above, since they are numbered sequentially.

31. Roy Nash, Special Commissioner, "The Indians of Louisiana" (1931), 5, ser. 4C, box 48, folder 7, Joe Jennings Bureau of Indian Affairs Records.

32. Reid cited an article from the Lake Charles newspaper called *Echo* from March 24, 1883, amended by her handwritten notations. Maude Reid Collection (hereafter MRC), scrapbook 4, ser. 1, box 2, p. 123, and box 4, p. 17.

33. De Caro and Jordan, *Louisiana Traditional Crafts,* 18. The Acadians, also known

as Cadiens or Cajuns, are descendants of the French who settled in Nova Scotia during the seventeenth century. By the mid-eighteenth century, after coming under attack by English colonists, they began migrating to Louisiana, where they established their own settlements or enclaves. Several Acadian families live around the Coushattas' Bayou Blue settlement, resulting in many Coushattas learning to speak French and enjoying Cajun music. For more on Cajun history, see Brasseaux, *Acadian to Cajun.*

34. Yvonne Jackson, interview with Linda Langley, September 24, 2009.

35. The two baskets are numbers 186 and 187 in the CTLA.

36. For more on Coushatta homesteading history, see Precht, "Coushatta Homesteading in Southwest Louisiana and the Development of the Community at Bayou Blue"; Langley, Oubre, and Precht, "Louisa Williams Robinson, Her Daughters, and Her Granddaughters"; and Bates, *Basket Diplomacy.*

37. Johnson and Leeds, *Patteran,* 18.

38. Kniffen, Gregory, and Stokes, *The Historic Indian Tribes of Louisiana,* 150.

39. Jamison Poncho and Doris Celestine Battise interview, June 26, 2009, transcribed and translated by Linda and Bertney Langley, CTLA. Doris mentioned going on several specific basket-selling trips with cousins who were also renowned basket makers, including Rosabel Sylestine, Madeline Celestine, and Margaret John, saying in classic understated Koasati style, "We really enjoyed it—since we were all kin, we stuck together." When Rosabel Sylestine was interviewed about her involvement with the Louisiana Handicraft Project, she remembered her mother going out in the wagon with a group of other tribal members to trade baskets and bringing home food such as potatoes and rice. Sylestine, interview with Pam Rabalais, September 2, 1995, transcribed by Camille Benoit, catalog no. 4700.0511, Lower Mississippi Valley Collections.

40. Poncho used the expression *toknaawa laana,* "gold money," to emphasize that early trading practices were entirely by barter, without the exchange of a single piece of coin. "Cane," November 18, 2009, CTLA, CKU05019-20.

41. Statement of Henry Buller, January 12, 1958, rpt. in Putnam, *A Town Named Elton,* 44.

42. Patricia Hall, personal communication with Linda Langley, July 22, 2019.

43. Handwritten note at bottom of page, box 4, 17, MRC.

44. Marie McGee Guillory, qtd. in Langley, LeJeune, and Oubre, eds., *Les Artistes,* 72.

45. Kniffen, Gregory, and Stokes, *The Historic Indian Tribes of Louisiana,* 153.

46. Harrington, "Among Louisiana Indians," 656.

47. In a letter to John Swanton dated March 11, 1930, Caroline Dorman noted, "There was a pile of cane, split for making baskets" (NMAI and CTLA, MS_4964).

48. For an example, see Usner, *Weaving Alliances with Other Women.*

49. Solomon and Adeline Battise, interview by Rose Goebel, April 5, 2000, CTLA. Oak and other hardwood trees are premium for loggers, making them harder to get for Coushatta weavers. Oak trees are also much heavier than split cane, making them more difficult to transport back to the community without wagons or cars. Coushatta weavers' preference for river cane was likely also based on the higher prices they received for cane baskets from area merchants.

50. Swanton Field Notes, 2 (NMAI and CTLA, MS 4658_14:2). Swanton made several visits to the community between 1906 and 1930, noting that he didn't observe the use of any other basket-making materials and that tribal weavers continued to produce these varieties of split-cane baskets. See Swanton's *Indian Tribes of the Lower Mississippi Valley and Adjacent Coast of the Gulf of Mexico* and "Early History of the Creek Indians and Their Neighbors."

51. Although Swanton did not record the weavers' names or itemize the prices paid for each basket, the 1917 Bureau of American Ethnology annual report records these "Seven baskets made by the Koasati Indians of Louisiana, collected by Dr. John R. Swanton (61315)" (39th Annual Report of the Bureau of American Ethnology, 27).

52. Harrington worked for George G. Heye as an archaeologist, ethnologist, field collector, and curator. In addition to having photographic skills, Harrington had received a BA and an MA in anthropology from Columbia University, where he studied under Franz Boas (NMAI biographical note, NMAI.AC.001.035, ead_collection:sova-nmai-ac-001-035). Photographs and objects from the Coushatta Tribe purchased by the Heye Museum of the American Indian were transferred to the Smithsonian Institution in 1989, along with the other Heye collections.

53. Harrington, "Among the Louisiana Indians."

54. The cover of Harrington's field notebook lists the tribes visited from February to September 1908 as "Seminole, Mohegan, Nanticoke, Nansoppard [*sic*], Pamunkey, Catawba, Choctaw, Chitimacha, Houma, Koasati, Cherokee" (NMAI and CTLA).

55. Harrington purchased a basket he described as "hasokpakkoli—diagonal basket open weave" from Jackson "Alabamu" for fifteen cents. This was likely a sunrise basket, a powerful medicine basket made using natural and red-dyed cane that had to be completed in a single day between sunrise and sunset.

56. Harrington field notebook, jpegs 22–36, items 506–542, NMAI and CTLA. This tool is like the one in the earliest photo of Coushatta weavers shown previously. The most common types of cane baskets bought by Harrington were for carrying, sifting/winnowing, storage, and cooking. The referenced basket made by Winnie Thompson appears as item E in the Harrington notebook, 24, and is still in the Coushatta Collection at the NMAI (ID 018557). Ceremonial uses of cane baskets by the Coushattas was documented by Lyda Averill Paz Taylor in "A Comparative Study of Southeastern Cultures." She included descriptions of corn processing (3), basketry production (11), and dances (38–40).

57. Kniffen, Gregory, and Stokes, *The Historic Indian Tribes of Louisiana*, 156. Paz-Taylor's notebook records an interview with "Alison Baptise" (Ellisor Battise, Solomon Battise's father) in which he described tribal members skinning the bark off a tree to make rope and tie logs together with a vine to make a raft (Paz-Taylor notebook 6, July 31, 1936, in MS_4658, NMAI and CTLA). Kimball's *Koasati Dictionary* has two entries that shed additional light on this use of bark. One explicatory sentence states: "When they looked for, cut, and brought back roundleaf brier stems, they tied the dead trees in the middle with them." Another reference states that "Long ago the Indians used to strip the basswood bark and sew baskets with it" (4 and 28).

58. Kimball, *Koasati Dictionary*, 48.

59. Paz-Taylor, "A Comparative Study of Southeastern Cultures," 11.

60. See Lee, "The Ties That Bind," where the author attributes the consistency of Chitimacha design elements, in part, to the preservation of heirloom pattern baskets handed down within the families of tribal weavers, 47.

61. De Caro and Jordan, *Louisiana Traditional Crafts*, 18; Gettys, "Choctaw Cane Baskets," 98; Poulsen, "Rim Forms on Historic Southern Cane Baskets," 166.

62. Kniffen, Gregory, and Stokes, *The Historic Indian Tribes of Louisiana*, 149.

63. Claude Medford Jr. to Marshall Gettys, August 14, 1987, emphasis in original. Gettys provided copies of this correspondence to Linda Langley in preparation for a basketry book that remained unwritten, noting that Medford "was one of the best versed scholars on SE basketry I have ever known" (Marshall Gettys to Linda Langley, June 25, 2014, CTLA).

64. Neuman, "Split Cane Items in Louisiana," 16.

65. Coushatta basket-weaver Leonard Battise has made each of these designs. See also examples in Lee, "The Ties That Bind," and Usner, *Weaving Alliances with Other Women*.

66. Darden, Darden, and Brown, "In the Family Tradition," 41.

67. Kniffen, Gregory, and Stokes, *The Historic Indian Tribes of Louisiana*, 150. Paz-Taylor observed Coushatta weavers using cane in the natural color, dyed black by boiling with black gum in water, and dyed red by boiling with a tree bark she was unable to identify ("A Comparative Study of Southeastern Cultures," 11).

68. The Harrington sketches are found in NMAI and CTLA, MS 4658, subfolder 15. The distinctive Coushatta design motif on basketry, beadwork, clothing, and jewelry includes a diamond pattern, sometimes coupled with a turtle and/or a dipper motif. The Coushatta Princess Committee publishes annual instructions for contestants that include samples of these patterns to be used in constructing traditional dresses.

69. Poncho and Battise interview, June 26, 2009, CTLA. Poncho may have been recalling the sawmill on Bayou Nezpique opened by Wilbur and Otis Putnam in 1906. Putnam, *A Town Named Elton*, 4.

70. Marion Robinson John, interview with Crystal Williams, July 22, 2008, transcribed and translated by Loretta Williams, CTLA binder 178-C.

71. Other common communal tasks included building homes or barns, harvesting crops, and butchering animals. See Paz-Taylor, "A Comparative Study of Southeastern Cultures."

72. Hasselbacher, "'Written in Indian.'" Although this work deals with communal review and authorship related to spoken and written language products, the same process of asking family members and tribal elders to critique one's work can be seen in basketry, dancing, and other cultural traditions. Even tribal elders prefer to work together in this way.

73. Raynella Thompson Fontenot, personal communication, March 28, 2019. See chapter 4 for interviews with young tribal weavers.

74. Kniffen, Gregory, and Stokes, *The Historic Indian Tribes of Louisiana*, 95–96.

75. Loris Abbott Langley, qtd. in Langley, LeJeune, and Oubre, eds., *Les Artistes,* 59.

76. For more on the Tupper General Merchandise Museum, see John St. Ores, "Tupper's Wares: The Life of a General Store," *Daily Advertiser,* June 2, 1996, 13.

77. A pine-needle wall basket by Elsie John has a 25 cent price tag, and a small pine-needle vase with a handle has a 10 cent price tag. CTLA, basket numbers 106 and 107. Information about the Tupper Museum can be found at www.tuppermuseum.com.

78. Marie McGee Guillory, qtd. in Langley, LeJeune, and Oubre, eds., *Les Artistes,* 70.

79. Gail Shuff Stevens, interview with Linda Langley, November 14, 2008. The Shuff baskets represent a number of tribal weavers, made of both river cane and pine needles, including two cane fanner baskets, an armadillo effigy basket made by Florence Robinson, two frog baskets made by Elsie John, and two dolls in cradleboard baskets made by Rosabel Sylestine. CTLA, basket numbers 26, 79, 80, 85, and 86.

80. Loris Abbott Langley, qtd. in Giovo, Turner, and Langley, *Vox Populi,* 20.

81. For scholarship on how racial discourse shaped the boundaries of Indian identity in Louisiana, see Klopotek, *Recognition Odysseys,* and "Indian Education under Jim Crow"; and Usner, "'They Don't Like Indians around Here.'" Also useful for this conversation, see Blu, *The Lumbee Problem;* Lowery, *Race, Identity, & the Making of a Nation;* Sider, *Living Indian Histories;* and Coleman, *That the Blood Stay Pure.* Finally, Theda Perdue's work provides a foundation from which to better understand the significance of Native peoples in the construction of southern historical narratives. See "Indians in Southern History" and "Native Americans, African Americans, and Jim Crow."

82. The ruling covered schools in both Lafayette and Jefferson Davis parishes. See "School Integration in Two Parishes Is Asked in Suits," *The Times,* March 6, 1965, 2.

83. For more on this point, see the work of J. Anthony Paredes, who argues that "mastery of white institutions depends to a significant degree on the success of Southeastern Indians in 'marketing' their distinctiveness" ("Paradoxes of Modernism and Indianness in the Southeast," 341).

84. This point draws from the emerging scholarship on Indigenous arts leadership as a way of contesting and reshaping public space and identity. See Evans et al., "Containing, Contesting, Creating Spaces." Katherine Osburn's study on the Mississippi Choctaws also looks at a similar phenomenon in how tribal leaders leveraged race (as well as class) in order to secure political allies; see *Choctaw Resurgence in Mississippi.* For works that also discuss this issue further in relation to the Chitimachas, see Usner, *Weaving Alliances with Other Women;* or the Coushattas, see Precht, "Coushatta Basketry and Identity Politics," and Bates, *Basket Diplomacy.*

85. Kniffen, Gregory, and Stokes, *The Historic Indian Tribes of Louisiana,* 153. Claude Medford Jr. stated, "When cane basketry dies, coiled pine needle basketry takes its place" in tribes throughout the Southeast. Medford to Gettys, November 22, 1982.

86. Loris Abbott Langley, qtd. in Langley, LeJeune, and Oubre, eds., *Les Artistes,* 59–60.

87. Leonard Battise, personal communication with Linda Langley, May 30, 2014. Leonard is the son of the late Solomon Battise, who produced most of the cane baskets

in the Coushatta tribal collection. He recalled his parents and other weavers describing that the Choctaw rims just did not feel authentic to the Coushatta artisans.

88. De Caro and Jordan, *Louisiana Traditional Crafts*, 20.

89. Leonard Battise, interview with Ernest Sickey, November 18, 2016, CTLA.

2. *Ithani Asaala Taathatilkaak Sfaiyalok, Choiyi Hissi Asaala Achoohilitǫ*
Transitioning to Pine-Needle Baskets

1. Literal translation of chapter title: "We stopped weaving cane baskets, then began sewing baskets with pine needles."

2. Roy Nash, "The Indians of Louisiana in 1931," 7, folder 7, box 48, ser. 4C, Jennings Records. Other reports on the Coushattas' living conditions in the 1930s include Ryan to Monahan, October 10, 1934, 806—Choctaw, box 482, Central Classified Files, 1907–39, record group 75, National Archives and Records Administration, Washington DC.

3. Coushatta Chief Jeff Abbey and Vice-Chief Kinney Williams to John Collier, Office of Indian Affairs, July 23, 1938, CTLA, DC.04.081.

4. Cutting and stripping river cane requires very sharp knives. One of Leonard Battise's major concerns in starting cane-basketry classes was the danger the practice posed to inexperienced weavers learning to cut and split cane, and he did sometimes have students cut themselves badly. Leonard Battise, interview with Ernest Sickey, November 18, 2016, CTLA.

5. Joyce Abbey Poncho, "Cane." November 18, 2009, CTLA, CKU05019–20.

6. Wallace Stroud, interview with Jay Precht, August 29, 2008, CTLA. Stroud was a longtime friend to the Coushattas, which was particularly beneficial for providing Ernest Sickey with office space during his fight for tribal re-recognition and reinstatement of services in the late 1960s and early 1970s.

7. Zeline Langley Sylestine, interview with Crystal Williams, July 22, 2008, transcribed by Heather Williams, CTLA. Sylestine's daughter Derethea also recalled watching her grandmother, Maggie John Langley, weaving cane baskets. She said that Langley had a way of spreading the cane through her fingers and "doing the math in her head," so that she could weave very quickly. She also recalled that long strips of cane were spread around the house and the children had to tiptoe around them. Raynella Thompson Fontenot, personal communication, February 2020.

8. Kniffen, Gregory, and Stokes, *The Historic Indian Tribes of Louisiana*, 156. According to Donald Hunter, Mrs. Paul King Rand Sr. of Alexandria, Louisiana, stated that "she had taught some of the Coushatta women how to make the pine needle baskets, because the cane was dying out." See Hunter, "Coushatta Basketry in the Rand Collection." We haven't been able to independently corroborate the connection between Mrs. Rand and tribal weavers, and none of the current tribal weavers recall their parents or grandparents learning basketry from non-tribal weavers, though many recall seeing photographs or

baskets made by other tribes. Rand's large collection of Coushatta baskets is still housed at the Williamson Museum at Northwestern State University, Natchitoches, Louisiana.

9. Barbara Williams Langley and Bertney Langley, personal communication with Linda Langley and Raynella Thompson Fontenot, January 22, 2019. Daniel Jacobson suggested that the Louisiana Coushatta first "learned of" pine-needle basketry when Mark Robinson purchased a pine-needle basket in Livingston, Texas, in 1919, but there is no evidence to support this reactive—rather than proactive—approach to basketry innovation. See Jacobson, "Koasati Culture Changes," 177.

10. Leona Williams Francis, interview with Crystal Williams, June 10, 2008, transcribed by Heather Williams, CTLA.

11. Margaret Williams John, interview Crystal Williams, July 22, 2008, translated and transcribed by Loretta Robinson Williams, CTLA. Linda Langley later found and purchased this basket on eBay; it still has the original tribal tag identifying Margaret Williams John as the weaver. This basket is shown in chapter 3.

12. Loris Abbott Langley, qtd. in "Getting Started: Collecting and Sorting the Pine Needles," in Langley, LeJeune, and Oubre, eds., *Les Artistes*, 54.

13. Jeanette Celestine Langley, interview with Crystal Williams, July 21, 2008, transcribed by Heather Williams, CTLA. The full text of Langley's prayer begins the introduction of this book.

14. Geraldine Sylestine Reed, "Basket Weaving at the Museum," March 2007, CTLA. Bertney Langley also recalled hearing this story from his uncle Bel Abbey.

15. Notes on "Oral History of Margaret Williams John, with Barbara Williams Langley, Paula Manuel, Lorenda John Poncho, and Crystal Williams," July 22, 2008. Extra information and commentary were provided by Barbara Williams Langley while listening to the oral history on January 22, 2019, all at the CTLA. Barbara's mother, Margaret Williams John, said that she also climbed the trees and bent them down.

16. Edith Sylestine Langley, interview by Crystal Williams, June 17, 2008, transcribed by Loretta Robinson Williams, CTLA.

17. Susie Sylestine Bond, interview with Crystal Williams, June 4, 2008, transcribed by Heather Williams, CTLA. Susie's exact words were "You almost have to go close to Texas," which suggests she was referring to traveling on Highway 190 toward the Alabama-Coushatta Reservation in Livingston, Texas (often referred to simply as "Texas" by those in the Louisiana Tribe).

18. Jeanette Celestine Langley, interview with Crystal Williams, July 21, 2008, transcribed by Heather Williams, CTLA.

19. Edith Sylestine Langley, interview by Crystal Williams, June 17, 2008, transcribed by Loretta Robinson Williams, CTLA.

20. Ernest Sickey, personal communication with Linda Langley, April 1, 2019.

21. Leona Williams Francis, interview by Crystal Williams, June 10, 2008, transcribed by Heather Williams, CTLA. The process of gathering enough pine needles to sell or gift to tribal members who cannot go on gathering trips continues today.

22. Marion Robinson John, interview with Jonas John, July 23, 2008, transcribed and translated by Loretta Robinson Williams, CTLA.

23. Jeanette Celestine Langley, interview with Crystal Williams, July 21, 2008, transcribed by Heather Williams, CTLA. Jeanette Celestine Langley and Margaret Williams John also mentioned gathering swamp grass to make baskets, though this was mainly done only when they observed clumps of long grass while gathering pine needles. Elizabeth Marie Abbott Thompson volunteered to demonstrate sedge-grass basket making in Oklahoma in 1983, so presumably she gathered this grass to weave baskets. Claude Medford Jr. to Marshall Gettys, December 5, 1983, CTLA.

24. Loris Abbott Langley, qtd. in "Getting Started: Collecting and Sorting the Pine Needles," in Langley, LeJeune, and Oubre, eds., *Les Artistes*, 54.

25. *Chofa* is defined as any sharp tool (needle, hook, fork, pin, and so forth). *Chofa stachooka* is a sewing needle (literally a needle used to sew). Although the English word for *pine needle* would be grouped into this definition, in Koasati pine needle is *choiyi hissi* (literally pine-tree hair) (Coushatta Tribe of Louisiana, *Koasati Dictionary*, 417). Loris Abbey Langley speculated that pine-needle basketry is called "sewing" because of the use of sewing implements like a needle and thimble (qtd. in "Getting Started: Collecting and Sorting the Pine Needles," in Langley, LeJeune, and Oubre, eds., *Les Artistes*, 56).

26. Jeanette Celestine Langley, interview with Crystal Williams, July 21, 2008, transcribed by Heather Williams, CTLA.

27. Coushatta Tribe of Louisiana, *Koasati Dictionary*, 444. Geoffrey Kimball also recorded an earlier word for raffia, *pahi stachooka*, which translates as "grass used to sew with." This term suggests that Coushatta weavers used the swamp grass described by Jeannette Langley to sew with before commercial raffia was available. Kimball, *Koasati Dictionary*, 534.

28. Elissa "Liz" John, interview with Darlene Langley Dunnehoo, November 17, 2016, translated by Bertney Langley, CTLA. The plant used for red dye might have been chokecherry or sumac. See US Department of Agriculture, "Native Plant Dyes." Jeanette Celestine Langley also remembered Jane Battise Poncho showing her how to take the bark off the back of a tree (possibly an elm tree) that could be cleaned and used for raffia, though she never used this material herself. Jeanette Celestine Langley, interview with Jonas John, July 23, 2008, translated and transcribed by Loretta Robinson Williams, CTLA.

29. The technique of using bark or wood is still taught within some tribes. See Native Tech, "Native American Basketry."

30. Susie Sylestine Bond, Darlene Langley Dunnehoo, and Zeline Langley Sylestine, personal communication with Raynella Thompson Fontenot and Linda Langley, July 1, 2019.

31. Marion Robinson John, interview with Crystal Williams, July 22, 2008, transcribed and translated by Loretta Robinson Williams, CTLA.

32. Langley, LeJeune, and Oubre, eds., *Les Artistes*, 55; Imperial Calcasieu Planning and Development Commission, "Coushatta Existing Land Use Study" (Spring 1981), 8–9, CTLA; Adrian Poncho Sylestine, interview with Crystal Williams, August 8, 2008, transcribed by Heather Williams, CTLA.

33. The plain stitch is also called the simple stitch. Because the first generation of Coushatta pine-needle weavers only used this type of stitch, there are no Koasati terms to

designate the different stitches, so the English terms are most commonly used. A young tribal weaver, Clarissa Wier, said that she never learned names for different stitches, and distinguished between them by using descriptions for each.

34. Heather Williams, personal communication with Linda Langley, June 2019. Her tribal seal basket is no. 27 in the CTLA.

35. The two notable left-handed weavers in the modern era are Loris Abbott Langley and Marjorie Battise. Jeanette Celestine Langley said she can recognize baskets and makers by both the stitching and the shape of the knobs.

36. Lora Langley's plain-stitch oval basket, no. 14 in the CTLA, is beautifully decorated with a pattern of closed-stitch geometric ascending triangles in tribal colors.

37. Marion Robinson John, interview with Jonas John, July 23, 2008, transcribed and translated by Loretta Robinson Williams. The oldest pine-needle baskets in the CTLA are all plain stitch.

38. Lorenda John Poncho interview, June 5, 2008, and Marion Robinson John interview, July 22, 2008, CTLA.

39. Susie Sylestine Bond, personal communication with Raynella Thompson Fontenot and Linda Langley, June 25, 2019. Bond recalled hearing of a time when her mother, Della Sylestine, was making baskets outdoors with Susie Williams, who had just finished a large eight- or ten-inch basket and put it too close to the fire to do the finishing, burning up the entire basket. Jeanette Celestine Langley demonstrated rubbing a finished basket with a soft cloth so the pine-needle ends wouldn't stick to her fingers, then quickly passing it over a flame to burn off the raffia ends and keep them from unraveling. "Basket Weaving at the Museum," March 2007, CTLA.

40. The CTLA has several examples of older covered baskets without knobs, including numbers 125 and 105 (from the Tupper Museum collections). Susie Sylestine Bond also remembered that knobs were a later addition to baskets.

41. Raynella Thompson Fontenot recalled her mother's stories of trying to sew with pine needles that had not been properly dried. The resulting baskets were deemed too loose to sell. Tribal basket makers still say they are too embarrassed to sell a basket that "doesn't look right." Raynella Thompson Fontenot, personal communication with Linda Langley, April 2019.

42. Marion Robinson John, interview with Crystal Williams, July 22, 2008, transcribed and translated by Loretta Robinson Williams, CTLA.

43. CTLA, basket numbers 139, 140, and 188. John said that she did not like the way the goblet looked and did not want to finish it; however, she was willing to donate it to the tribe in 2009 since none of the other weavers were making baskets with dyed pine needles. John also explained that the technique was very time-consuming, as the pine needles had to be dried, then dyed, then dried again, and then dyed again. The process had to be repeated at least two or three times for the needles to take a good color. To date this technique is still not widely practiced in the tribe.

44. Marjorie Abbey Battise, interview with Jonas John, July 23, 2008, transcribed and translated by Loretta Robinson Williams, CTLA.

45. Raynella Thompson Fontenot, personal communication with Linda Langley, April 2019.

46. Numerous researchers have described and documented unique Indigenous ways of teaching and learning. For example, see Chávez, Ke, and Herrera, "Clan, Sage, and Sky"; Cajete, "Indigenous Education and the Development of Indigenous Community Leaders"; and Lomawaima and McCarty, *To Remain an Indian.*

47. For example, see the photo of Emily and Bruce Abbey (fig. 4); "Dr. Mary Mims to Work with Coushatta Indians," *Lake Charles American Press,* September 17, 1949; "Koasati Indians To Sell Wares Here," *Lake Charles American Press,* March 18, 1951, 16; "Koasati Indians Plan Sale Here," *Lake Charles American Press,* May 23, 1951, 41; and "Koasati Indians To Appear Here," *Lake Charles American Press,* February 22, 1952.

48. Langley, LeJeune, and Oubre, eds., *Les Artistes,* 60.

49. Edith Sylestine Langley, interview with Crystal Williams, June 17, 2008, transcribed by Loretta Robinson Williams, CTLA. Langley described her mother Rosabel's basket box as "just a regular box she had her sewing stuff in." Barbara Williams Langley said her grandmother Suzie Williams's basket box always had all the supplies she needed to sew every day, including her pine needles, raffia, thimble, cloth, and knife. Many basket makers also kept scissors, an apron or cloth to cover their lap, and several basket centers waiting to be completed in their boxes. Susie Sylestine Bond explained that wrapping the raffia around pine needles to make basket centers is time-consuming and difficult, so weavers often make several centers at a time. The best basket centers would be continued and ultimately finished into complete baskets. The remaining centers would be saved for another time, or sometimes given to children to practice stitching techniques. Susie Sylestine Bond, personal communication with Raynella Thompson Fontenot, July 1, 2019.

50. Margaret Williams John interview, July 22, 2008, CTLA.

51. Rosabel Robinson Sylestine, qtd. in "Coushatta Pine Needle Coiled Basketry by Rosabel Robinson Sylestine," September 9–December 30, 1973, CTLA.

52. Marion Robinson John, interview with Crystal Williams, July 22, 2008, translated and transcribed by Loretta Robinson Williams, CTLA.

53. Leona Williams Francis, interview with Crystal Williams, June 10, 2008, transcribed by Heather Williams, CTLA.

54. Darlene Langley Dunnehoo, interview with Crystal Williams, July 23, 2008, translated and transcribed by Loretta Robinson Williams, CTLA. Dunnehoo used the habitual past tense, *Anok naahohchoolik maamak achoolin hiichaliifookok naaholihchoolik tathalaichit staatalihchoolik.* In Koasati, this tense indicates a persistent state of being, that is, "When I always used to see my mother sew, I always used to try to sew." This concept is not easily translated into English.

55. Lorenda John Poncho, interview with Jonas John, July 23, 2008, Loretta translated and transcribed by Robinson Williams, CTLA.

56. In 1799, Hawkins noted this practice among Coushattas still living among the Creek Nation: "The men work with the women and make plenty of corn. All labor is done by the joint labor of all" (Grant, *Letters, Journals, and Writings of Benjamin Hawkins,* 296). In 1828, the Swiss-trained botanist Jean Louis Berlandier encountered the Coushattas in his travels through Texas and observed that "the women are quite willing to do the heavy work in the fields and to help with the flocks. . . . the wife becomes a comrade to her husband, willingly sharing his sorrows and his labors" (*The Indians of Texas in 1830,*

35, 124 and 174). Paz-Taylor observed that the shared division of labor continued in the Bayou Blue community, noting "Both men and women work in the field" ("A Comparative Study of Southeastern Cultures," 6).

57. The closest expressions in Koasati are *naanik iltohnoos* (a man was working) or *taiyik iltohnoos* (a woman was working). Coushatta Tribe of Louisiana, *Koasati Teaching Grammar,* 28.

58. Susie Sylestine Bond, interview with Crystal Williams, June 4, 2008, transcribed by Heather Williams; Edith Sylestine Langley, interview with Crystal Williams, June 17, 2008, translated and transcribed by Loretta Robinson Williams, CTLA. Langley recalled Rosabel teaching her techniques to her son-in-law, a member of the Mississippi Band of Choctaw. She said that his sewing was "pretty good," and family members who observed him sewing wanted to buy baskets he made.

59. Adrian Poncho Sylestine, interview with Crystal Williams, August 8, 2008, transcribed by Heather Williams, CTLA.

60. Jeanette Celestine Langley, interview with Crystal Williams, July 21, 2008, translated and transcribed by Loretta Robinson Williams, CTLA.

61. Marion Robinson John, interview with Crystal Williams, July 22, 2008, translated and transcribed by Loretta Robinson Williams, CTLA. Lorenda John Poncho, Susie Sylestine Bond, and Adrian Poncho Sylestine all remembered learning to sew easier baskets like hot pads and wall baskets, then working up to small bowls, and finally learning to make covered baskets.

62. For example, Adrian Poncho Sylestine is known for her miniature baskets, Susie Sylestine Bond for her vases, and Marjorie Abbey Battise for her left-handed wheat stitch.

63. Jeanette Celestine Langley, interview with Crystal Williams, July 21, 2008, transcribed by Heather Williams, CTLA.

64. Susie Sylestine Bond, personal communication with Raynella Thompson Fontenot, April 5, 2019.

65. Coushatta Tribe of Louisiana, *Kowassaati Nasmathahli Asaala* (Coushatta Animal Baskets).

66. Literal translation of heading: "How We Lived Changed."

67. For more on the "basket craze" of the late nineteenth century, as well as the rise in tourism in the early decades of the twentieth century, see Smith-Ferri, "The Development of the Commercial Market for Pomo Indian Baskets"; Hutchinson, *The Indian Craze;* Cahill, "Making and Marketing Baskets in California"; Wilkins, *Patterns of Exchange;* Hill, *Weaving New Worlds* and "Marketing Traditions"; and Usner, "From Bayou Teche to Fifth Avenue," "'They Don't Like Indian around Here,'" and *Weaving Alliances with Other Women.*

68. "Allen 4-H Club Day Set April 30," *Weekly Town Talk,* March 26, 1928, 10.

69. "Indian Basket Show and Sale Set Near Elton," *Lake Charles American Press,* April 4, 1950, 18; "Koasati Indians Plan Sale Here," *Lake Charles American Press,* May 23, 1951, 41; "Indians to Hold Sale in Elton," *Lake Charles American Press,* June 18, 1951, 33; "Allen Parish Church Is Tribute to Man Who Converted Keasati [*sic*] Indian Tribe," *Town Talk,* February 3, 1951, 3.

70. Superintendent McMullen to Chief Jeff Abbey, June 19, 1942, CTLA. See also Superintendent Harvey Meyer to Elizabeth Lansden, April 4, 1939, CTLA, DC.04190.

71. For example, see photo of Mrs. Wanda Johnson and a group of women dressed visiting the community to buy baskets, May 2, 1963, CTLA, PH.02.95.

72. In 1952, Daniel Jacobson observed that pine-needle baskets sold for a price up to $3.50, and cane baskets could bring as much as $4.50 ("Koasati Culture Changes," 176).

73. Marion Robinson John, interview with Crystal Williams, July 22, 2008, translated and transcribed by Loretta Robinson Williams, CTLA.

74. "4 Kosati Indians Will Appear at Crowley Festival," *Beaumont Enterprise,* October 15, 1950, box 4, 5, MRC.

75. Chief Abbey to Dugas, October 4, 1950, CTLA, DC.04.232.

76. "Elect Chief for Koasati Indian Tribe," *Lake Charles American Press,* March 13, 1951, 3.

77. "Koasati Indians to Sell Wares Here," *Lake Charles American Press,* March 18, 1951, 16; "Indian Chief Will Be Presented with Headdress Here," *Lake Charles American Press,* March 21, 1951, 1.

78. Deloria, *Playing Indian,* 109.

79. "Koasati Indians to Visit Pack 3," *Lake Charles American Press,* March 20, 1957, 40; Barbara Williams Langley, interview with Denise E. Bates, April 4, 2016, CTLA; "Indians to Hold Sale in Elton," *Lake Charles American Press,* June 18, 1951, 33; "Three Graduate From Cubs, Three Get Wolf Badges," *Lake Charles American Press,* September 1, 1951, 5.

80. Bertney Langley, personal communication with Linda Langley, July 3, 2019.

81. Ernest Sickey, interview with Denise E. Bates, October 28, 2016, CTLA. Also see "Cub Scouts to Hold Program to Help Indians," *Lake Charles American Press,* December 8, 1954, 31. Bertney Langley, personal communication with Linda Langley, July 3, 2019. Langley recalled Tim Dugas helping raise enough money for their family to get their own water well, so they no longer had to carry water buckets from a neighbor's well.

82. The initial letter cannot be located, but the response to Dugas's letter indicates its contents. See Robert M. Cullum (Choctaw Agency) to Tim Dugan [*sic*], April 9, 1952, CTLA. "Indian Basket Show and Sale Set near Elton," *Lake Charles American Press,* April 4, 1950, 18; "Koasati Indians Plan Sale Here," *Lake Charles American Press,* May 23, 1951, 41; "Indians to Hold Sale in Elton," *Lake Charles American Press,* June 18, 1951, 33.

83. *Rural Louisiana,* Jeff Davis Electric Co-op edition, April 1955, 2, CTLA.

84. Louisiana News Digest, *Louisiana Indians,* 3. The two baskets in the photo are a wall basket and a small covered basket, both decorated with flowers. The covered basket does not have a knob.

85. Marion Robinson John, interview with Crystal Williams, July 22, 2008, translated and transcribed by Loretta Robinson Williams, CTLA.

86. Adrian Poncho Sylestine, interview with Crystal Williams, August 8, 2008, transcribed by Heather Williams, CTLA.

87. "Allen Parish," *Lake Charles American Press,* October 8, 1954, 2.

88. "Two Tourist Couples Are Feted at Elton," *Lake Charles American Press,* May 7, 1959, 35; "Tourists Are Entertained at Elton," *Lake Charles American Press,* May 8, 1958, 33.

89. Marjorie Abbey Battise, interview with Jonas John, July 23, 2008, translated and transcribed by Loretta Robinson Williams, CTLA.

90. Ernest Sickey, personal communication with Linda Langley, June 19, 2019. Sickey recalled a woman from the St. Martinville Museum named Mrs. Despit buying baskets and bringing raffia to weavers once a month.

91. Piazza, "Loulou," 22.

92. A 1995 interview with Rosabel Robinson Sylestine about her involvement with the Louisiana Handicraft Project references meetings and correspondence between the two women in 1952, but that correspondence has not yet been located. Sylestine, interview with Pam Rabalais, September 2, 1995, transcribed by Camille Benoit, catalog no. 4700.0511, Lower Mississippi Valley Collections.

93. Edith Sylestine Langley, interview with Crystal Williams, June 17, 2008, transcribed by Loretta Robinson Williams, CTLA. Ernest Sickey also recalled Rosabel Robinson Sylestine placing bulk orders for raffia, then supplying the raffia to other tribal weavers. Sickey, personal communication with Linda Langley, June 19, 2019.

94. Lorenda John Poncho, interview with Crystal Williams, June 5, 2008, translated and transcribed by Loretta Robinson Williams, CTLA. This statement was also made of anthropologists, such as John Swanton, Lyda Averill Paz Taylor, and Daniel Jacobson, as well as linguists such as Eugene Burnham and Geoffrey Kimball.

95. In 1990, Linda Langley invited the "best basket makers" to a photo shoot to publicize the new tribal gift shop, but none of the weavers came because they didn't want to appear to be bragging or agreeing to the Western-style concept of "best."

96. Marjorie Abbey Battise, interview with Jonas John, July 23, 2008, translated and transcribed by Loretta Robinson Williams, CTLA.

97. For example, coauthor Langley is often asked to price river-cane baskets by Leonard Battise and pine-needle baskets by his sister Glenna Battise Robinson, both of whom express discomfort with setting their own prices.

98. Battise's efforts were supported by Wanda Johnson, who along with her husband Rev. Don Johnson, helped to run the school attached to St. Peter's Indian Church, and brought wealthy local ladies into the community to buy baskets. See CTLA, PH.02.095.

99. Leonard Battise, interview with Denise E. Bates, November 18, 2016, CTLA.

100. Ernest Sickey, personal communication with Linda Langley, April 1, 2019.

101. For a discussion on the movement of some tribes to incorporate as nonprofit organizations in order to qualify for funding during the Johnson administration, see Paredes, "Paradoxes of Modernism and Indianness in the Southeast," 353; and Deloria, "The Era of Indian Self-Determination," 198.

102. This name was used interchangeably with "The Coushatta Indians of Allen Parish, Inc.," in personal narratives about this period.

103. In the mid-1960s, the gravel road that led into the Coushatta settlement was paved, permitting the tribe to emphasize that the Trading Post was accessible via a "hard surfaced road." See Trading Post advertisement, *Basile Weekly,* July 3, 1968, 4.

104. Ella Mitchell, "Coushatta Indian Lauds Non-Profit Tribal Charter," *Lake Charles American Press,* June 21, 1972, 12.

105. Winston De Ville, "Louisiana . . . En Passant," *Town Talk*, March 29, 1967, 25.

106. Ernest Sickey to William Byler, 1975, folder 4, box 245, Association on American Indian Affairs (hereafter AAIA) Records, Seeley G. Mudd Manuscript Library, Princeton University, Princeton, NJ.

107. "Elton Indian Tribe to Open Trading Post," *Lake Charles American Press*, January 28, 1967, 6. For more on Indians in popular culture, see Berkhofer, *The White Man's Indian*, 71–111. For examples of educational programs carried out at the Trading Post, see "Kindergarten Tots Go on Field Trip," *Daily World*, April 21, 1967, 15; "Scouts, Cubs Make Totem Poles, Meet Real Indians," *Daily World*, May 21, 1967, 27; "Kindergarten Enthused at Trading Post," *Daily World*, May 16, 1968, 6; "Eunice Cub Scouts Visit Indian Post," *Daily World*, November 29, 1968, 18; "Elton Receives Homestead Roll," *Daily World*, February 7, 1969, 11; "Nursery Tots Visit Indian Trading Post," *Daily World*, May 1, 1969, 6; "Nursery School Students Visit Indian Village," *Daily World*, May 5, 1970, 6; "Indian Hills Nursery Tots Visit Indians," *Daily World*, April 1, 1971, 6; and "Elton Group Tours School," *Daily World*, March 5, 1972, 18.

108. "Tepee Going Up to Welcome Visitors," *Daily World*, June 28, 1967, 20; and "Newest Attraction," *Daily World*, July 18, 1967, 9.

109. "Indian Craft Shown at Smithsonian," *Daily World*, December 3, 1968, 7.

110. Edna Redlich, "Beadwork Rejuvenated: Indian Art Gets New Life," *Daily World*, June 9, 1968, 21; and Oris Redlich, "Indian Artifacts Gain Recognition," *Daily World*, February 1, 1970, 17.

111. Eloise M. Fruge, "Trading Post," *Lake Charles American Press*, February 18, 1967, 4.

112. Mary Alice Fontenot, "En Passant: Again the Indians," *Daily World*, September 26, 1969, 16.

113. Ernest Sickey, personal communication with Linda Langley, April 4, 2019; Precht, "Coushatta Basketry and Identity Politics," 152.

114. Hosea Hebert, "Around Town," *Basile Weekly*, August 28, 1968, 1. Hebert (1923–2009) was an Army veteran, self-employed notary, and tax professional who worked in the Basile area for over fifty years. He had many strong friendships within the Coushatta community and actively promoted tribal basketry. He also collected photographs and news clippings about the tribe throughout his lifetime, which he asked his nieces and nephews to return to the tribe after his death.

115. *Basile Weekly*, June 25, 1969, 2.

116. "To Demonstrate Basketry," *Opelousas Daily World*, October 27, 1968, 31; and Ernest Sickey, personal communication with Linda Langley, August 27, 2019.

117. "Claiborne, Concordia, Allen Youth Corps Plans Okayed," *The Times*, December 15, 1965, 33; "Pretty Indian Maid Manages Trading Post," *Daily World*, September 21, 1967, 12; "Indian Trading Post Manager Assumes Duties," *Lake Charles American Press*, September 21, 1967, 24.

118. "Elton Indians Open Trading Post All Day Saturday," *Daily World*, March 17, 1967, 5. Between 1967 and 1971, the Trading Post was advertised over 150 times. This is an estimate based on a search of the databases from the *Daily World*, *The Times*, *Town Talk*, and the *Lake Charles American Press*. The most detailed coverage can be found

in "Elton Indians to Start Handcraft Trading Post," *Daily World,* July 24, 1966, 1; "Elton Indian Tribe to Open Trading Post," *Lake Charles American Press,* January 28, 1967, 6; "Elton Indians to Open Trading Post," *Daily World,* January 31, 1967, 12; "Indian Trading Post Opens," *Town Talk,* January 31, 1967, 7; "Elton Indians Open Trading Post All Day Saturday," *Daily World,* March 17, 1967, 5; and "Louisiana's Only Indian Trading Post," *Daily World,* July 31, 1969, 16.

119. Bertney Langley, personal communication with Linda Langley, July 15, 2019. Gatherings at the Trading Post and use of the telephone are mentioned in numerous oral histories gathered by the tribe.

120. Lorenda John Poncho, interview with Crystal Williams, June 5, 2008, translated and transcribed by Loretta Robinson Williams, CTLA.

121. "Indians Seeking Artifacts for Post," *Daily World,* March 26, 1968, 11.

122. Mary Doran, "Coushatta Indians: River Cane Basket Weaving Taught," *Lake Charles American Press,* July 28, 1973, 19.

123. Edna Redlich, "Beadwork Rejuvenated: Indian Art Gets New Life," *Daily World,* June 9, 1968, 21; and Ernest Sickey, interviews with Denise E. Bates, July 28 and November 16, 2015, CTLA.

124. Joanne Putnam, "'Forgotten' Craft Revived as Indians Learn Weaving," *Daily World,* May 28, 1973, 10.

125. Ernest Sickey, personal communication with Linda Langley, April 1, 2019.

126. Ernest Sickey, personal communication with Linda Langley, April 1, 2019.

127. Edna Redlich, "Beadwork Rejuvenated: Indian Art Gets New Life," *Daily World,* June 9, 1968, 21; Stephen M. Richmond to Carl Wilkins (Louisiana Inter-Government Relations), April 7, 1976, CTLA.

128. Zeline Langley Sylestine, interview with Crystal Williams, July 22, 2008, transcribed by Heather Williams, CTLA; and personal communication with Raynella Thompson Fontenot, June 19, 2019.

129. Ernest Sickey, personal communication with Linda Langley, April 1, 2019.

130. Rosabel Robinson Sylestine, interview with Pam Rabalais, September 2, 1995, transcribed by Camille Benoit, LSU Archives, Lower Mississippi Valley Collections.

131. Leona Williams Francis, interview with Crystal Williams, June 10, 2008, transcribed by Heather Williams, CTLA. Prior to that time, she received only four dollars for a basket this size.

3. *Asaala Schoolpak Komawiichito̱*
Selling the Baskets Helped Us

1. Claude H. Heyer, "Report: The Coushatta" (July 1959): 1, folder 2, box 245, AAIA.

2. Ernest Sickey during Leonard Battise interview, November 18, 2016, CTLA.

3. Ellis Byers, "Acadiana Trail: 'Trail' Prospects Aired at Assn. Meet," *Opelousas Daily World,* January 11, 1970, 22.

4. "Tourist Bureau Will be Indian Day Site," *Lake Charles American Press,* November 10, 1971, 13.

5. Ernest Sickey, qtd. in Ella Mitchell, "Elton Tribe Has Unlimited Growth in Tourism Industry," *Daily World,* June 9, 1972, 5.

6. Translation of heading: "More Basket Buyers Came." This is the Koasati explanation for the establishment of the Coushatta Cultural Center on Highway 190 in Elton, rather than a literal translation in English.

7. "Railroad to Give Depot," *Daily World,* December 6, 1973, 2.

8. "Rep. Breaux Speaker at Supper in Elton," *Daily World,* December 30, 1973, 13. See also "Elton May Become 'The Indian Capital,'" *Jennings Daily News,* December 27, 1973, n.p. According to the *Lake Charles Associated Press,* the Louisiana Senate passed a resolution declaring Elton the "Indian Capital of Louisiana" in 1974. "Senate Moves to Honor Coushattas," *Lake Charles Associated Press,* July 10, 1974, n.p.

9. "Elton Seeks New Vehicles," *Daily World,* June 16, 1974, 23.

10. "Donation for Indian Center Given," *Daily World,* July 3, 1974, 12; "Bank Presents Donation for Indian Museum," *Lake Charles American Press,* July 8, 1974.

11. Bertney Langley, "Coushatta Indian Cultural Center," *Coushatta Smoke Signal,* March 25, 1977, 1, CTLA.

12. Stephen M. Richmond to Ernest Sickey, May 6, 1975, CTLA.

13. "Coushatta Tribal Bicentennial Proposal," submitted by the Coushatta Tribe of Louisiana, June 16, 1975, 2–3, CTLA.

14. Stephen M. Richmond to Judy McKee (Alison, Los Angeles), July 23, 1974, CTLA.

15. Ernest Sickey to William Byler, July 1974, AAIA.

16. Ernest Sickey, personal communication with Linda Langley, April 4, 2019.

17. By 1978, this total grant from the EDA reached $42,000. Sandra Lantz, "Coushatta Indians: Basket Weaving Trade Changes," *Daily World,* June 18, 1978, 17. Ernest Sickey to William Byler, July 14, 1975, AAIA.

18. "America the Beautiful Fund" brochure, ca. 1975, AAIA. This image of Battise also appears in a tribal publication, "The Struggle Has Made Us Stronger."

19. Ann Muchison, "Calcasieu Imperial Commission: Bicentennial Funds Distributed," *Lake Charles American Press,* February 17, 1976, 46. Funding from the Bicentennial Commission was also used to print brochures. Ernest Sickey, interview with Denise E. Bates, September 30, 2015, CTLA.

20. Ernest Sickey, interview with Denise E. Bates, July 28, 2015, CTLA.

21. Stephen W. Tabasko Jr. (Bibb Co.) to Daphne E. Hardoon (Drucilla Handy Co.), June 7, 1974, and Stephen W. Tabasko to Ernest Sickey, April 15, 1977, AAIA. For more on the Coushatta tribal seal, see Bates, "What's in a Seal?" Discussing the development of the tribal seal with Leonard Battise nearly a half-century after these events, Sickey recalled that the tribal council all got together and talked about which elements of their traditions to use on the seal. They met with tribal elders to gather their opinions. He remembered Solomon Battise telling them: "Don't ever forget our clans. Those are ours. . . . The colors represent the seasons and the times of day, when you should plant—don't forget that either." The council discussed several possible animals to use in the center of the seal, but finally agreed that the garfish was the right animal to honor. Sickey said that tribal elders remembered the gar being used for food, and they recalled being disciplined by

being scratched on the backs of their legs with the gar teeth and scales. Leonard Battise, interview by Ernest Sickey, November 18, 2016, CTLA.

22. "Coushatta Indians Open Cultural Center in Elton," *Lake Charles American Press*, September 11, 1974.

23. Photo, CTLA.PH.06.06, Loris Abbott Langley Collection, CTLA.

24. Photos CTLA.PH.01.45, CTLA.PH.01.48, and CTLA.PH.01.49, Ernest Sickey Collection, CTLA.

25. Ernest Sickey, interview with Denise E. Bates, September 16, 2015, CTLA.

26. Bertney Langley, "Report from Cultural Center," *Coushatta Smoke Signal*, March 25, 1977, 4, CTLA.

27. Hosea Hebert, "The Forgotten Tribe," qtd. in Putnam, *A Town Named Elton*, 138.

28. Lorenda John Poncho, interview with Crystal Williams, June 5, 2008, transcribed and translated by Loretta Robinson Williams, CTLA.

29. Jeanette Celestine Langley, interview with Crystal Williams, July 21, 2008, transcribed by Heather Williams, CTLA.

30. Marion Robinson John, interview with Crystal Williams, July 22, 2008, transcribed and translated by Loretta Robinson Williams, CTLA.

31. Johnson, *The Coushatta People*, 96.

32. Sandra Lantz, "Coushatta Indians: Basket Weaving Trade Changes," *Daily World*, June 18, 1978, 17; Claude Medford Jr. to Stephen Richmond, May 23, 1975, and Stephen M. Richmond to Ernest Sickey, December 3, 1975, CTLA.

33. Dr. Jan Van der Poll (assistant director, Louisiana Division of Arts) to Ernest Sickey, October 22, 1976, and Ernest Sickey, "Chairman's Report," *Coushatta Smoke Signals*, February 28, 1977, 2, CTLA.

34. Bertney Langley, "Cultural Center," *Coushatta Smoke Signals*, February 28, 1977, 1, CTLA. Ena Mae Robinson Sickey won the first of these contests in the covered-basket category with an eight-inch basket that was "perfectly round." The Jennings American Bank manager was one of the contest judges who bought the winning basket and then donated it back to the tribe.

35. Bertney Langley, personal communication with Linda Langley, July 3, 2019. Langley said he would put the more common baskets, ones that were less in demand by locals, in the storeroom. When traders came from out-of-state, they would ask him, "What do you have in the back?" assuming the highest-quality baskets were those not on display. He also trained CETA interns on how to buy, sell, and manage the basket inventory.

36. Photographs of the exhibit are in the CTLA, though not the original display. Bertney Langley, personal communication with Linda Langley, August 28, 2019. Langley traveled with Lovelin Poncho, Mona Abbey, and Tribal Princess Roxanne John. He recalled one woman agreeing to purchase $1,000 of baskets if they would help her set up a similar display in her store.

37. Adrian Poncho Sylestine, interview with Crystal Williams, August 8, 2008, transcribed by Heather Williams, CTLA.

38. Loris Abbott Langley, personal communication with Linda Langley, 2007. Lang-

ley's "Man in the Maze" basket is no. CTLA.OB.02.170 in the CTLA collections. When coauthor Langley visited the NMAI in 2007 to inventory the tribal collections housed there, she was told that this design showed the diffusion of both southwestern motifs and tribal cosmology/religious beliefs into the Coushatta; however, Loris Abbott Langley said that she did not know the meaning or story behind the "Man in the Maze" motif. Rather, she chose to copy the design because it seemed elaborate and difficult. After successfully making it once, she didn't ever feel the need to make a similar basket again.

39. In 1986, Claude Medford Jr. said that Elsie John was the only active cane basket maker among the Coushattas in Louisiana. He said that poor health kept Ivey Obe Thompson, Minnie Obe, and Martha John from making cane baskets, and kept Solomon Battise from making both cane and white oak baskets. Claude Medford Jr. to Marshall Gettys, January 6, 1986, CTLA.

40. Literal translation of heading: "The Basket Makers Got Good at Their Sewing and People Came Looking for Them."

41. Ernest Sickey, interview with Denise E. Bates, September 2, 2015, CTLA.

42. Ernest Sickey to Stephen Richmond, March 4, 1975 and Sickey interview with Bates, April 29, 2015, both in CTLA.

43. NMAI accession information states that the Indian Arts and Crafts Board purchased this owl basket from Sylestine in 1976 for fifty-one dollars. NMAI catalog no. 25/5387. For additional inventory and acquisition information on the baskets that were transferred from the Indian Arts and Crafts Board to the National Museum of the American Indian, see Smithsonian Institution, www.nmai.si.edu/searchcollections/results.aspx?catids=0&cultxt=Coushatta&src=1-1&size=75&page=1 (accessed May 31, 2017).

44. Sickey to Richmond, September 29 and October 20, 1976; Richmond to Sickey, October 28, 1976, CTLA.

45. Haynes, "Constructing Authenticity," 19; Sickey to Richmond, August 18, September 29, and October 20, 1976; Richmond to Sickey, October 28, 1976, CTLA.

46. *Indian and Eskimo Organizations Marketing Native American Arts and Crafts: Source Directory 1.* Washington, DC: US Department of the Interior, Indian Arts and Crafts Board, 1976, 2, CTLA.

47. Ernest Sickey, personal correspondence with Linda Langley, April 1, 2019.

48. "Coushatta Pine Needle Coiled Basketry by Rosabel Robinson Sylestine," exhibition, September 9–December 30, 1973, CTLA.

49. Edith Sylestine Langley, interview with Crystal Williams, June 17, 2008, transcribed by Loretta Robinson Williams, CTLA.

50. Richmond to Sickey, March 28, 1973, CTLA.

51. Sickey to Johnson, March 22, 1973; Johnson to Richmond, October 19, 1973, CTLA.

52. US Department of the Interior Indian Arts and Crafts Board and the Coushatta Tribe of Louisiana, "Exhibition on Pine Needle Coiled Basketry by Rosabel Robinson Sylestine," 1973. Accession #P95-72, Indian Affairs, Governor's Commission, Louisiana State Archives (hereafter Indian Affairs, LSA). Richmond to Garrison, July 3, 1973, CTLA. Also, Sylestine's basket exhibition appeared in several news outlets; see "Elton Indian

Basketry Exhibit in Jackson Square," *Daily World,* July 13, 1973, 2; "Coushatta Indian Basket Exhibition to Open Sunday," *New Orleans States-Item,* July 11, 1973; and "Coushatta Indian: Elton Artist Has N.O. Show," *Lake Charles American Press,* July 14, 1973, 22.

53. For further details, see Bates, *Basket Diplomacy.*

54. Richmond to Robert G. Hart (General Manager), July 18, 1973, CTLA. Also, additional discussion on the media coverage of the Sylestine exhibit appears in Adalie Brent (addressed as Mrs. Allan R. Brent) (Louisiana Arts and Science Center) to Stephen Richmond, September 13, 1973, CTLA. Regarding the basket sales, see Frieda Morford (Louisiana State Museum) to Stephen Richmond, August 13, 1973, CTLA. Based on an itemized invoice prepared by Richmond at the start of the exhibit, the total value of the pine-needle baskets that Sylestine initially presented for sale was approximately $650; however, the demand prompted her to offer more pieces, resulting in over $1,000 worth of sales as reflected in a note produced after the exhibition ended. See Louisiana State Museum Receipt of Objects, Coushatta pine needle coiled basketry by Rosabel Robinson Sylestine for exhibit, July 15–Aug. 31, 1973, and "Geoff" to Stephen Richmond, October 18, 1973, CTLA.

55. Indian Arts and Crafts Board Regional News Release, "Louisiana Arts and Science Center to Show Indian Basketry Exhibit," September 9, 1973; and Stephen M. Richmond to Bob Ferguson, October 15, 1973, CTLA.

56. Press release, "Special Exhibition of Indian Crafts to Open at the Cabildo," November 23, 1973, CTLA.

57. Lorena Abbott Langley to Stephen M. Richmond, January 21, 1974, CTLA.

58. US Department of the Interior, Indian Arts and Crafts Board, "Crafts by the Langley Family," December 20, 1972–January 17, 1973, folder 3, box 245, AAIA.

59. "Coushatta Indian Crafts by Edna Langley," brochure for exhibition, December 9, 1973–January 31, 1974, LSU, Lower Mississippi Valley Collections; "Contemporary Coushatta Fashions by the Langleys," press release, May 1–28, 1978, folder 3, box 245, AAIA; "Lorena Abbott Langley Sews Best of Both Worlds," *Houston Chronicle,* May 3, 1978; Stephen M. Richmond to Edna Lorena Abbott Langley, September 6, 1977, CTLA. Langley's basket is a remarkably complex twill-plaited cane basket, NMAI catalog no. 25/5564.

60. Lorena Abbott Langley, qtd. in "Contemporary Coushatta Fashions by the Langleys," press release, May 1–28, 1978, folder 3, box 245, AAIA.

61. Richmond prematurely sought help for Langley from an outside source with clothes construction; however, she made it clear that she wanted her exhibit to be Coushatta-made and -created. Stephen M. Richmond to Ruth Fontenot, July 28, 1976, CTLA.

62. Claude Medford Jr.'s (1941–1989) biographical information can be found at *Folklife in Louisiana: Louisiana's Living Traditions,* www.louisianafolklife.org/LT/Virtual_Books/Splittin/splittin_on_the_grain.html. See also Medford, Gregory, and Sepulvado, *The Old Ways Live;* "Basket Classes Planned," *Town Talk,* May 15, 1981, 17; and "Folklife Center to Honor Artists," *Town Talk,* June 15, 1983, 29. During a five-day class in 1998, an audio recording was taken of Medford describing the process of harvesting and processing river

cane in the production of Choctaw baskets using diagonal plaited basket patterns. See "Choctaw Diagonal Twill Plaiting." Some of Medford's publications include "Things of Cane," "Coushatta Baskets and Basketmakers, and "Split Cane Basketry."

63. De Caro and Jordan, *Louisiana Traditional Crafts*, 23.

64. Marion Robinson John's biographical sketch draft was included with a letter from Michael Scott (editor of *The Crafts Report*) to Marion Robinson John, September 15, 1976, CTLA; Marion Robinson John, qtd. in "Coushatta Indian Pine Needle Basketry by Marion Robinson John," August 5–September 15, 1974, CTLA. See also "Baskets Full of Art: Coushatta Indian Basketweaver," *Houston Post*, August 4, 1974, 3.

65. Richmond to Johnson, May 6, 1974; Richmond to Margaret Prince (Contemporary Arts Museum), June 5, 1974, CTLA.

66. Sickey to Richmond, April 5, 1974, CTLA.

67. Richmond to H. E. Long (Louisiana State Exhibit Museum), October 11, 1974, CTLA.

68. Sickey to Richmond, August 7, 1974, CTLA.

69. Marion Robinson John, interview with Crystal Williams, July 22, 2008, transcribed and translated by Loretta Williams, CTLA.

70. Marion Robinson John to "Sir" (National Endowment for the Arts, Visual Arts Program), May 11, 1976, CTLA.

71. John's wastebasket is still housed at the Renwick, NMAI catalog no. 1975.140. The accession information states that the Renwick exhibit "highlighted the work of production craftsmen who created utilitarian objects in multiples of ten or more."

72. "Baskets from Pine," *Shreveport Women's Times*, June 16, 1975, B1. John also discussed her children helping her in the oral history conducted by the tribe. John interview, July 22, 2008, CTLA. Mention of John's honor from the Renwick Gallery was in correspondence from Ernest Sickey to Stephen Richmond, March 17, 1975, CTLA. John, qtd. in "Coushatta Indian Pine Needle Basketry by Marion Robinson John," August 5–September 15, 1974, CTLA. Richmond to Elena Canavier (Visual Arts Program, National Endowment for the Arts), November 20, 1974; Peg Bolton to Stephen M. Richmond, October 24, 1974, CTLA. In 1975, John was one of the headlining attractions at the First United Methodist Church's Ninth Annual Art Festival. "Pine Needles Baskets," *Town Talk*, April 4, 1975, 18. She was also invited to become part of Shreveport's Creative Craft Alliance Invitational Show. "Calendar of Events," *The Times*, June 1, 1975, 119.

73. William A. Reedy (Eastman Kodak Company) to Ernest Sickey, December 5, 1974, CTLA.

74. John interview, July 22, 2008, CTLA.

75. "Three Indian Artists to be at Gate House," *The Times*, November 12, 1983, 19.

76. Shana Walton, "Folklife Fest Begins," *Town Talk*, August 2, 1985, 23.

77. Governor Edwin Edwards to Ernest Sickey, November 3, 1976, CTLA.

78. Richmond to Bob Hart, November 16, 1976, CTLA.

79. Richmond to Carl Wilkins (Director, Commission of Local Affairs, State of Louisiana Inter Government Relations), April 7, 1976, CTLA.

80. Richmond to Wilkins, April 7, 1976; Richmond to Carl H. Aiken, September 13, 1977, CTLA.

81. De Caro and Jordan, *Louisiana Traditional Crafts*, 19–21.

82. William A. Reedy to Ernest Sickey, January 24, 1975, and January 24, 1975; Richmond to Sickey, March 7, 1975; Allie C. Peed Jr. (Manager, Advertising, Promotion and Publications) to Sickey, April 27, 1976, CTLA.

83. Richmond to Georganne Fletcher, June 14, 1979, CTLA.

84. Stephen M. Richmond retired as field representative for the federal Indian Arts and Crafts Board on March 31, 1983. He wrote that "this retirement is rather sudden, but, with my physical problems, I find it necessary." He was succeeded in his position by Meredith Stanton. Stephen M. Richmond to Nicholas Spitzer (Louisiana Folklife Program), March 21, 1983, CTLA. The names of the Coushatta exhibitors in the Southeastern Indian Basketry exhibition are listed in the exhibition flyer, CTLA; Richmond to Sickey, March 30, 1981, CTLA.

85. Richmond to Sickey, October 10, 1975, and July 1, 1976, CTLA.

86. Richmond specifically pointed out how Marion Robinson John's basket prices were "extremely low" when she first began her exhibitions but, following her Houston show, she "was able to derive greatly increased prices for her creations." Stephen M. Richmond to Elena Canavier, November 20, 1974; Ernest Sickey to Nancy Hanks (National Endowment for the Arts), July 1, 1977; Sickey to Richmond, September 18, 1973, CTLA.

87. Sickey to Richmond, November 4, 1975, CTLA.

88. Elvin Reed, "Candidates for Anti-Poverty," *Daily World*, September 13, 1964, 17; Elvin Reed, "Tribe Facing Dispersal: One Ray of Hope Left for Coushattas," *Sunday Advocate*, June 20, 1965, 3E; "Elect Tate to Congress," *Daily World*, August 29, 1965, 24. For more on Shriver's role in Johnson's Anti-Poverty Programs and his position on Indian affairs, see Cobb, *Native Activism in Cold War America*, 89, 120–21, 122–23, and 134–35.

89. Sickey interviews with Bates, November 16 and December 15, 2015, CTLA.

90. Ernest Sickey, presentation at Arizona State University, February 8, 2018, personal notes collected by Denise E. Bates.

91. Sickey interview with Bates, April 29, 2015, CTLA.

92. Sickey, personal communication to Linda Langley, August 22, 2019.

93. Bonner Miller Cutting, interview with Denise E. Bates, November 18, 2015, CTLA.

94. Blume frequently appeared in Louisiana newspapers because of her role in bringing millions of dollars into the state for arts workshops, performances, and exhibitions. See Mary Catherine Bounds, "Premiere of LODA Play 'A Magnificent Thrill,'" *The Times*, June 20, 1976, 1; and "Arts Workshop Set in B.R.," *Town Talk*, June 16, 1977, 38. Sickey interview with Bates, November 16, 2015, CTLA.

95. "Indian Arts Show Opens at Museum," *Lake Charles American Press*, October 13, 1973, 8.

96. Sickey interview with Bates, November 16, 2015, CTLA.

97. The Bel Estate acquired segments of Coushatta homesteads as early as 1909, as reported by Jacobson ("Koasati Culture Changes") based on information supplied to him in a letter by C. L. Marcantel, mayor of Elton. Regarding the resentment of tribal

members toward the Bel Estate, see Sickey interview with Bates, July 28, 2015, CTLA. J. A. Bel left a sizeable estate to his children, Marie, Katherine, and Ernest, upon his death in 1918. Bel's heirs organized the estate into three separate companies: Bel Oil, Bel Estate, and Quatre Parish Company. The history behind the three companies is detailed in an unpublished professional report for the fulfilment of an MBA degree by one of the Bel heirs, Della Bel Blake, "Bel Oil Corporation."

98. Accounts indicate that the initial two acres for the Coushatta School were donated by the Bel Estate. See Thos J. Griffin (Allen Parish School Board Superintendent) to L. W. Page (Superintendent of the Choctaw Agency), September 26, 1938, CTLA. Then, in 1960, the Bel Estate donated approximately five acres to the Indian Church to use as a parsonage and cemetery. Johnson, *The Coushatta People,* 81. Reference to Battise signing for the land on behalf of the tribe also appears in a letter from David Garrison Jr. to William Byler (AAIA), May 15, 1973, folder 3, box 245, AAIA.

99. "State Unit Created for Indian Affairs," *Lake Charles American Press,* June 8, 1972, 18.

100. For more on the origin and early development of the Louisiana Office of Indian Affairs see Bates, *The Other Movement* and *Basket Diplomacy;* also see Klopotek, *Recognition Odysseys.*

101. Garrison to Edwards, June 6, 1972, Indian Affairs, LSA.

102. David L. Garrison Jr. to Mitchell Wilder, July 19, 1974; Richmond to Garrison, July 3, 1973, CTLA. US Department of Interior, Indian Arts and Crafts Board, "Exhibition on Pine Needle Coiled Basketry by Rosabel Robinson Sylestine," 1973, Indian Affairs, LSA.

103. The 20.8 acres donated to the tribe from the Bel Estate became the second reservation. The first 15 acres located in the eastern part of the community were acquired and approved as federal trust land just a month prior. See Richard E. Gerard to William Byler, June 30, 1976; "Act of Donation Inter Vivos," July 2, 1976; Knapp to Dean, November 6, 1975; Dean to Knapp, November 10, 1975; US Department of Interior, Regional Solicitor to Eastern Area Director, BIA, May 13, 1976; Dean to Sickey, December 16, 1976; Dean to W. D. Wesley (John A. Bel Estate), December 7, 1976; and Dean to Sickey, January 19, 1977. All sources from folder 5, box 245, AAIA.

104. Sickey interview with Bates, July 28, 2015, CTLA. Sickey, personal communication with Langley, April 1, 2019.

105. Sickey, personal communication with Langley, April 1, 2019.

106. Sickey interview with Langley, April 1, 2019.

107. Bertney Langley, qtd. in tribal exhibit "We Are Still Here," Grand Hotel lobby, April 2016, CTLA. In a 1993 interview, Langley further explained that Coushatta women typically were responsible for passing the Koasati language on to their children. "The ladies are the backbone because they have access to the kids more than the father would. But now because of a family having two jobs we start to see the impact on the language" ("Tribal Folklore," *Lake Charles American Press,* December 26, 1993, 13).

108. Bertney Langley, interview with Linda Langley, April 1, 2019. The washing machine and dryer were purchased for the Sickeys in spring 1982.

109. Ernest Sickey, personal communication with Linda Langley, August 29, 2019.

110. Anne Searborough, "Made by Coushatta Indians: Baskets from Pine," *Women's Times*, June 16, 1975, B1.

111. Byler held this position with the Bibb Company until May 1976, after which time he became president of merchandising at Dan River Home Furnishings, Inc. "Byler Named to New Position Within Danville Division of DR," *The Bee*, May 4, 1976, 9.

112. Paul McClung, "Kiowas to Benefit from Sale of Items," *Lawton Constitution*, November 3, 1974, 20.

113. Byler to Sickey, December 10, 1973, AAIA.

114. Stephen W. Tabasko Jr. (Bibb Co.) to Daphne E. Hardoon (Drucilla Handy Co.), June 7, 1974, AAIA.

115. Tabasko to Hardoon, June 7, 1974, AAIA; Stephen W. Tabasko to Ernest Sickey, April 15, 1977, AAIA.

116. Ernest Sickey, interview with Bates, November 19, 2015, CTLA.

117. Tribal seal basket weavers to date include Rosabel Robinson Sylestine, Florence Robinson, Lora Langley, and Heather Williams. Several tribal members have also beaded and/or sewn tribal seal emblems.

118. Loretta Robinson Williams, personal communication with Bertney Langley, April 17, 2019, CTLA.

4. *Ittoiyat Ittillokoolit Intoliino̱ Maththit*
We Had to All Stand Together and Work Together

1. Ernest Sickey, personal communication with Linda Langley, April 1, 2019.

2. Stephen M. Richmond to Dallas Johnson, December 1, 1982, Cherokee Field Office Records, 1968–83, record group 435, box 12, folder 76B, Bureau of Indian Affairs Records, US Department of the Interior, Records of the Indian Arts and Crafts Board, record group 435, National Archives at Atlanta.

3. Ernest Sickey, interview with Bertney Langley, March 7, 2007, CTLA. Sickey talked about getting a $10,000 grant to build the first tribal building and using those funds to buy construction materials while tribal members did the work themselves. In discussing how hard it was to stretch their limited health-care funds, Langley recalled: "We didn't have anything, and even Indian Health Service used to commend us. One of them told me, 'How did y'all come this far? Because we would give you a small amount of money and we thought y'all wouldn't be able to handle it, but y'all would always have more.'" They laughed about shared memories of Crest sending an eighteen-wheeler with toothbrushes and toothpaste to the reservation and lifting a broom to measure the height of a backstop for the ballpark they built. See also Bates, *Basket Diplomacy*, 182, 196; Record Collections CTLA.DC.05, Re-recognition Era (1965–75); and CTLA.DC.06, Pre-Casino Era (1976–94).

4. Coushatta Tribe of Louisiana, Tribal Ordinance no. 84-1: Bingo Operations Authorization, January 18, 1984, CTLA. For a complete discussion of the historical context of Coushatta gaming, see Precht, "The Lost Tribe Wanders No More."

5. These agencies included the Allen Parish Sheriff's Department, which conducted

a raid on the tribe's bingo hall in October 1984, challenging their sovereignty. Bertney Langley, previously the Cultural Center director, then the tribal health director and bingo hall manager, responded by filing a lawsuit against Allen Parish. See *Langley v. Ryder*, 602 F. Supp. 335 (US District Court, Western District of Louisiana, Lake Charles Division, 1985). On December 18, 1985, the Fifth Circuit Court of Appeals upheld the lower court's decision that the state had no jurisdiction on the Coushatta Reservation. *Langley v. Ryder*, 778 F. 2d 1092 (5th Cir. 1985).

6. Precht argued that the Bureau of Indian Affairs did more than offer the requested technical assistance in the tribal election process, instead paternalistically making decisions for the Coushattas ("The Lost Tribe Wanders No More," 117). Thirty years later, this sentiment was echoed by Ernest Sickey, who always believed the federal government was motivated to cause upheaval in the Coushatta Tribe in order to settle outstanding land-claims litigation at a fraction of the price the tribe was seeking (interview with Linda Langley, March 7, 2007, CTLA).

7. Without tribal funds to purchase baskets, weavers got frustrated and ultimately asked to take over management of the Cultural Center. Bernita Sickey Baker, Leola Sylestine, Madeline Robinson Celestine, and other weavers attempted to keep the Cultural Center open, but weavers could not afford to leave their baskets on consignment and had to find other marketing venues.

8. Literal translation of heading: "Starting Up a Store to Sell the Baskets Again."

9. In the 1930s, Folsom-Dickerson noted the apparent "disappearance" and then resurgence of dance traditions among the Koasati living with the Alabama Indians on their reservation in Texas (*The White Path*, 34). For a discussion of nonlinear social change models, see also Richards, "Nonlinear Modeling."

10. Qtd. in Langley, LeJeune, and Oubre, eds., *Les Artistes*, 63.

11. The Jazz & Heritage Festival featured a "Native American Village" that advertised two weeks of "demonstrations of traditional indigenous crafts from many of the Louisiana Native tribes such as the art of basket weaving." See New Orleans Jazz & Heritage Festival.

12. Rosabel mentioned traveling to New Orleans several times to sell her baskets. She said she met Louise Olivier and got involved with the Louisiana Handicraft Project on one such trip. She also mentioned her sister, Madeline Robinson Celestine, and Bel Abbey as being active in the basketry trips to New Orleans. Rosabel Robinson Sylestine, interview with Pam Rabalais, September 2, 1995, transcribed by Camille Benoit, catalog no. 4700.0511, Lower Mississippi Valley Collections.

13. Bel Abbey was honored as a "Koasati Craftsman & Storyteller," Marjorie Abbey Battise for "Koasati Cooking," and Myrna Abbey Wilson as a "Koasati Pinestraw Basket Maker." Lorena Abbott Langley was honored for her "Koasati Indian Crafts" in 1993, and Doris Celestine Battise as a "Coushatta Pine-needle Basket Weaver" in 2011.The complete list of inductees can be found at Northwestern State University of Louisiana, "Hall of Master Folk Artists." In 2019, when the tribe used the designation of "Master Artisan," weavers joked that they had been given a master's degree.

14. In a 1991 interview, Poncho expressed his hope that new ventures, such as gaming

and grocery sales, would "give our reservation an economic boost." "State Signs Compact with Coushatta Tribe," *Daily Advertiser,* September 18, 1991, 3. Poncho was elected in a special election held after several challenges to the tribal election ordinance and process. For more background on this process, see Interior Board of Indian Appeals, *Anna Thompson et al. v. Area Director, Easter Area Office, Bureau of Indian Affairs,* IBIA 88-31-A, decided January 23, 1989.

15. Public Law 93-638, 88 Stat. 2203.

16. Bertney Langley served as the health director for the Narragansett Indian Tribe and secured funding for this training. He invited Poncho and introduced him to Parker, then working on her PhD dissertation at Brown University.

17. See Parker et al., "Traditions and Innovations."

18. Jeanette Celestine Langley, interview with Crystal Williams, July 21, 2008, transcribed by Heather Williams, CTLA.

19. "Coushatta to Share Way of Life With Others," *Lake Charles American Press,* September 28, 1991, 9.

20. "Coushatta Cling to Rich Culture," *Lake Charles American Press,* October 6, 1991, 31 and 41. Also see "Grand Opening Held at Coushatta Complex," *Basile Weekly,* October 31, 1991, 10.

21. "Coushatta Cling to Rich Culture," *Lake Charles American Press,* October 6, 1991, 31.

22. Rachel Lemoine, "Coushatta Reservation Is 'Time Machine,'" *Oakdale Journal,* April 19, 1990, 64.

23. Bertney Langley, personal communication with Linda Langley, September 9, 2019. News of the grand opening can be found in Jerry Hoffpauir, "Saturday Events Worth the Trip," *Eunice News,* July 25, 1991, 4.

24. "'Lost Tribe' Takes Spotlight in Elton," *Lake Charles American Press,* July 20, 1991, 7.

25. State of Louisiana, Office of the Lieutenant Governor, issued July 20, 1991, CTLA. Also see "Hardy Invited to Smoke Peace Pipe," *Oakdale Journal,* May 30, 1991, 8.

26. State of Louisiana, Office of the Lieutenant Governor, issued July 20, 1991, CTLA.

27. *Basile Weekly,* January 23, 1992, 1; "Awards Received at Travel Summit," *Eunice News,* January 19, 1992, 1.

28. "Tribe Shares Centuries-Old Customs," *Lake Charles American Press,* August 12, 1992, 47.

29. The lease agreement was amended from a previous one to clarify that the town wasn't obligated to pay for any improvements on the building if the need arose. See "Lease Proposals on Buildings Approved by Elton Council," *Basile Weekly,* September 15, 1994, 1.

30. "Bertney Langley Gives Presentation on Tribal Culture and Customs," *Basile Weekly,* May 5, 1999, 12.

31. Loris Abbott Langley, qtd. in Langley, LeJeune, and Oubre, eds., *Les Artistes,* 59.

32. "Coushatta Tribe Powwow," *Lake Charles American Press,* September 25, 1992, 29.

33. "Coushatta Heritage," *Lake Charles American Press,* March 19, 1994, 5.

34. "Vermilionville Plans Exhibit on Native American Groups," *Daily World,* November 20, 1991, 8.

35. "Learning About Indians," *Eunice News*, October 31, 1990, 3.

36. "Louisiana Folklife Festival: Native American Crafts," *Eunice News*, September 29, 1991, 86. In addition to this grant, Lorena Langley received funding to teach her daughter, Trudy Fontenot, basketry traditions and assist in the preservation of pine-needle basketry. See Louisiana Folklife Program. "Folklife Apprenticeships."

37. Bel Abbey, recording by Linda Langley, April 7, 1990, CTLA; "Saturday Festival," *Oakdale Journal*, April 5, 1990, 1; and "Antique Car Show Set in Elton," *Eunice News*, April 6, 1990, 2.

38. "Indian Fest Attracts ABC-TV," *Ville Platte Gazette*, June 18, 1992, 12; "Bayou Indian Festival Begins Friday in Elton," *Basile Weekly*, June 18, 1992, 1.

39. "Schwegmann Opening Festival," *Daily Advertiser*, June 19, 1993, 6.

40. "Touristic Destinations Cajun Country," 1991, CTLA. All production information, including direct quote from Linda Harkness, can be found in Barbara Doyle, "Local Tribe on National Promo," *Oakdale Journal*, September 26, 1991, 1.

41. A reference to a film of Coushatta traditional dances being shown to an elementary school class appears in "Kindergarten Students Celebrate Thanksgiving with Coushatta Indians," *Crowley Post-Signal*, December 2, 1990, 7. See also "Cultural Enrichment," *Eunice News*, December 2, 1993, 2. For presentations given by Jeanette Celestine Langley utilizing film footage from the tribe, see "Bayou Belles Take Field Trip," *Basile Weekly*, July 30, 1992, 5, and "International Tea to Feature Coushatta Indians," *Basile Weekly*, September 10, 1992, 5.

42. Reference to the tribally produced video appears in "International Tea: Coushatta Indians Are This Year's Topic," *Ville Platte Gazette*, September 24, 1992, 13.

43. *A Taste of Louisiana with Chef John Folse & Company*, produced by Louisiana Public Broadcasting, episode first aired on June 14, 1992, and episode first aired August 5, 2006. Reference to Langley's appearance with John Folse appears in "Bayou Indian Festival This Weekend in Elton," *Basile Weekly*, June 17, 1993, 1.

44. Qtd. in basketry section of "Coushatta Heritage: Louisiana's Hidden Treasure," Coushatta Tribe of Louisiana, 1990. In Koasati, Langley said: *Hinaap, chalbaksotok haikat, chalbifa stahobaachifookap!* or literally, "My finger nail polish is faded and they're taking my picture!" In addition to several weavers doing pine-needle demonstrations, Solomon Battise demonstrated cane-basket weaving for the video and Bel Abbey demonstrated making blowguns and toys from cane.

45. *Parlez Vous* recording, Spring 1991, OWL-TV, Carola Ann Andrepont (interviewer), CTLA. Andrepont picked up on Abbey's use of the term "Lost Tribe" to refer to the Coushattas. At the end of the program, Abbey told her, "I'm sure glad you found us!"

46. See Folklife in Louisiana, *Swapping Stories: Folktales from Louisiana*, for a discussion of the book, film, and links to related curriculum materials. Bel Abbey and Bertney Langley each contributed several stories to this work. Reference to the video premier appears in "Library Premiers Video," *Oakdale Journal*, April 23, 1998, 1. Bel Abbey also contributed to the handfishing documentary entitled *Anything I Catch* (Pat Mire Films), as well as a documentary about the Coushattas produced by Fred Kniffen that has not been located as of this writing. Abbey was also a featured performer at the Smithsonian

Institution's 1985 Festival of American Folklife. See Smithsonian Institution, Center for Folklife and Cultural Heritage, CFCH.SFF.1985, Series 3, CTLA.

47. "Tribal Folklore," *Lake Charles American Press,* December 26, 1993, 13.

48. Louisiana State University at Eunice performance, September 1996 and September 1997, recordings courtesy of CTLA. "Langley to Meet WWII Code Talkers," *Jennings Daily News,* May 15, 2002, 1–2.

49. Literal translation of heading: "We Made Gaming Money Work for Us."

50. See Precht, "The Lost Tribe Wanders No More," 132–41, for a discussion of key factors in the Coushattas' decision to open a casino, including the 1988 passage of the IGRA, the economic and social climate within Louisiana, and the tribal council's perception that their future lay in gaming. See also Sarah Sue Goldsmith, "Sudden Prosperity Brings Concerns About Future," *The Advocate,* June 9, 1996, 18.

51. DeAdrian Alexander, "Allen Parish Has Hit the Jackpot with Casinos, Outdoors," *Town Talk,* February 28, 1998, 54.

52. Kevin Sickey was one of the tribe's first police officers. He later became the tribal police chief, then served as tribal chairman from 2005 to 2013. He is credited with incorporating the basket design onto the new badge design.

53. Jeanette Celestine Langley made a twelve-inch covered basket in tribal colors, using all three forms of stitching, which the casino bought in 1995 for $1,200 (CTLA, OB.012).

54. Imperial Calcasieu Planning and Development Commission, "Coushatta Existing Land Use Study," Spring 1981, 6–8, CTLA.

55. "Many Returning to Indian Heritage," *Lake Charles American Press,* January 27, 1995, 7. The tribe built ten housing units on the reservation in 1997 to accommodate the increased number of younger members returning to the area to work at the casino. Within three years, they added twenty-three new housing units. There is currently a waiting list for tribal housing, with average wait times of approximately two years. Jill Gradney (Tribal Housing Director), personal communication with Linda Langley, September 12, 2019.

56. The early years of the tribe receiving gaming revenues were not without difficulties and internal dissent. For more on the economic and political discord within the tribe during this time, particularly related to the Abramoff scandal, see National Public Radio, "Indian Casinos and Lobbying, After Abramoff"; Brotherton, *A Fistful of Kings;* and Bertney Langley, interview with Bill Moyers.

57. "History of the Coushatta Tribe of Louisiana," April 2003, CTLA. Also see "Native Pride & Prejudice" on the *Snap Judgment* podcast for an interview with Bertney and Linda Langley about the early years of their relationship.. In a 1997 presentation to the American Folklore Society, Langley commented, "My wife, when she first started coming out there, nobody would trust her. She was a white person. They would be nice to her, but they wouldn't let her into the inner circles. It took a while. I had to marry her. See what I do for you folks." For a complete transcript of Langley's presentation, see "A Storyteller's Perspective," *Louisiana Voices.*

58. Bates, "The Coushatta Tribe of Louisiana."

59. The National Science Foundation provided funding for both the training at AILDI and five years of the Koasati language project (grant nos. 0651290 and 1065334). Special thanks are due to Dr. Susan Penfield, whose support at both AILDI and NSF started the tribe on this journey, and Dr. Jack Martin whose support and guidance were invaluable throughout the project. See also Bischoff and Jany, eds., *Insights from Practices in Community-Based Research,* and Langley and Langley, "Kowassaaton Ilhaalos."

60. Bates, "The Coushatta Tribe of Louisiana."

61. The ending of this interview was never translated until 2018, when it was translated by Bertney Langley.

62. Knowledge of *chawahka*-making was traditionally kept within families. Steven was the grandson of Solomon Battise, who had been gifted Solomon's cane baskets used in making *chawahka* and had always adhered to the way he had been taught without sharing this information. Even in the previous century, when so many anthropologists, linguists, and ethnographers visited the tribe, no one had fully documented this process.

63. Steven Robinson, interview with Ernest Sickey, March 7, 2007, translated by Ernest Sickey and transcribed by Linda Langley, CTLA.

64. Steven Robinson, interview with Ernest Sickey, March 9, 2007, translated by Ernest Sickey and transcribed by Linda Langley, CTLA. Steven demonstrated the use of the *kihcho* and *kistapi* (log and pounder used to pound corn), the three types of cane baskets used to sift the corn, building the fire, and the different steps involved in the cooking process. The process of making this soup is so specialized that it requires the use of a different verb in Koasati, that is, *chawahka chawahlit* instead of the more common words for cooking, *libaatlit* and *hopoonit.* Coushatta Tribe of Louisiana, *Koasati Dictionary,* 40.

65. Robinson interview with Sickey, March 7, 2007.

66. Ernest Sickey, personal communication to Linda Langley while translating interview with Steven Robinson, July 23, 2019.

67. "Coushatta Slow Cooked Corn Soup," *Indian Country Today,* May 23, 2013.

68. See US Department of Fish and Wildlife Services, "Woven from the Landscape." The tribal longleaf pine tree tract is named *Choiyi Achihka,* "Longleaf Ridge" (literally "place where the pine trees are planted").

69. Her mother, Loretta Robinson Williams; grandmothers, Florence Robinson and Leona Williams; and great-grandmothers, Maggie Langley and Lizzie Robinson, were all highly respected tribal weavers. Her weaving lineage extends further back into the nineteenth century, but weaving records are less accurate from this earlier period.

70. Coushatta Tribe of Louisiana, *A Koasati Conversation.*

71. *Kinder Courier News,* August 8, 2013, 3; "Revitalizing the Coushatta Heritage," *Jennings Daily News,* November 14, 2014, 1–2.

72. The ending sequence of the tribe's *Hidden Treasures* video shows Battise explaining his techniques to Linda Langley, CTLA.

73. Leonard Battise, interview with Ernest Sickey, November 18, 2016, Bertney Langley (translator), CTLA.

74. Battise, interview with Sickey, November 18, 2016, CTLA.

75. Battise used the Koasati word *boklit* to describe this process, which literally translates to "beating." However, his accompanying hand gestures make it clear that the English term "thunking" is a better description of the process he uses to test the cane to see if it makes the right sound.

76. Coushatta Tribe of Louisiana, *The Last Coushatta Cane Basket Maker*, film, 2016, CTLA.

77. Battise, interview with Sickey, November 18, 2016, CTLA.

78. See Langley et al., LSUE vol. 3, 85, CTLA, for an example of an anthropologist criticizing the "costumes" of tribal dancers because they were constructed from modern materials. Recent scholarship has helped to expand the discussion, emphasizing that "traditional" material culture should be defined by Indigenous practitioners. For example, see Rangel's discussion of ways that the Museum of Contemporary Native Arts encourages the recognition of Indigenous ways of knowing, Indigenous models of representation, Indigenous aesthetics, and the delivery of knowledge pertaining to Native arts and culture. Additionally, contemporary Native people produce cultural art forms as a way of connecting to and preserving generations of creativity and tradition. Rangel's analysis of basketry and other material culture needs to take into consideration the stories, songs, genealogies, oral histories, and Indigenous aesthetics inherent in these forms. Rangel, "Moving Beyond the Expected," 41. See also Lonetree, "Continuing Dialogues," for a discussion of the NMAI's collaborative model for developing exhibitions.

79. Marianna Luquette, personal communication with Linda Langley, July 26, 2019.

80. The picnic-basket maker is unknown. It was traded at the Tupper Museum around 1930 (CTLA, OB.101). The scrapbook cover was made by Arzile Langley around 1930 (CTLA, OB.250).

81. Lorenda John Poncho has described trying new techniques for dyeing raffia.

82. Battise, interview with Sickey, November 18, 2016, CTLA.

83. Clifford is the son of Jane Poncho, who was in the first weaving workshop held at the Trading Post in 1973. Lorenda John Poncho was also a participant in this first workshop. Loretta Robinson Williams is the granddaughter of cane weavers Maggie Langley and Lizzie Robinson.

84. Battise, interview with Sickey, November 18, 2016, CTLA.

85. Bertney Langley, personal communication while translating Battise-Sickey interview, July 16, 2019.

86. Lorenda John Poncho, interview with Crystal Williams, June 5, 2008, translated and transcribed by Loretta Robinson Williams, CTLA.

87. The makers of each of these baskets are Marion Robinson John, Julia Robinson Lowe, Heather Williams, Lorenda John Poncho, and Leonard Battise.

88. For example, Loretta Robinson Williams brings her siblings, daughters, and grandchildren to the annual Vermillionville demonstrations. Also, Raynella Thompson Fontenot brings her children to Moundville and other annual events.

89. Linda Langley, photographs, notes, and discussions during the visit.

90. "Sickey Meets with U.N. Ambassador," *Lake Charles American Press*, November 13, 2014, A6; "Native American Tribe Signs Friendship Treaty with Israel," *Native Village Youth and Education News*, January 1, 2009; "Coushatta," *Lake Charles American Press*, January 6, 2013, B1 and B4; "Coushatta Bridge a Gap," *Lake Charles American Press*, March 31, 2016, A10. The pine needles were bundled in the Coushatta tribal seal and bore the inscription, "Dear Senator McCain, On behalf of Native Americans and the Coushatta Tribe of Louisiana, you taught us that fame is mist, honor is granite," CTLA.

91. Jeanette Celestine Langley, interview at museum, March 7, 2007, CTLA.

92. Notes, Koasati Language Committee, June 12, 2009, CTLA.

93. Ernest Sickey, interview with Linda Langley, July 24, 2019, CTLA.

94. Coushatta Tribe of Louisiana, *The Last Coushatta Cane Basket Maker*, film, 2016, CTLA.

95. Gwyneth Thompson (aged nineteen), interview with Linda Langley, August 27, 2019, and Clarissa Wier (aged sixteen), interview with Linda Langley, August 28, 2019, CTLA. Weavers often point to the accomplishments of Sophia John Daigle, Marion Robinson John's granddaughter, who markets her creations as "Sophia's Pine Needle Baskets" on Facebook. Older weavers say that her small, precise stitches are reminiscent of her grandmother's weaving.

96. Clarissa Wier interview, August 28, 2019, CTLA. Eli Langley described utilizing a similar "Master-Apprentice" method of taking a tribal language class, then finding elders to converse with after class to become conversationally fluent in Koasati.

97. Clarissa Wier interview, August 28, 2019, CTLA.

98. Daigle thinks the basket was started by Paula Abbey Manuel and recalls that he was taught the basic plain-stitch and shaping techniques by Lorenda John Poncho. He says that the first basket he finished was "a big ugly thing that looked like a hornet's nest." Landon Daigle, personal communication with Linda Langley, March 27, 2020.

99. Daigle, personal communication with Langley, March 27, 2020. The old house belonged to Roy and Fern Abbey, and the materials Daigle found likely belonged to Fern Williams Abbey. Daigle also found a small pair of rusty scissors and a thimble, so this was likely Abbey's "basket box." The box also contained a few small baskets partially started, which were given to other young family members interested in learning to weave.

100. Daigle recalled Poncho basically "re-teaching" him, and says he had a much greater understanding because he was older.

101. Daigle wanted to finish his basket with pine cones in order to "bring back the more traditional, older looking baskets." Adrian Poncho Sylestine helped Daigle complete the basket decorations, showing him her signature way of adding pinecones and raffia. Tribal elders were very moved by Daigle's determination to learn this stitch himself with advice given over the phone rather than demonstrations in person. They saw his dedication as a powerful affirmation that the younger generation cared about continuing their cultural traditions and suggested that he be invited to join the Language and Cultural Committee. At the time of this writing, Daigle is working on a twelve-inch wheat-stitch basket, which is unheard of among younger weavers. He plans to eventually

develop an online market for his beadwork and basketry. Lorenda Poncho John and Landon Daigle, personal communication with Linda Langley, March 27, 2020.

102. Ronnie Abbey, correspondence with Raynella Thompson Fontenot, March 10, 2020. Abbey recalled that the group included Adele Williams, Isabel Robinson, Liz John, and Shirley Sylestine.

103. Elliott Abbey, interview with Linda Langley, March 30, 2020.

104. Gwyneth Thompson interview, August 27, 2019. Gwyneth also took the tribal language class and became conversationally fluent in Koasati.

105. Clarissa Wier interview, August 28, 2019.

106. Elliott Abbey interview, March 30, 2020. Abbey attended a basketry class held on the Alabama-Coushatta Reservation, taught by weaver Joyce Abbey Poncho. See Elliott Abbey's basketry and gallery website.

107. Gwyneth Thompson interview, August 27, 2019.

108. Jackson, "Containers of Tradition."

109. "Basket Weaving at the Museum," March 2007, CTLA. The casual setting prompted a lot of discussion, interspersed with laughter and teasing while the weavers sewed and observed each other's baskets. Weavers present were (in alphabetical order): Marjorie Abbey Battise, Sharon Crosby, Darlene Langley Dunnehoo, Marion John, Barbara Langley (interviewer), Jeanette Celestine Langley, Loris Abbott Langley, Lorenda John Poncho, Geraldine Sylestine Reed, Adrian Poncho Sylestine, Elizabeth Marie Abbott Thompson, and Loretta Robinson Williams.

110. "Basket Weaving at the Museum," March 2007, CTLA.

111. Lorenda John Poncho, Kaitlynn Nichols Courville, and Hannah Nichols Boudreaux demonstrated cane basketry, and master weavers Myrna Abbey Wilson, Glenna Battise Robinson, Adrian Poncho Sylestine, and Darlene Langley Dunnehoo demonstrated pine-needle basketry. Jonas and Dakota John demonstrated stickball racquet and ball making, and students Avery and Aerwyn Fontenot demonstrated basketry and beadwork.

112. Lorenda John Poncho, interview with Crystal Williams, June 5, 2008, transcribed and translated by Loretta Robinson Williams, CTLA. Elliott Abbey also expressed the value of allowing his children to be present when he is sewing baskets, even if they play with his needles or made a mess with the raffia. "I want to take my memories as a kid and give it to my kids, let them learn to make baskets." Interview with Linda Langley, March 30, 2020.

Bibliography

ARCHIVAL SOURCES

American Missionary Association Photographs, 1887–1952. Amistad Research Center, Tulane University, New Orleans.

Association on American Indian Affairs Records. Seeley G. Mudd Manuscript Library, Princeton University, Princeton, NJ.

Bureau of Indian Affairs Records. US Department of the Interior. Central Classified Files, 1907–39, Record Group 75. National Archives and Records Administration, Washington, DC.

———. Cherokee Field Office Records, 1968–83. Records of the Indian Arts and Crafts Board, Record Group 435. National Archives at Atlanta, Morrow, GA.

Coushatta Tribal Archives. Coushatta Tribe of Louisiana Heritage Department. Elton, LA.

Harrington Field Notebook. National Museum of the American Indian. Washington, DC.

Joe Jennings Bureau of Indian Affairs Records. Archives of Appalachia. East Tennessee State University, Johnson City.

Louisiana Indian Affairs. Governor's Commission. Louisiana State University Archives, Baton Rouge.

Lower Mississippi Valley Collections. Louisiana State University Archives, Baton Rouge.

National Museum of the American Indian. Washington, DC.

Pickett Family Papers. Alabama Department of Archives and History. Montgomery.

Maude Reid Collection. Scrapbook 4, ser. 1. On loan from Calcasieu Parish Public Library. Archives and Special Collections Department, Frazar Memorial Library, McNeese State University, Lake Charles, LA.

Ashbel Smith Papers. Dolph Biscoe Center for American History, University of Texas, Austin.

NEWSPAPERS

The Advocate (Baton Rouge, LA)
Basile Weekly (LA)
Beaumont Enterprise (TX)
The Bee (Danville, VA)
Coushatta Smoke Signal (Elton, LA)
Crowley Post-Signal (LA)
Daily Advertiser (Lafayette, LA)
Daily World (Opelousas, LA)
Eunice News (LA)
Houston Chronicle
Houston Post
Indian Country Today (Washington, DC)
Jennings Daily News (LA)
Kinder Courier News (LA)
Lake Charles American Press (LA)
Lake Charles Associated Press (LA)
Lawton Constitution (OK)
New Orleans States-Item
Oakdale Journal (LA)
Opelousas Daily World (LA)
Shreveport Women's Times (LA)
Sunday Advocate (Baton Rouge, LA)
The Times (Shreveport, LA)
Town Talk (Alexandria, LA)
Ville Platte Gazette (LA)
Weekly Town Talk (Alexandria, LA)

WEB SOURCES

Abbey, Elliott. Basketry and Gallery. pineneedleworkbyera.com/.

ABC News. "NAIDOC Week: Indigenous Languages Aren't Dead, Just Sleeping—and This Is Why They Matter." www.abc.net.au/news/2017-07-08/naidoc-week-not-dead-just-sleeping-indigenous-languages-matter/8681076.

"Choctaw Diagonal Twill Plaiting: A Workshop with Claude Medford, Jr." CD, 1988. *The Basket Maker's Catalog.* www.basketmakerscatalog.com/ps/dvds-and-cds/952-cd-choctaw-diagonal-twill-plaiting-a-workshop-with-claude-medford-jr.html (accessed October 10, 2017).

Folklife in Louisiana. *Swapping Stories: Folktales from Louisiana.* www.louisiana folklife.org/LT/Virtual_Books/Swapping/creole_books_swapping_sto .html.

Koasati Heritage. koasatiheritage.org.

Langley, Bertney. Interview with Bill Moyers. *Spotlight,* 2006. billmoyers.com/ content/moyers-on-america-capitol-crimes/.

Louisiana Folklife Program. "Folklife Apprenticeships Awarded by the Louisiana Division of the Arts." www.louisianafolklife.org/awards.html#tab2.

Louisiana Public Broadcasting. *A Taste of Louisiana with Chef John Folse & Company.* www.lpb.org/shop/items/taste-of-louisiana-folse-episodes.

Martin, Howard N. "Coushatta Indians." In *Handbook of Texas Online,* Texas State Historical Association, tshaonline.org/handbook/online/articles/ bmcag (accessed July 5, 2019).

———. "Alexander Hamilton Washington." In *Handbook of Texas Online,* Texas State Historical Association, tshaonline.org/handbook/online/articles/ fwa61 (accessed July 5, 2019).

Medford, Claude, Jr. "Crafts from the 'Back Days.'" In *Folklife in Louisiana: Louisiana's Living Traditions.* www.louisianafolklife.org/LT/Virtual_Books/ Splittin/splittin_on_the_grain.html (accessed October 12, 2019).

National Conference of State Legislatures. "Federal and State Recognized Tribes." www.ncsl.org/research/state-tribal-institute/list-of-federal-and-state-recognized-tribes.aspx#State.

National Public Radio. "Indian Casinos and Lobbying, After Abramoff." *Talk of the Nation.* www.npr.org/templates/story/story.php?storyId=5160734. Aired January 17, 2006.

"Native Pride & Prejudice." *Snap Judgment* podcast. snapjudgment.org/native-pride-prejudice. Aired June 14, 2013.

Native Tech. "Native American Basketry." www.nativetech.org/basketry/ (accessed November 3, 2019).

New Orleans Jazz & Heritage Festival. www.nojazzfest.com.

Northwestern State University of Louisiana. "Hall of Master Folk Artists." louisianafolklife.nsula.edu/hall-of-master-folk-artists/.

Pat Mire Films. *Anything I Catch: The Handfishing Story.* patmire.com/films/ anything-i-catch/.

Smithsonian Institution. "Collection Search Center." collections.si.edu/search/.

"A Storyteller's Perspective." *Louisiana Voices.* www.louisianavoices.org/Unit5/ edu_ss_storytellers_perspective.html.

Tupper Museum. www.tuppermuseum.com.

US Department of Agriculture. "Native Plant Dyes." www.fs.fed.us/wildflowers/ ethnobotany/dyes.shtml (accessed November 3, 2019).

US Department of Fish and Wildlife Services. "Woven from the Landscape." www.fws.gov/southeast/articles/woven-from-the-landscape/ (accessed January 23, 2018).

OTHER SOURCES, PUBLISHED AND UNPUBLISHED

Abel-Vidor, Suzanne, Dot Brovarney, and Susan Billy. *Remember Your Relations: The Elsie Allen Baskets, Family & Friends.* Berkeley, CA: Grace Hudson Museum; Oakland Museum of California; Heyday Books, 1996.

Abernethy, Francis E. *Tales from the Big Thicket.* Austin: University of Texas Press, 1966.

Barrett, Samuel A. *Pomo Indian Basketry.* 1908. Rpt. Ukiah, CA: Grace Hudson Museum, 1996.

Bates, Denise E. *The Other Movement: Indian Rights and Civil Rights in the Deep South.* Tuscaloosa: University Press of Alabama, 2012.

———. "Reshaping Southern Identity and Politics: Indian Activism during the Civil Rights Era." *Native South* 9 (2016): 125–51.

———. "What's in a Seal? How a Fish Came to Represent the Coushatta Tribe of Louisiana." *Southern Cultures,* Fall 2017, 128–33.

———. "The Coushatta Tribe of Louisiana: Preserving the Past to Make Way for the Future." *64 Parishes,* Winter 2019.

———. *Basket Diplomacy: Leadership, Alliance-Building, and Resilience among the Coushatta Tribe of Louisiana, 1884–1984.* Lincoln: University of Nebraska Press, 2020.

Bentley, Amy, and Hi'llei Hobart. "Food in Recent U.S. History." In *Food in Time and Place: The American Historical Association Companion to Food History,* ed. Paul Freedman, Joyce E. Chaplin, and Ken Albala, 165–87. Oakland: University of California Press, 2014.

Berger, R., M. Bendat, and A. Parker. "America's Oldest Basketry." *Radiocarbon* 40, no. 2 (1998): 615–20.

Berkhofer, Robert F., Jr., *The White Man's Indian: Images of the American Indian from Columbus to the Present.* New York: Vintage Books, 1978.

Berlandier, Jean Louis. *The Indians of Texas in 1830.* Ed. John C. Ewers. Washington, DC: Smithsonian Institution Press, 1969.

Bernstein, Bruce. *The Language of Native American Baskets: From the Weavers' View.* National Museum of the American Indian, 2003.

Binkley, William C. *Journals of the Fourth Congress of the Republic of Texas, 1839–1840, to Which Are Added the Relief Laws.* Ed. Harriet Smither. Vol. 1: *The Senate Journal.* Vol. 2: *The House Journal.* Vol. 3: *Reports and*

Relief Laws. Austin, TX: Von Boeckmann-Jones Co., 1930, 1931. In Texas Library and Historical Commission, State Library.

Bischoff, Shannon T., and Carmen Jany, eds. *Insights from Practices in Community-Based Research: From Theory to Practice Around the Globe*. Berlin: Walter de Gruyter GmbH & Co., 2018.

Blake, Della Bel. "Bel Oil Corporation: A Five Generation Experience." MBA thesis, University of Texas, Austin, 1981.

Blu, Karen I. *The Lumbee Problem: The Making of an American Indian People*. Lincoln: University of Nebraska Press, 1980.

Boyd, Mark F. "Expedition of Marcos Delgado, 1686." *Florida Historical Quarterly* 16 (1937): 3–32.

Brasseaux, Carl A. *Acadian to Cajun: Transformation of a People, 1803–1877*. Jackson: University Press of Mississippi, 1992.

Brotherton, John. *A Fistful of Kings*. Humble, TX: Shear Group, Ltd., 2000.

Cahill, Cathleen. "Making and Marketing Baskets in California." In *The Women's National Indian Association: A History*, ed. Valerie Sherer Mathes, 126–49. Albuquerque: University of New Mexico Press, 2015.

Cajete, Gregory A. "Indigenous Education and the Development of Indigenous Community Leaders." *Leadership* 12, no. 3 (2016): 364–76.

Chávez, Alicia Fedelina, Fengfeng Ke, and Felisha A Herrera. "Clan, Sage, and Sky: Indigenous, Hispano, and Mestizo Narratives of Learning in New Mexico Context." *American Educational Research Journal* 49, no. 4 (2012): 775–806.

Child, Brenda J. *Holding Our World Together: Ojibwe Women and the Survival of Community*. New York: Penguin, 2012.

Cobb, Daniel M. *Native Activism in Cold War America: The Struggle for Sovereignty*. Lawrence: University Press of Kansas, 2008.

Coleman, Arica L. *That the Blood Stay Pure: African Americans, Native Americans, and the Predicament of Race and Identity in Virginia*. Bloomington: Indiana University Press, 2013.

Conrad, G. R., ed. *The Historical Journal of the Establishment of the French in Louisiana, 1698–1723*. Rpt. Lafayette: University of Southwestern Louisiana, 1971.

Cooper, Karen Coody. *Oklahoma Cherokee Baskets*. Charleston, SC: History Press, 2016.

Coushatta Tribe of Louisiana. "The Struggle Has Made Us Stronger." Elton, LA: Coushatta Tribe of Louisiana, 1977.

———. *A Koasati Conversation*. Elton: Coushatta Tribe of Louisiana, 2012.

———. *Koasati Dictionary*. Elton, LA: Coushatta Tribe of Louisiana, 2017.

———. *Koasati Teaching Grammar.* Elton, LA: Coushatta Tribe of Louisiana, 2017.

———. *Kowassaati Nasmathahli Asaala* (Coushatta Animal Baskets). Elton: Coushatta Tribe of Louisiana, 2017.

Darden, John Paul, Scarlett Darden, and Melissa Darden Brown. "In the Family Tradition: A Conversation with Three Chitimacha Basketmakers." In *The Work of Tribal Hands,* ed. Lee and Gregory.

Davis, William C. *The Pirates Lafitte.* Austin, TX: Harcourt Press, 2005.

De Caro, F. A., and R. A. Jordan. *Louisiana Traditional Crafts.* Baton Rouge: Louisiana State University Union Gallery, 1980.

Deloria, Philip J. *Playing Indian.* New Haven, CT: Yale University Press, 1998.

Deloria, Philip S. "The Era of Indian Self-Determination: An Overview." In *Indian Self-Rule: First-Hand Accounts of Indian-White Relations from Roosevelt to Reagan,* ed. Kenneth R. Philip, 191–207. Logan: Utah State University Press, 1995.

Estes, James R. and Rahmana A. Thompson, "Cane: Its Characteristics and Identification in Baskets." In *Basketry of the Southeastern United States,* ed. Marshall Gettys, 44–57. Idabel, OK: Museum of the Red River, 1984.

Ethridge, Robbie. *Creek Country: The Creek Indians and Their World.* Chapel Hill: University of North Carolina Press, 2003.

Evans, Michelle, Amanda Sinclair, Rachel Wolfgramm, Chellie Spiller, and Cora Voyageur. "Containing, Contesting, Creating Spaces: Leadership and Cultural Identity Work among Australian Indigenous Arts Leaders." *Leadership* 12, no. 3 (2016): 270–92.

Fariello, M. Anna, *Cherokee Basketry: From the Hands of Our Elders.* Charleston, SC: History Press, 2009.

Flores, D. L. *Southern Counterpart to Lewis & Clark: The Freeman & Custis Expedition of 1806.* Norman: University of Oklahoma Press, 1984.

Fogelson, Raymond. *Handbook of North American Indians.* Vol. 14: *Southeast.* Washington, DC: Smithsonian Institution, 2004.

Folsom-Dickerson, W. E. S. *The White Path.* San Antonio, TX: Naylor Co., 1965.

Franco, Jere. "The Alabama-Coushatta and Their Texas Friends." *East Texas Historical Journal* 27, no. 1 (1989): 31–43.

Geib, Phil R., and Edward A. Jolie. "The Role of Basketry in Early Holocene Small Seed Exploitation: Implications of a ca. 9,000 Year-Old Basket from Cowboy Cave, Utah." *American Antiquity* 73, no. 1 (2008): 83–102.

Gettys, Marshall. "Choctaw Cane Baskets, 1830 to 1950: An Oklahoma Perspective." In *The Work of Tribal Hands,* ed. Lee and Gregory.

Giovo, J., I. B. Turner, and L. Langley. *Vox Populi: The Voice of the People, An*

Oral History of Jefferson Davis Parish. Jennings, LA: Jeff Davis Arts Council, 2000.

Grant, C. L., ed. *Letters, Journals, and Writings of Benjamin Hawkins.* Vol. 2. Savannah, GA: Beehive Press, 1980.

Gregory, H. F. "Pete." "Pieces and Patches—A Whole from Many Parts." *Splittin' on the Grain, Louisiana Folklife* 8, no. 1 (1983): 9–11.

———. "The Louisiana Tribes: Entering Hard Times." In *Indians of the Southeastern United States in the Late 20th Century,* ed. J. Anthony Paredes, 162–82. Tuscaloosa: University Press of Alabama, 1992.

———. "Asá:la Koasati Cane Basketry." In *The Work of Tribal Hands,* ed. Lee and Gregory.

Hahn, Steven C. *The Invention of the Creek Nation, 1670–1763.* Lincoln: University of Nebraska Press, 2014.

Harrington, M. Raymond. "Among Louisiana Indians." *Southern Workman* 37 no. 12, (December 1908): 656–61.

Harvison, C. Renée, and Maida Owens. "Bel Abbey: Koasati Stories: Elton, Jefferson Davis Parish." In *Swapping Stories: Folktales from Louisiana,* ed. Carl Lindahl, Maida Owens, and C. Renée Harvison, 80–104. Jackson: University Press of Mississippi, 1997.

Hasselbacher, Stephanie. "'Written in Indian': Creating Legitimized Literacy and Authorized Speakership in Koasati." PhD diss., College of William and Mary, 2015.

Haynes, Joshua S. "Constructing Authenticity: The Indian Arts and Crafts Board and the Eastern Band of Cherokees, 1935–1985." *Native South* 3 (2010): 1–38.

Hill, Sarah H. *Weaving New Worlds: Southeastern Cherokee Women and Their Basketry.* Chapel Hill: University of North Carolina Press, 1997.

———. "Marketing Traditions: Cherokee Basketry and Tourism Economics." In *Selling the Indian: Commercializing & Approaching American Indian Cultures,* ed. Carter Jones Meyer and Diana Royer, 2001. Tucson: University of Arizona Press. 212–35.

Hunter, Donald G. "Coushatta Basketry in the Rand Collection." *Florida Anthropologist* 28 no. 1 (March 1975): 27–37.

Hutchinson, Elizabeth. *The Indian Craze: Primitivism, Modernism, and Transculturation in American Art, 1890–1915.* Durham, NC: Duke University Press, 2009.

Jackson, Jason Baird. "Containers of Tradition: Southeastern Indian Basketry." *Gilcrease Journal* 17, no. 2 (Winter 2000): 4–25.

Jacobson, Daniel. "Koasati Culture Changes." PhD diss., Louisiana State University, 1954.

———. "The Origin of the Koasati Community of Louisiana." *Ethnohistory* 7, no. 2 (Spring 1960): 97–120.

James, George Wharton. *Indian Basketry: Forms, Designs, and Symbolism of Native American Basketry.* New York: Dover Publications, 1972.

Johnson, Bobby H. *The Coushatta People.* Phoenix, AZ: Indian Tribal Series, 1976.

Johnson, Kathryn S., and Reverend Paul Leeds. *Patteran: The Life and Works of Paul Leeds.* San Antonio, TX: Naylor Co., 1964.

Kimball, Geoffrey D. *Koasati Dictionary.* Lincoln: University of Nebraska Press, 1994.

Klopotek, Brian. *Recognition Odysseys: Indigeneity, Race, and Federal Tribal Recognition Policy in Three Louisiana Indian Communities.* Durham, NC: Duke University Press, 2011.

———. "Indian Education under Jim Crow." In *Indian Subjects: Hemispheric Perspectives on the History of Indigenous Education,* ed. Brenda J. Child and Brian Klopotek, 48–72. Santa Fe, NM: School for Advanced Research Press, 2014.

Kniffen, Fred B., Hiram F. Gregory, and George A. Stokes. *The Historic Indian Tribes of Louisiana: From 1542 to the Present.* Baton Rouge: Louisiana State University Press, 1987.

Langley, Bertney, Linda Langley, Jack B. Martin, and Stephanie Hasselbacher. "The Koasati Language Project: A Collaborative, Community-Based Language Documentation and Revitalization Model." In *Insights From Practices in Community-Based Research,* ed. Bischoff and Jany, 132–50.

Langley, Linda. "The Tribal Identity of Alexander McGillivray: A Review of the Historical and Ethnographic Data." *Louisiana History* 46, no. 2 (Spring 2005): 231–39.

———. "Koasati (Coushatta) Literature." In *A Listening Wind: Native Literature from the Southeast,* ed. Marcia Haag, 263–68. Lincoln: University of Nebraska Press, 2016.

Langley, Linda, and Bertney Langley. "Kowassaaton Ilhaalos: Let Us hear Koasati." In *Languages in Louisiana: Community and Culture,* ed. Nathalie Dajko et al., 28–36. Jackson: University Press of Mississippi, 2019.

Langley, Linda, Claude Oubre, and Jay Precht. "Louisa Williams Robinson, Her Daughters, and Her Granddaughters (1855–1932): Recognizing the Contributions of Three Generations of Coushatta Women in Louisiana." In *Louisiana Women: Their Lives and Times,* ed. Janet Allured and Judith F. Gentry, 155–74. Athens: University of Georgia Press, 2009.

Langley, Linda, Susan G. LeJeune, and Claude Oubre, eds. *Les Artistes: Crafters Tell Their Tales.* Eunice: Louisiana State University, 1996.

Le Page du Pratz, [Antoine-Simon]. *The History of Louisiana, or of the Western Part of Virginia and Carolina. . . .* Translated from the French. London: T. Becket Pub., 1774.

Lee, Dayna Bowker. "The Ties That Bind: Cane Basketry Traditions among the Chitimacha and the Jena Band of Choctaw." In *The Work of Tribal Hands,* ed. Lee and Gregory.

Lee, Dayna Bowker, and Hiram F. Gregory, eds. *The Work of Tribal Hands: Southeastern Indian Split Cane Basketry.* Natchitoches, LA: Northwestern State University Press, 2006.

Lomawaima, K. Tsianina, and Teresa L. McCarty. *To Remain an Indian: Lessons in Democracy from a Century of Native American Education.* New York: Teachers College Press, 2006.

Lonetree, Amy. "Continuing Dialogues: Evolving Views of the National Museum of the American Indian." *Public Historian* 28, no. 2 (2006): 57–62.

Louisiana News Digest. *Louisiana Indians.* Baton Rouge, LA: Dept. of Commerce and Industry, April 1951.

Lowery, Malinda Maynor. *Race, Identity, & the Making of a Nation.* Chapel Hill: University of North Carolina Press, 2010.

Mason, Otis Tufton, *American Indian Basketry.* New York: Dover Publications, 2012.

Medford, Claude, Jr. "Things of Cane." *Eagle Wing Press,* Fall 1984, 5.

———. "Coushatta Baskets and Basketmakers." In *Basketry of the Southeastern United States,* ed. Marshall Gettys, 51–56. Idabel, OK: Museum of the Red River, 1984.

———. "Split Cane Basketry." *Louisiana Folklife* 13 (1989): 5–12.

Medford, Claude, Jr., H. F. Gregory, and Don Sepulvado. *The Old Ways Live: The Claude Medford, Jr. Collection.* Natchitoches: Northwestern Louisiana State University, Williamson Museum, 1990.

Mier y Terán, Manuel de, Jack Jackson, Scooter Cheatham, and Lynn Marshall. *Texas by Terán: The Diary Kept by General Manuel de Mier y Terán on His 1828 Inspection of Texas.* Vol. 2. University of Texas Press, 2000.

Miller, Mark Edwin. *Forgotten Tribes: Unrecognized Indians and the Federal Acknowledgment Process.* Lincoln: University of Nebraska Press, 2004.

———. *Claiming Tribal Identity: The Five Tribes and the Politics of Federal Acknowledgment.* Norman: University of Oklahoma Press, 2013.

Mueller, Timothy, Sarah Sue Goldsmith, and Risa Mueller. *Nations Within: The Four Sovereign Tribes of Louisiana.* Baton Rouge: Louisiana State University, 2003.

Neuman, Robert. "Split Cane Items in Louisiana: A View from Archaeology and Ethnology," in *The Work of Tribal Hands,* ed. Lee and Gregory 6–26.

Osburn, Katherine M. B. *Choctaw Resurgence in Mississippi: Race, Class, and Nation Building in the Jim Crow South, 1830–1977.* Lincoln: University of Nebraska Press, 2014.

Paredes, J. Anthony. "Paradoxes of Modernism and Indianness in the Southeast." *American Indian Quarterly* 19, no. 3 (Summer 1995): 341–60.

Parker, L., M. Jamous, R. Marek, and C. Camacho. "Traditions and Innovations: A Community-Based Approach to Substance Abuse Prevention." *Rhode Island Medical Journal* 74 (1991): 281–86.

Perdue, Theda. "Indians in Southern History." In *Indians in American History: An Introduction,* 2nd ed., ed. Frederick Hoxie and Peter Iverson, 121–39. Wheeling, IL: Harlan Davidson, Inc., 1998.

———. *Cherokee Women: Gender and Culture Change, 1700–1835.* Lincoln: University of Nebraska Press, 1998.

———. "Native Americans, African Americans, and Jim Crow." In *indiVisible: African-Native American Lives in the Americas,* ed. Gabrielle Tayac, 21–33. Washington, DC: Smithsonian Institution, Nation Museum of the American Indian, 2009.

Piazza, Marianna. "Loulou: Louise Olivier's Career of Cultural Activism in Louisiana." MA thesis, University of Louisiana at Lafayette, 2018.

Poulsen, Tom. "Signatures: Rim Forms on Historic Southern Cane Baskets." In *The Work of Tribal Hands,* ed. Lee and Gregory.

Precht, James "Jay" H. "'The Lost Tribe Wanders No More': Indian Gaming and the Emergence of Coushatta Self-Determination." PhD diss., Arizona State University, 2007.

———. "The Nine from the Pines: High-Stakes Bingo and Federal Intervention in Coushatta Tribal Affairs in the 1980s." *Native South* 6 (2013): 142–69.

———. "Coushatta Basketry and Identity Politics: The Role of Pine-Needle Baskets in the Federal Rerecognition of the Coushatta Tribe of Louisiana." *Ethnohistory* 62 (2015): 145–67.

———. "Coushatta Homesteading in Southwest Louisiana and the Development of the Community at Bayou Blue." *Journal of Southern History* 84, no. 1 (February 2018): 113–38.

Putnam, Joanne. *A Town Named Elton.* Opelousas, LA: Bodemuller Printers, 1977.

Rangel, John Paul. "Moving Beyond the Expected: Representation and Presence in a Contemporary Native Arts Museum." *Wicazo Sa Review* 27, no. 1 (2012): 31–46.

Richards, Diana. "Nonlinear Modeling: All Things Suffer Change." *Political Complexity: Nonlinear Models of Politics.* Ann Arbor: University of Michigan Press, 2000, 1–20.

Shoemaker, Nancy, ed. *Negotiators of Change: Historical Perspectives on Native American Women*. Abingdon, UK: Psychology Press, 1995.

Shuck-Hall, Sheri M. *Journey to the West: The Alabama & Coushatta Indians*. Norman: University of Oklahoma Press, 2008.

———. "Alabama and Coushatta Diaspora and Coalescence in the Mississippian Shatter Zone." In *Mapping the Mississippian Shatter Zone: The Colonial Indian Slave Trade and Regional Instability in the American South*, ed. Robbie Ethridge and Sheri M. Shuck-Hall, 250–71. Lincoln: University of Nebraska Press, 2009.

Sibley, John. "A Report from Natchitoches in 1807." New York: Museum of the American Indian, Heye Foundation, 1922.

Sider, Gerald. *Living Indian Histories: Lumbee and Tuscarora People in North Carolina*. Chapel Hill: University of North Carolina Press, 1993.

Smith-Ferri, Sherrie. "The Development of the Commercial Market for Pomo Indian Baskets." *Expedition* 40, no. 1 (1998): 15–22.

Smither, Harriet. "The Alabama Indians of Texas." *Southwestern Historical Quarterly* 36, no. 2 (1932): 83–108.

Swanton, John Reed. *Indian Tribes of the Lower Mississippi Valley and Adjacent Coast of the Gulf of Mexico*. Washington, DC: US Government Printing Office, 1911.

———. "Early History of the Creek Indians and Their Neighbors." *Bureau of American Ethnology Bulletin* 73. Washington, DC, 1922.

Taylor, Lyda Averill Paz. "A Comparative Study of Southeastern Cultures." MA thesis, Yale University, 1937.

Trammell, Camilla Davis. *Seven Pines: Its Occupants and Their Letters, 1825–1872*. Houston, TX: Southern Methodist University Press, 1986.

Turnbaugh, William A., and Sarah Peabody Turnbaugh. *American Indian Baskets: Building and Caring for a Collection*. West Chester, PA: Schiffer Publishing, 2013.

Usner, Daniel H., Jr. "From Bayou Teche to Fifth Avenue: Crafting a New Market for Chitimacha Indian Baskets." *Journal of Southern History* 79, no. 2 (May 2013): 339–74.

———. *Weaving Alliances with Other Women: Chitimacha Indian Work in the New South*. Athens: University of Georgia Press, 2015.

———. "'They Don't Like Indians around Here': Chitimacha Struggles and Strategies for Survival in the Jim Crow South." *Native South* 9 (2016): 89–124.

Washington, Alexander H. "The Friendly Indians of Trinity River, in Texas." *Texas Almanac*, 1861, 126–31.

Weltfish, Gene. "Prehistoric North American Basketry Techniques and Modern Distributions." *American Anthropologist*, new ser., vol. 32, no. 3, pt. 1 (July–September 1930): 454–95.

Wilkins, Teresa. *Patterns of Exchange: Navajo Weavers and Traders.* Norman: University of Oklahoma Press, 2008.

Winfrey, Dorman H., and James M. Day, eds. *The Indian Papers of Texas and the Southwest, 1825–1916.* Vols. 1–5. Austin: Texas State Historical Association, 1995.

Winfrey, Dorman H., and Jack Bryant. *Indian Tribes of Texas.* Waco, TX: Texian Press, 1971.

Wrede, Friedrich W. von. "Sketches of Life in the United States of North America and Texas." Waco, TX, 1970.

Index

Note: Page numbers in italics refer to illustrations; those followed by "n" indicate endnotes.

Printed in the USA
CPSIA information can be obtained
at www.ICGtesting.com
LVHW041726170124
769199LV00003B/14

9 780807 171240